JN058570

JAPANORAMA

JAPANORAMA
NEW VISION ON ART SINCE 1970

editorial supervisor **YUKO HASEGAWA**

wind rose – suiseisha

Tokyo, 2021

Centre
Pompidou-Metz

This book is based on the French-language publication *Japanorama. Nouveau regard sur la création contemporaine*, published by the Centre Pompidou-Metz to accompany the exhibition curated by Yuko Hasegawa and presented from October 20, 2017 to March 5, 2018 in Metz, France.

Contents

Preface

—

Yuko Hasegawa

The present volume, *Japanorama: Contemporary Japanese Art since 1970*, is the book version of the catalogue for the *Japanorama* exhibition (published in French) that was held at the Centre Pompidou-Metz (in the city of Metz), a branch of the Centre Pompidou in Paris, in 2017. Consisting of texts by eleven Japanese and French writers as well as introductions to the artists and exhibition materials, it is my hope that this book will go beyond the catalogue and become an important reference that discusses and introduces audiences to contemporary Japanese art and visual culture. The *Japanorama* exhibition drew some 100,000 visitors over a three-month period and was highly acclaimed, winning a full page of coverage in the New York Times. This is the first time in thirty years that an exhibition has sought to showcase the history of contemporary Japanese art, since *Japon des avant gardes, 1910-1970* was held at the Centre Pompidou in Paris in 1986. Considering that the catalogue for this earlier exhibition was only available in French, the fact that the content of this exhibition is being introduced in Japanese and English is also significant in terms of archival value.

The texts by each writer, which offer not just introductory outlines or expla-nations but a unique, critical perspective on contemporary Japanese art, have an archipelago-like diversity to them that connects the contemporary art of this country, with its complex cultural background, to its visual culture, thinking, and political and economic contexts. How can contemporary Japanese art and visual culture, the transmission of which is lagging behind the globalized world, be showcased to a foreign audience? We received many requests from foreign audiences for an English-language edition of this book, and this Japanese-English publication hopes to respond to the expectations of art professionals, students, researchers, as well as art lovers in general, both Japanese and foreign. In addition to all the writers who have kindly agreed to having their texts reprinted here, the Centre Pompidou-Metz, and all participating artists, I would also like to express my sincere gratitude to all those who provided images and plates, and Kotaro Shimada and Mio Harada for their editorial assistance. I would also like to thank Soichiro Fukutake, the Japanese Friends of Centre Pompidou chaired by Takeo Obayashi, and Richard Colas of Chanel for their generosity and understanding as patrons of culture.

This book is dedicated to Emma Lavigne, former director of the Centre Pompidou-Metz and current president of the Palais de Tokyo.

Translated from Japanese by Darryl Jingwen Wee

Preface for French version

—

Serge Lasvignes
President, Centre Pompidou and Centre Pompidou-Metz

Emma Lavigne
Director, Centre Pompidou-Metz

In her novel, *The Silence Museum*, Yoko Ogawa tells the story of a young museographer who takes up his duties in a mansion on the edge of the world, where he must record, arrange and exhibit a collection of objects, relics of daily life and the imprints of the passage of time, composing a reflection on the memory, the accumulation and the obsessions that underlie the elaboration of any exhibition. "Japanorama," orchestrated by curator and artistic director of the Museum of Contemporary Art Tokyo (MOT) Yuko Hasegawa, is an embodied, organic and sensuous crossing that makes audible and palpable the pulses of creation in contemporary Japan. A seasoned museographer who took part in the foundation of the 21st Century Museum of Contemporary Art, Kanazawa, a place where present time and the reality of an artistic scene animated by perpetual movement pulsate, Hasegawa offers us a unique panorama of creative activities in Japan that allows us to challenge some generally accepted ideas. On the one hand, Japanese art today cannot be circumscribed as a well-defined entity of its own. It is in exciting dialogue with fashion, architecture, music, the art of manga and anime, and the performing arts that a contemporary Japanese "visual culture" has emerged with vigor since the end of the 1960s. A culture so special that it immediately gives rise to deep feelings of attraction and fascination, still intact. On the other hand, the little we think we know about this contemporary Japan is quickly overturned by a wealth and profusion of practices and visions, which Hasegawa has articulated with brilliance. It was necessary to look from within in order to take into account this extreme diversity and to understand the relationship between art and society in Japan today. She has thus selected some one hundred and ten artists, many showing work for the first time in France, and organized the two floors of the museum that encompass the exhibition using an archipelago motif in the image of the country, with the help of architects from the firm SANAA (Kazuyo Sejima and Ryue Nishizawa).

This exhibition is all the more important because it is part of a prestigious line of events that have formed the history of the Centre Pompidou. In 1986, the institution organized the exhibition "Avant-Garde Arts of Japan 1910-1970." Designed by a team with a wide range of skills, this multidisciplinary event continued the great dialogues "Paris-New York" (1977), "Paris-Berlin" (1978), "Paris-Moscow" (1979), and "Paris-Paris" (1981). The Centre Pompidou-Metz salutes this heritage with its Japanese season, inaugurated in September 2017 on the occasion of the opening of "Japan-ness. Architecture and urbanism in Japan since 1945," and "Japanorama" (October 2017-March 2018) takes over from "Avant-Garde Arts of Japan," placing its cursor at 1970, where the previous exhibition left off. The friendship between our two countries has thus clearly grown over the years. The collection of the National Museum of Modern Art at the Centre Pompidou now includes more than twelve hundred Japanese works. The Centre Pompidou-Metz, designed by Japanese architect Shigeru Ban, with Jean de Gastines, had already staged an exhibition of the artist Tadashi Kawamata in one of its galleries in 2016. Finally, the Japanese season planned by the teams of the Centre Pompidou-Metz does not stop with "Japanorama," since, from January 2018, a gallery will be used for an exhibition of the art collective Dump Type, pioneers in multimedia arts, while the spaces dedicated to the performing arts will be enlivened by the Japanese atmosphere throughout the season thanks to an exceptional program designed by independent curator Emmanuelle de Montgazon, who has invited leading figures in performance, dance, music and theatre. This season also promises to be a prelude to the program Japonismes 2018. As part of this large-scale event, the Centre Pompidou in Paris will host a retrospective of the film director Naomi Kawase and an exhibition dedicated to the artist Ryoji Ikeda.

The history of this friendship therefore continues, with the help of remarkable artists and lenders, such as the Museum of Contemporary Art Tokyo, and with the support of an unfailing partner whom we would like to warmly thank, The Japan Foundation, co-organizers of "Japanorama." Thanks to this shared energy and precious collaboration, the Centre Pompidou-Metz is very happy to make perceptible, for one season, the metabolism of the Archipelago, the constant reinvention of creation permeated by the concept *ma*, defined by Arata Isozaki: "Space = void + ma. The word *ma* originally meant the 'natural distance/time between two things existing in a continuity'; it has come to designate 'the in-between, the space between object and object.'" Thanks, also, to the richness of the work of the artists, whom

we of course wish to thank as well, their reflections, emotions and impressions acti-
vate a memory put back in motion. This collective poetry intervenes in the invisible
space of our identities, comes to qualify this void and make it meaningful, inviting
rich crossings in this panorama of the Japanese archipelago.

Translated from French by Kenjiro Matsuda

Preface for French version | Emma Lavigne

Japanorama:
An archipelago of perpetual change

—

Yuko Hasegawa

Japan is, in a certain sense, a singular country. This archipelago in the Far East, rich in a cultural heritage of more than two thousand years, was one of the first Asian nations to modernize itself at the end of the 19th century. Japan modeled its own history by escaping from the cultural colonization of the West, notably of its language. It is a country where tradition and cutting-edge technology coexist, where harmonious coexistence with others rests on the concept of a loose and supple "subject." A country that establishes an organic relationship between man and nature, all the while deconstructing traditional perceptions of nature as well as the environment that surrounds us — Japan is a composite entity that also maintains a certain ambiguity.

In this era of globalization, there are numerous reasons that might lead one to be interested in Japan. The exhibition *Japanorama*, which opened in the autumn of 2017, poses the question of how this Asian country, a former site of experimentation for Western "modernism," can represent a cultural stimulus and a source of inspiration for Europe today as it faces rupture and an uncertainty that obscures the future. The experimental process of modernization, launched at the end of Japan's isolationist policy (*sakoku*) after the country opened itself up to the world at the end of the 19th century, did not take the form of a "revolution," but rather a "restoration," and was marked by two wars. In 1945, two Japanese cities served as laboratories for the technology of mass destruction represented by the dropping of the atomic bomb. Numerous democratic experiences took shape under the American occupation — notably the constitution — and Japan became a model of reconstruction and industrialization. Against the backdrop of the experiments brought about by modernization, Japan underwent a unique process of hybridization, fusion, and coming-and-going between two cultures: it survived and adapted itself to these experiences of modernization, in order to arrive at its current state.

As a result, Japan has become an ensemble of paradoxes that manifest themselves in terms of a kind of coexistence between tradition and technology, or even through a sort of discrepancy: that which exists between the profound Japanese respect of nature and their cold indifference to its destruction during the economic miracle. This is an attitude that can appear contradictory, indeed schizophrenic. During his studies of "nature" in Japan, the orientalist and philosopher Augustin Berque remarked that this term did not merely refer to all kinds of natural environments. As the social also permeates "nature," Berque saw that the respect for a natural state of harmony in this collectivity that includes society was what was responsible for its destruction.[1]

1.

Japanorama as a future vision/archipelago

Japanese contemporary art or the Japanese visual arts have only rarely been the subject of historical exhibitions and retrospectives abroad. In France, practically the only example of an exhibition offering such an overview was *Japon des avant gardes, 1910-1970*, held at the Centre Pompidou in Paris in 1986. This was an important exhibition that outlined the way in which modernism developed in Japan under the influence of avant-garde art from Europe and America. In a certain sense, however, this exhibition had sought to establish links between the context of the Japanese avant-garde and that of Western modernism. Exhibitions devoted to Japan that have been held in Europe and America for some thirty years have mainly dealt with the postwar period dating up until the 1970s.[2] All of them focused on the avant-garde, sticking to a formulation that starts with Gutai, Jikken Kobo, the Yomiuri Independent, Anti-Art, and the 1970s period of Mono-ha. The objective was to observe the development of a modernism that was particular to Japan, different from that of the West, by analyzing the relationship that the artists maintained with Western art and the ways in which they appropriated all the Western "isms," art informel, Anti-Art, or even Dadaism. In the preface entitled "Japanese Art after 1945" for the catalogue of the exhibition *Japanese Art after 1945: Scream Against the Sky*, which covered the postwar period up until the 1990s, curator Alexandra Munroe states that "this exhibition presents the confluence of international 'isms' and Japanese activity in a comparative context focusing on the artists' individual and cultural experience as the source of expression."[3]

This exhibition, *Japanorama: A New Vision of Japanese Contemporary Art*, inherits the spirit of *Japon des avant gardes* as it had taken place in Paris, focusing on the period from the 1970s up until the present, in 2017. The title "Japanorama" stems from a certain desire to present a panoramic overview of the Japanese visual arts while also encompassing the visual culture that underlies them. During the 1970s, Japan temporarily put the postwar period behind it: the "new vision" in the subtitle alludes to an image of Japan that follows this one, at the moment when the country started to seek out its own cultural identity. Various heterogeneous elements came into play during this period, when Japan, one of the first countries to realize a "post-avant-garde," saw its economy grow rapidly before falling victim to a spectacular decline. For this exhibition, which mixes art with other forms of visual expression, we have opted to organize it according to themes rather than a chronological order.

As shown by the architecture exhibition *Japanness: Architecture and Urbanism*

Japanorama: An archipelago of perpetual change | Yuko Hasegawa *in Japan since 1945*, held concurrently at the Centre Pompidou-Metz, design and architecture have taken the form of a national culture in the modernist context, and developed in a structural manner. Contemporary art, on the other hand, developed in a chaotic manner, in relation to diverse cultures, situations or real events, without the presence of a consistent, all-encompassing theory or discourse. Japan's inability to construct a coherent discourse, such as one would find in Western art history, facilitated the emergence of many unique forms of expression. In contrast to their predecessors who, until the 1960s, took a clear position that critically deconstructed all the Western -isms, it has not always been easy for many of these post-avant-garde artists to create something unique in the name of art. After his exhibition *Little Boy: The Arts of Japan's Exploding Subculture*, Takashi Murakami criticized and proposed a new point of view on Japanese culture and society in *Superflat*, testifying to the difficulty of creating in a place where the word "art" has neither an established framework nor definition.

> The reason I create works of art — and this may appear illogical — is that I seek to integrate undifferentiated contexts into the heart of my works, in the hope of seizing upon 'miraculous instants,' so that I can store them, just as they are, on a shelf in my head. I have so far been unable to discern what is 'Japanese' about this mental shelf, however. I cannot encounter the real 'me.' Nothing allows us to discover what our 'art' is.[4]

Murakami turned his back on this going around in circles, a situation he was unable to break out of through verbal means. He lined up all these images and opened an endless stream of windows one at a time, and attempted to explain Japanese art in terms of the "superflat" landscape that appeared all at once at the moment that they became joined to each other.

Koki Tanaka, an internationally active conceptual artist, made a similar comment regarding the flimsiness of this foundation in Japan, saying that "it does not seem that so-called 'art history' exists as a common, shared foundation for artists, and that they go about creating their works based on that premise."[5]

2.
An archipelago of unique conceptions of the "body" and "subject": the six themes of the exhibition

Japanese artists did not see art history as the platform of their activity: instead, they sought to locate a certain unique base or framework, thereby arriving at a new form of creation. They also erased the boundaries and opened up the field of possibilities for art for other genres, such as design or architecture. We can identify two characteristics or catalysts common to these artists: firstly, a singular conception of corporeality, and secondly, the presence of a loose and supple "subject."

Let us first look at this distinctive "corporeality." The Japanese react directly to reality and their environment, with an embodied intelligence through which bodily experiences give rise to knowledge. They tend to be equipped with sensors that perceive the external world (environment) with the same density and intensity, while transcending the boundaries between material and immaterial, physical and virtual. This straightforward bodily reaction to things and spaces can be seen in the artistic practices of Gutai and Mono-ha, while delicate and complex bodily reactions to the atmosphere and environment that surround us are present in the dance of Butoh, for example. In architecture, after the exercise in incorporating and blending modernism and the postmodern period came to an end, the 1990s saw the emergence of a certain physicality that read situations in a direct and straightforward manner, and translated them into a unique and distinctive architectural program.

Since the 1990s, in a world where ideologies tended to become attenuated, artists became increasingly inclined to seek out alternative standards for criticism in experiences, events, and the physical body. The following quote from Toyo Ito, in his criticism of Kazuyo Sejima, clearly illustrates this turning point.

> Her enthusiasm and independence, unconstrained by our society, give her the capacity to understand the reality of our society with unerring accuracy, without being imprisoned by the force of custom. The schematizations found in her work are not abstract, as the experiments of numerous architects can be. Sejima's work is an act of describing reality through her own body, which lives out reality in a liberated fashion. In a society where ideology no longer holds any value, it is this straightforward, embodied act that seeks to schematize reality itself without making any detours that holds the greatest critical potential.[6]

This assertion is not limited to the particular brand of corporeality found in Sejima: it highlights the fact that the embodied, corporeal acts of the 1990s offered the opportunity to discover new possibilities, or values that had previously been overlooked.

This high level of embodied intelligence and sensitivity is not limited to special events: it is also exercised in everyday life. The aesthetics of one's behavior in situations involving the tea ceremony or flower arrangement, for instance, as well as kimonos and everyday items, demonstrate a finely honed level of aesthetic awareness. The fact that daily life and aesthetics were integrated with each other meant that there was no distinction between pure art and the applied arts before the modern era. Taking a cue from this historical context, the distinction between high culture and low culture is loose and fluid in Japan. There is a tendency to view all cultural phenomena in terms of a horizontal equality — something that could also be linked to the unique development of Pop Art in this country. Art critic Junzo Ishiko argues that "expressions that we do not need to call, and which have no need of being called art flourish in diverse forms, as one style of a 'history' that pertains to one's corporeality."[7] For Ishiko, an attitude that is open to the possibilities offered up by the miscellany of urban visual culture relies on the body as a mediating presence.

Derrick de Kerckhove, a sociologist of art, argues that the Japanese are unfamiliar with the Western concept of empty space, and that space has never actually been empty in traditional Japanese culture.

> For the Japanese, space is a continuous flow, animated by mutual interaction and defined by a delicate conception of intervals and pacing. This is what is meant by the word *ma*… For the Japanese, *ma* refers to the entire, complex network of people and things. Space in Japan is not empty…it is this sensation that assesses distance, the generator of complex networks between people and objects, and beautiful resonances akin to chords. This conception leads to exemplary designs for interfaces.[8]

Kerckhove then quotes the French Japanologist Michel Random, and emphasizes that the notion of *ma* is behind everything, as a sensation of pause that creates a beautiful resonance, like a chord. He believes that this concept of *ma* can be effectively applied to the electronic *ma* that exist in the networks of electronic technology. These electronic intervals, which enliven the interplay and bridge the gap between mind and technology and between human and machine, contributes to the exploration and creation of interface patterns. This is an area in which Japanese media artists and designers excel. As a network of meaning that comprehensively connects the body, senses, and knowledge, *ma* exists in the space between subjects. As a site where the exterior and interior overlap with each other, it blurs the boundary between the subject and the exterior, a situation that leads to a loose subjectivity.

The second point pertains to the unique configuration of the subject. In Japan, the "subject" is not the starting point for the "reconstruction of the world through thought" as it is in the West, nor is it clearly separated by the boundary between the self and the other. Rather, it can be called a "loose subjectivity" that is defined in relation to its surroundings.

According to Claude Lévi-Strauss, the Japanese, "instead of a cause, make the subject a result." "Western philosophy of the subject is centrifugal: everything emanates from it," he argues, whereas "the way that Japanese thought conceives the subject seems more centripetal." Lévi-Strauss cites Japanese syntax as an example. Similar to how sentences are constructed by limiting the general to the particular, Japanese thinking puts the subject last, thereby making this subject the final site for reflecting on one's belonging and affiliations. This is a way of constructing the subject from the outside, and there is a strong tendency to define oneself by one's family, professional group, geographical environment, and status in the country or society. This is not the rejection of the subject or self-renunciation found in Eastern thought, but rather the materialization of the subject in a particular way that allows self-consciousness to exist as an individual, a "loose subject" within the social structure. As Lévi-Strauss sees it, the Japanese do not reject the Western idea of logos and discourse, but simply pick and choose what suits them. This is expressed in their scientific awareness and an attitude that values intuition, experience, and practice (Masao Maruyama), which does not take the view that natural phenomena and human actions depend on a single, logical necessity. According to Lévi-Strauss, these unique positions are linked to the distinctiveness of Japanese culture.[9]

On the other hand, Augustin Berque analyzes this looseness in terms of a collective unity or fusion between human beings and "nature" (defined in a broad sense, including moods, atmosphere, and climate), even going so far as to say that the environment can constitute a subject. "Their culture has an aversion to extracting the individual subject from its environment, thereby leaving the subject relatively open to the summoning of a larger subject (called nature)."[10] Strong relationships with the aspects that pertain to a particular location or site, as well as the things that go with it, eventually come to accompany such a subject, and manifest themselves in terms of culture. The spiritual climate of this country — where the frontiers between exterior and interior, society and individual, and self and other are ambiguous — render "expression" weak and fragile: it has a tendency to annihilate the distance from the self, which makes it possible to analyze the object. What does the private or intimate mean in Japan? The particular subjectivity of "I" traces its origins to the autobiographical novels produced in modern Japan oriented towards the self, severing its relationship to Western history and literature. Thanks to its profoundly centripetal nature, but also its peculiarly introverted contemplation, the "I," even as it is directed towards the self, manages to produce an "expression" imbued with a universal force — exactly as if individual intention had vibrated, infiltrated that particular place, and created some sort of magnetic field.

The subject is also an extended concept that transcends the idea of the human. Amid cautionary warnings of the advent of the era of the Anthropocene,[11] the problems engendered by subject-object dualism and anthropocentrism, which have caused a rift to appear between humans and nature, are becoming more grave. Expectations of a reevaluation of Asian de-anthropocentrism and animism, as well as an updating of these notions, have been heightened. In effect, this is a proposal to recalibrate the relation between humans and the environment so that the same value might be attributed to both humans and the non-human (things, animals, and plants). The propensity for Japanese artists and creators to treat bodies and things (information, technology, media) in an organic and integral manner alludes, whether through the design of objects or methods of obtaining and interpreting information, to a new way of negotiating and coexisting with the environment and its phenomena.

While visualizing the correlation between these two catalyzing elements, Japanorama has been configured to create relationships between the different genres that highlight the sense of reality and awareness of the times embodied by each of them, such as art and architecture, design (including fashion), music, or subcultures like manga. The uniqueness of these forms of visual expression has been organized according to these two catalyzing elements, while the exhibition itself is divided into six conceptual themes that, like the islands of an archipelago, are linked to each other in an organic way. The first island has the theme "Strange Object: Post-human Body"; the second, "Pop Art: before/after the 1980s"; the third, "Collaboration/ Participation/Sharing"; the fourth deals with the "Poetics of Resistance"; the fifth examines the concept of "Soft, Floating Subjectivity/Private Documentary"; while the sixth and final island looks at the subject of "Relationships between Materials, and Reductionism." Works dating from before 1970 serving as references have also been integrated into the exhibition in order to clarify each of these concepts.

These six themes intentionally highlight the "symbolic aspects" of the ter- minology often seen in the foreign critical discourses of the past that dealt with contemporary Japanese art and culture. In a cultural sphere built on the logos, and to facilitate the transmission of Japanese forms of artistic expression which are precisely beyond the logos, we have introduced symbolic emblems that might serve as an guiding framework for visitors, providing certain cues for this guidance and encouraging free interpretation. The metaphor of islands comes from the fact that Japan is an archipelago. These small islands, each of which possesses an ecosystem of its own, maintain an organic relationship among themselves and exert a recip- rocal influence on each other. Let us take the islands "Collaboration/Participation/ Sharing" and "Soft, Floating Subjectivity/Private Documentary" as an example. These islands deal with two concepts that are apparently opposed to each other, but they express a certain coexistence between the state of being open to the other and the centripetal aspect. The first island, "Strange Object: Post-human Body," and the sixth, "Relationships between Materials, and Reductionism," were inspired by the indivisible link that unites the body and the spatial concept of *ma*.

The relationships between the meanings of each "island" are indicated by the configuration of the exhibition space and the constellations of artworks. To give a brief overview of this configuration: first of all, "Strange Object: Post-human Body" (the beginning of the exhibition) and "Relationships between Materials, and Reduc- tionism" (the end) address the uniquely Japanese spatial concept of *ma*, and have a strong relationship to each other. The special sensitivity that is capable of respond- ing directly to the media and technology that surround us, as Kerckhove points out, is linked to how relationships between objects in the Mono-ha works of the sixth and final island are formed, in the form of a "sensitivity that measures intervals," as well as the *ma* filled with the materiality and vibrations of the digital symbols of Ryoji Ikeda and Tatsuo Miyajima.

The second island titled "Pop Art: before/after the 1980s," as Junzo Ishiko points out, addresses the diversity and complexity of Pop Art as a device that transforms everything around us, from everyday objects including our physicality to everyday items, waste, and pop culture icons, starting from our aesthetic relationships with these things. This second island is also intended to reveal the aesthetics of "design" that translate the active responses of our bodies and sensibilities to a shifting visual environment into a sophisticated form.

In terms of the second catalytic element, the "subject," "Collaboration/Participation/Sharing" and "Soft, Floating Subjectivity/Private Documentary," which examine the concept of a loose subjectivity, are paired with each other. What does it mean to be "private" in Japan? The self and the other are not separate, and the self can exist expansively in a magnetic field of collective consciousness. As such, the expression of this self can have a strong impact despite its extremely private nature. The fifth island showcases subjectivist photography starting with Provoke, as well as private documentary photography and video.

The sharing of this magnetic field underlies both the "collaboration" of "Collaboration/Participation/Sharing" and "Soft, Floating Subjectivity/Private Documentary," which seems opposite to it at first glance. The Fluxus artists of the 1960s are combined with the socially engaged conceptual artists of the 2000s. Audience participation and collaboration does not entail a simple collectivism, but rather a more self-aware form of interdependence and involvement. Yoko Ono created instruction, a score that is re-enacted by others, as an exploration of the relationship between art and the simple, habitual actions of daily life. Koki Tanaka's collaborative and constructive experimental performances are based on the theme of how we might share in the experiences of others. The skill and delicacy with which the parameters of these situations are constructed serve to make invisible sites of co-creation visible. Each of these cases makes a proposal for empathy, symbiosis, and co-creation, based on a loose individualism.

The fourth island, "Poetics of Resistance," unfolds in a similar fashion while remaining the most resistant to existing conceptual frameworks. It has often been said that the most elusive aspect of Japanese contemporary art is that which has a political and social nature. The illogical, loose subjectivity, which emphasizes sensibility and feeling over logos, seems to lack a sense of criticality and a dialectical, analytical attitude. Behind the expressions described as kawaii (innocent, naive) are acts of social resistance and social statements. While these things are difficult to perceive as signs or symbols within the space of logos, this island has been created to highlight the unique nature of the politics of expression in Japan.

Evolution from the 1970s up until the present

1970, the year of the Osaka World Expo and the culmination of Japan's postwar modernism, is one of the starting points for this exhibition. The Tokyo Biennale, "Between Man and Matter" (curated by Yusuke Nakahara), which saw the participation of many contemporary conceptual artists, was held that same year. This was the start of a transitional period during which Japan sought to break away from the postwar system, and establish its autonomy from the "avant-garde" cultural influence of the West. During the 1950s and 60s, a period of emancipation after the end of the war, a diverse range of experiments were carried out in the name of the avant-garde and Anti-Art. In a certain sense, they were put into practice through the free interpretations of Japanese artists. These experiences, which took the form of visual scandals, created more of a stir in the society columns than the art columns of the mass media. As we discover in the essay by Manabu Miki, also included in this catalogue, many avant-garde artists participated in the Osaka World Expo, undertaking multiple interdisciplinary experiments with a view to establishing a link between antiquity and the contemporary, and between tradition and technology. An anti-Expo movement also appeared, however: after the Expo ended, results were mixed, with some participating artists coming to consider the subject of the Expo as taboo, for example. The World Expo is a symbolic event in which art is absorbed within a festival. One might even go so far as to say that the very nature of art and culture began to slowly shift after the Osaka Expo.

The 1970s, which were more subdued, were marked by the oil crisis. The tendency to deny and relativize Anti-Art was interiorized and connected to reductionism. In the domain of art, the Mono-ha movement ("school of things"), which reduced things to their material substance, and the Nippon Gainen-ha movement ("Japanese conceptual school"), which reduced things to their concepts, sought to create a culture of their own by maintaining their distance from grand Western theories or artistic currents. Mono-ha, which took its starting point from experiments in perception and a curiosity about the relationships between things, expressed certain ontological doubts. Their ideology, which consisted in having the material itself speak, rather than projecting human intention onto it, led to the concept for the exhibition Between Man and Matter (1970), organized by the art critic Yusuke Nakahara, who had studied theoretical physics at Kyoto University under the physicist and Nobel laureate Hideki Yukawa.

It was during the 1980s that Japan emerged onto the international cultural map as a country of postmodern futurist culture, with Tokyo at its center. Thanks to the profound relationship between the economic prosperity of the "bubble" and consumer culture, subculture, art, and academic thought were mutually exchanged on the same level in the name of "culture," giving birth to an itinerant culture of playful surfaces and symbols. 1979 saw the advent of techno-pop, triggered by the formation of YMO (Yellow Magic Orchestra), while Rei Kawakubo shocked the fashion world with her black parade at Paris Fashion Week in 1981. YMO, which deployed deconstruction and remix as their methods, came to prominence during the 80s with their stunning brand of originality. This group created cute, stylized fusions of Asian and Western symbols, and post-human hybrids of non-human bodies and digital presences. Kawakubo presented a new image of the body by effecting a deconstruction that was at once dialectical and reformative, in contrast to the Western conception of that body. There was something about this process that amounted to the purification of a corporeality burdened with the weight and emotional detritus of the postwar: it was in this rebooting that they were innovative.

The strategy of the Seibu department store chain, which sought to forge a connection between culture and consumer society, relied on having graphic designers enter into the realm of art: the visual impact of advertising swallowed up any metaphysical or social issues. Here, the shared foundation that used to be based on art history began to crumble, and a new platform of interdisciplinarity and equality emerged. In a certain sense, the culture of the 1980s was an era of excessive self-consciousness, where the act of accentuating the difference between the self and the other was seen as "creative." In his study of the 1980s, Akio Miyazawa points out the vacuity of the information produced during this time, while simultaneously extolling the results of the cultural originality of this same period. Even the orthography of the term otaku, one of the keywords of Japanese visual culture from the 1990s up until the present, underwent a shift in passing from the hiragana syllabary おたく to katakana オタク, thereby marking its transition towards body theory. "Subculture" was no longer subordinate to a high culture: it came to designate an autonomous culture known as sabukaru. In other words, hierarchies based on high culture were also disappearing.

For their part, the 1990s were marked by the collapse of the speculative bubble and economic malaise, which produced an atmosphere of ambiguous stasis in Japan, full of uncertainty about the future. Young people went in search of straightforward realities that could not be reduced to symbols. This situation produced flat individuals who were uniform, almost to the point of having an excess of non-consciousness. Uncertainty and ambiguity were combined with transience, the instability of life, and hope: taken together, they manifested themselves in terms of an art of transparency and fragile forms, testifying to an absence of references and frameworks as well as the decline of ideology. During the early 1990s, Takashi Homma's photographs of suburban areas, with their transparent, neutral, yet straightforward and unadorned perspective, sought to fully exploit the possibilities concerning their subject. The constructions of Kazuyo Sejima, which transcend conventional notions of architectural grammar, relinquish their meaning and significance, as well as decisions pertaining to how they should be programmed, to people who find themselves within transversal spaces that exist somewhere between the public and the private. Neo-Pop, distinct for how it borrows imagery from anime or figurines, as in the work of Takashi Murakami or throughout the history of modern art, is spectacular and strongly discursive. At the same time, however, it reflects a certain darkness, as well as psychological and pathological uncertainties caused by the chaos of environmental problems and the socio-political situation. The otaku culture, influenced by anime, video games, and figurines, acquired depth and underwent an almost pathological diversity of changes. The anime born of this vision has spread throughout the world since 2010 as "Cool Japan."

The otaku phenomenon emerged as a result of this country's inherent tendency toward "Galapagosization." However, it can also be seen as a form of self-defense based on an awareness of imminent crisis and sense of the gradually spreading uncertainty of our existence threatening our survival since the end of the 20th century. While otaku culture is self-referential, closed, and fragmented, the sharing of its conspicuously obsessive topics has produced an alternative circuit of visual communication that can gain access to contemporary issues. As a result, otaku culture has spread all over the world through manga, anime, and games.

At the end of the 1990s, in the wake of the Kobe earthquake and the Sarin gas attack in the Tokyo metro in 1995, a climate of profound suspicion in relation to "politics and society" emerged, and the Japanese came to place a higher premium on small-scale communication in the service of mutual aid and assistance. This was a transition towards a mode of expression that was personal, quotidian, and modest. The expression of personal emotion and a consciousness of the self, through a certain kind of improvisation and amateur practices, sought to reproduce and reconstitute a symbolic, imaginary sphere as a medium for communication. Numerous forms of expression that could easily establish a direct connection to the body and its sensations appeared: video, drawing, photography, performance.

Politics consisted in the engagement of each person in society, but at the level of the individual or small communities. The direction that was taken was not a matter of going in search of grand changes or reforms, but of exploring what possibilities lay just beneath our eyes, through free and supple crossings of the border between subject and object, interior and exterior. This tendency, which persists even today, can be found in different means of expression such as images (with photography or personal documentary), architecture, or even the "narrative" mode. After the catastrophe of March 11, 2011 (or "3.11"), the social engagement of artists intensified. As Yoshitaka Mōri's essay emphasizes, the deployment of social networks or even activist movements were significantly implicated in the programming of emotions, such as the analysis of information, the determination of one's practice, and communication. As the artist Koki Tanaka has it, 3.11 saw the emergence of a new shared "foundation" — which might be considered a democratic question more important than that of art history.[12] On the other hand, in a global economy, and in the name of the creative industry, the tendency for art to become commoditized is becoming stronger, giving rise to critical conflicts and negotiations. Kohei Nawa and Rhizomatiks, representatives of the New Materialism, a movement born out of the digital environment that fuses information with the material, shuttle back and forth between the domain of capital that governs the information industry and the realm of art, in search of a direction to take.

4.

In conclusion

This exhibition does not limit itself to a conventional symbolic understanding of zen or kawaii. Japanorama seeks to highlight the contemporary art and visual culture of Japan as a kind of structural model of a singular culture and ensemble of profound sensibility and knowledge. A unique archipelago with no center, where the contexts that underlie its organization cannot be seen, reacting to the present and exerting its influence upon it, exploiting the past and future in a supple fashion, all the while never ceasing to change its forms and relationships. On this moving earth, links and networks between a diverse range of things come into force through a process of exploration and renovation of uncertain references and frameworks, rewriting the established categories of art, art history, and cultural value. In this archipelago, art plays an active role in relation to the environment or the unfolding of events, or else functions as a symbol that can be shared in a spiritual or psychological sense. Accordingly, distinctions between high culture and low culture, or among genres, make no sense. Works that have resisted the passage of time and go down in history demand to be evaluated and discovered continually in the present, instead of being considered complete, having been described as belonging to history. In this era of uncertainty, in this epoch of diversification of value systems and cultures, the state of being a supple subject, which accords importance not to an ideal concept but rather physical reality or knowledge, and which forms an open relationship with the non-human (objects, information, or animals, for instance), is not a preponderant model in global culture. The supple subject, however, functions as a stimulating island: in constantly returning to it, one gains access to alternative points of view. This island possesses a "signification," like a magnetic field that serves as a catalyst for the production of new norms.

All of us who share in this era of crisis must contribute, from each of our own positions, to this cultural ecology that emerges out of the circulation and exchange of cultures. At the heart of the multicultural global network, this exhibition offers us an index that allows each of us to profit from the resources and possibilities contained within the visual culture of contemporary Japan.

Translated from Japanese by Darryl Jingwen Wee

Notes

[1] Augustin Berque, Fudo no Nihon—Shizen to bunka no tsutai, translated into Japanese by Katsuhide Shinoda of Le Japon dans son milieu. La trajection de la nature et de la culture), Chikuma Gakugei Bunko, 1992, p. 262.

[2] Examples of this are Reconstructions: Avant-Garde Art in Japan 1945-1965, held at the Museum of Modern Art in Oxford, UK in 1985, Japanese Art After 1945: Scream Against the Sky, which traveled to the Yokohama Museum of Art, Guggenheim Museum in New York, and San Francisco Museum of Modern Art from 1994-95, and Tokyo 1955-1970: A New Avant-garde at the Museum of Modern Art in New York in 2015.

[3] Alexandra Munroe, "Japanese Art After 1945," translated into Japanese by Atsumi Yamada, Japanese Art after 1945: Scream Against the Sky, Yokohama Museum of Art, 1994, p. 15.

[4] Takashi Murakami, Superflat, Madra Publishing Co., Ltd., 2000, p. 12.

[5] From a July 2017 conversation between the author and Koki Tanaka.

[6] Toyo Ito, "Diagram architecture," Kazuyo Sejima 1988-1996, monographie issue of El Croquis, 77(I), 1996, pp. 22-23.

[7] Junzo Ishiko, Yoshitaka Uesugi, Seigo Matsuoka, Kitsch: Magaimono no jidai, Diamond-sha, 1971, p. 302.

[8] Derrick de Kerckhove, Postmedia Theory: Towards a Collective Intelligence, NTT Publishing, translated into Japanese by Miiko Kataoka and Yutaka Nakazawa, 1999, pp. 200-201.

[9] Claude Lévi-Strauss, The Other Face of the Moon, translated into Japanese by Junzo Kawada, Chuo Koron Shinsha, 2014, p. 38.

[10] Berque, ibid., p. 374.

[11] The "Anthropocene" is a new epochal classification that means "the age of mankind," representing the next geological era after the Holocene. It advocates the criticism and amelioration of anthropocentric Western rationalism and capitalism by sharing the fact that in the 200 years that have passed since the Industrial Revolution, an era in which humans have come to exert a significant impact on the Earth's ecosystem and climate through deforestation and air pollution, for example, has become the default setting.

[12] From a July 2017 conversation between the author and Koki Tanaka.

An archipelago of six concepts

—

Yuko Hasegawa

Strange Object: Post-human Body

After the war, the search for a cultural identity particular to Japan had led physicality to become reflected in art in unique ways: a system that detects the external world and reacts directly to it, transforming existing knowledge and imagery into something new through the circuits of the body, or even a liberation of the identity and the body of the individual that welcomed the prospect of transformation. Exchanges and fusions with legends, animals, monsters, robots, the other (other cultures), and immaterial elements such as energy or information: this first island reveals how physicality developed and came to be expressed in all its diversity. The postwar period was the era of Gutai, neo-Dadaism, Butoh and other movements with animistic tendencies that sought out organic connections with non-human elements. The body is a medium that allows one to visualize, in a contemporary form, this animism that sees the presence of a spiritual force in all things, even non-human ones. These strange physical performances and objects that appear indigenous, surrealist, or grotesque prefigure the post-human bodily expression (bodily expressions that are open to entities other than human ones) of the 1980s and later. With its explosion of information and technological progress, the postmodernism of the 1980s gave birth to forms of bodily expression that were immaterial, fragmentary, ludic, and deconstructive: techno-pop music, new media, or even fashion. The evolution of the digital environment spurred further informatization and dematerialization, and the organic fusion of the physical and the digital ushered in futuristic developments.

On the other hand, the body as an anti-establishment critique of the system has gone into decline, shifting towards a model of the body as product, more realistic and affirmative, which integrates technological evolution in a form that is aesthetically refined. In addition, information shared in the space of the Cloud and a collective consciousness based on a conception of nature that encompasses things, animals, and the Earth have emerged as a kind of new metaphor for the body.

1.

A strange, prophetic, and allegorical body

Thanks to its intense impact on the spectators, a single photograph forever changed the meaning of the "body of the dancer." With his Butoh dance *Revolt of the Body* (1968), Tatsumi Hijikata shocked the Western world with this "cadaver that only stands at the risk of its own life," his excesses, his sense of vernacular darkness, and his passion. His aesthetic, meticulously developed out of the physicality of the Japanese, with their short, bow-legged limbs, became a completely new norm. The dancer draws inspiration from the spiritual and cultural destruction of the war and the postwar period. In this way, the body bears the weight of this trauma with all its being, generating non-human and superhuman movements and traces, as if its nervous system had been amputated, and it was functioning thanks to the connection of other circuits.

The asymmetrical fissures that Shozo Shimamoto introduces into his paintings are symbols of the "concrete." They seem to resemble the rifts and tears of a gaze that allows us a glimpse of some unknown beauty, even as they make us aware of these traces of a raw and violent gesture. Tetsumi Kudo's baby carriages are metaphors for mutated bodies that have become one with objects alienated by radioactive contamination. These are cautionary warnings, bodily poems that embrace the inevitable mutation in a sensuous way. Kudo's series of garden and birdcage works wield a vividly allegorical evocative power even today because they anticipated our contemporary awareness of the problem of "dark ecology."[1] The same might be said of Natsuyuki Nakanishi's figures of men made out of clothes pegs: as strange objects, they bring infection and a state of agitation to the city like a virus.

In 1952, while other Gutai artists were grappling with concrete objects such as mud and paper, Atsuko Tanaka stood alone in creating *Denkifuku*, which made use of immaterial elements such as electricity and light. By putting on this flickering outfit, the electric dress became Tanaka's metaphorical body, overlapping with the biological rhythms and cycles of her own body of flesh and blood. Subsequently, she would return to this physical experience in paintings where she would reproduce circles and lines again and again in the form of abstract paintings. During the 1950s, Tanaka conceptualized futuristic works that resonate with the internet-based society of today, and networks that established links between concentric circles and these works.

Rei Kawakubo demonstrated the relationship between fashion and the body of the future. *Body Meets Dress, Dress Meets Body* (S/S 1997), more commonly known as "Lumps and Bumps," was a collection of dresses dotted with bumps on the backside and shoulders that sought to challenge conventional ideas of beauty, and the proposition of a beauty based on a deformed body — in other words, an encounter between the dress and the body in its capacity as a strange object. In a certain sense, Comme des Garçons transformed the act of consumption into a kind of ideology. During the late 1970s, as if to echo the process by which visual forms had been replaced by discourse in the field of art, Comme des Garçons attempted, through the intermediary of the body, to insert fashion into the domain of the discursive. Craig Owens called the act of reading one meaning from something completely different, however fragmentary and imperfect, an "allegory"[2] — in other words, the re-reading of a text, with a new meaning, through another text. This can be linked directly to Comme des Garçons' statement.

"This is not a repetition of what you have previously seen, but a new discovery oriented towards a vivid, free future. This is Comme des Garçons' new approach to making clothing."[3] Rei Kawakubo performs a discursive deconstruction in relation to existing Western modes of making clothing. Instead of negating the past, she adds a palette of alternative options. A "new text" is written by the clients themselves who select and wear these additional options. These strange bodies were able to harness an allegorical power that allowed us to imagine new forms of corporeality and humanity, precisely because of their deficiency, ugliness, fragmentation, and incompleteness.

2.
Metamorphoses

The heightened interest of the Japanese in the notion of metamorphosis can also be seen in the many cosplays, metamorphosed heroes, kabuki, or Takarazuka theater troupe. During the 1980s, Yasumasa Morimura created self-portraits where he substituted himself for famous Western figures in paintings. The imitation of the subject is one method of becoming one with that which one aspires to. Using his own body, Morimura stages *tableaux vivants* where he makes everything, from the costumes to the makeup and backgrounds. Morimura becomes one with all things, not just humans: he even becomes the apples in Cezanne's paintings. Becoming part of his subject is a process of conjugation: Morimura himself is alienated, as is his subject. It is, in effect, a critical gesture that is filled with love and affection. It is the rawness of that "gaze" that constitutes proof of his existence. His series inspired by the historical figures of the 20th century attempts a critique of the notion of "modern history."

In Mariko Mori's *Link of the Moon (Miko no inori)*, how does an extraterrestrial sorceress (the artist's avatar) that has landed on Earth see contemporary Japan? With the futuristic space of Kansai Airport in the background, Mori orchestrates an ironic mise-en-scène that lies somewhere between futurism and shamanism. Sputniko!, who studied mathematics and critical design at the Royal College of Art in London, plays the character of Takashi, a young man with a strong desire to experience menstruation. He creates a menstruation machine that he wears while he roams the streets dressed as a woman. This double gender switch allows Sputniko! to go straight to the heart of reality, that of lived experience, with no regard for the ideological criticisms of society surrounding conventional notions of gender. Her new vision of the body, where an artificial device takes the place of metamorphosis, converts the centripetal impulse of Morimura where one can become anything, into the dispersal of the space of the Cloud, where one can become anyone.

3.
Camouflage, prosthesis, fragment, skin: towards the disappearance of the body

In addition to being the era of postmodernism, the 1980s were also a period that saw the appearance of anthropomorphic sculptures that were hybrid, schismatic, absurd, and ludic. The sculpture *Viridian Adaptor + Kodai's Morpho II* by Kodai Nakahara (1989), constructed out of the supple material of knitting yarn, expands throughout the space, partially made up of a hypertrophied human body, cranial nerves, and eyeballs. This form, reminiscent of Gilles Deleuze's rhizome, seems to be connected to a sensory anomaly. Nakahara integrates private and corporeal connections into his works, under the concept of possessions.

During the second half of the 1990s, Motohiko Odani expressed the uncertainty of reality and floating physical sensations through sculpture and video. Odani expressed these notions by exploring the nature of a sculpture that would be capable of incarnating the conflicts between physicality and virtuality in a material form. The title of *Phantom-Limb* (1997) is a psychoanalytic term describing the sensations felt in a hand that ought to have been lost. A young girl who seems to have lost her hands floats, limb-like, in an in-between state, suspended between waking and awakening, woman and child (undifferentiated gender), floating and landing, loss and presence. Her dress made of hair (itself a part of the body), intertwined like the wave-like surface of a baroque sculpture, is a representation of a disincarnated body, made up of the only sensation felt when touching skin.

Yuko Mohri builds organic connections between found objects, including musical instruments. Inspired by the "wallpaper music" of Erik Satie, she sees the spatial element of wallpaper as a sensor, sensing the surrounding environment and turning the resulting reactions, such as the activation of musical instruments, into artworks. This is the world of things after humans have vanished from it: a vision of a "post-human" body.

4.
Digitization and posthumanism

The bubble economy during the 1980s was accompanied by technological advances and the advent of an information society. Faced with this situation, the multimedia artist group Dumb Type (formed in 1984) and the musical collective YMO (formed in 1978, made up of Ryuichi Sakamoto, Haruomi Hosono, and Yukihiro Takahashi) offered a new vision of humanity that deployed technology in a way that was both creative and critical. Dumb Type critiqued our overdependence on information in a state of dumbness, without having recourse to speech. In its place were images (written and visual), sounds, lights, mechanical spatial devices, and theatrical performances by living bodies reacting to these elements. The relationships with the world that surrounds us, the encounters, domination, and authority produced every day are things that we do not typically notice under normal temporal conditions. Dumb Type deploys a sophisticated program of images, sounds, and other sensorial elements in spatial installations that function as scenographies, disrupting our daily routines with their minimalist repetitions, their shocks, and their unplanned suddenness. In *pH* (1990), the entire space is nothing but a gigantic photocopier that scans the bodies of the performers. For *OR* (1997), which deals with that which lies in between life and death in a space of electronic sounds and blinding white light, the perception of this border and the awakening of one's consciousness leads us towards a knowledge of this relationship. The discrepancies and lags, the contradictions, the fragility of these bodies of flesh and blood that belong to the performers are exposed by the machines and the digital space. This work marked the emergence of a radical mode of expression that explores the relationship between machine and body at the level of perception and consciousness.

YMO are the pioneers of techno-pop. Through the use of new technologies like synthesizers and computers, they took the exotic Asian musicality that Haruomi Hosono had previously explored in a different direction, bringing it to a new level. Their minimalist non-physicality and sense of disembodied cleanness represented a departure from the anti-authoritarian passion and enthusiasm of the 60s — a kind of rite of passage with the objective of resetting our relationship to the body.

Listeners of techno-pop music give themselves over to the rhythm in a space filled with undulations of sound, without ever touching each other. Through the phenomenon of resonance, each individual self experiences a sophisticated sort of kinship or empathy, in a moment of communion. This intermediate state that is neither white nor black — "yellow" culture — is a minimal and anti-expressionist format in which the intensity of emotions is modulated. The non-physicality of the YMO musicians lacks the stiffness of Kraftwerk: it is in fact soft and organic. Their physical sensibilities are mysterious and tender, harmoniously fusing the boundaries between computer and body, digital and physical, as if the nerves were naturally connected to cables, not muscles. This phenomenon anticipated the pliable, uniquely Japanese sense of a "commons" that exists between the digital and the human.

The futuristic post-human of the 2010s that exists somewhere in between the digital and the physical: the musical group Perfume emerges, as a form of mediatized corporeality. The gentle images of these bodies mingle freely in the space of reality, in the form of a digital mosaic. This is a visual experience where the digital, physicality, and materiality meld with each other in a fluid manner. The words of the Rhizomatiks artist and programmer Daito Manabe, who is in charge of the visual design of Perfume, call to mind Derrick de Kerckhove's argument that "the bodies at the center of the performance are not a display: they are interfaces between external data and internal data (memories, sensations)."

Pop Art: Before/After the 1980s

Pop Art is created by integrating the local culture and vernacular elements through modernist modes of expression, and a process of compromise and transformation, thereby serving to recuperate values that have been neglected or abandoned by the principal currents of modernism. Accordingly, it plays an essential role in the formation of alternative, local modernisms. In Japan, the diversity and dynamism of Pop Art is linked to the richness of its pre-modern culture and various subcultures. During the 1960s, Japanese Pop Art, born under the influence of American Pop and its critique of consumer society and mass culture, incorporated within itself popular images and expanded its scope by conveying political messages, or those related to the underground culture. With advancing informatization during the 80s, Japan saw the emergence of an eclectic Pop Art through a diversification of media and the maturity attained by manga, illustration, and "Parco culture" (an approach to mixing high and low culture pioneered by the department store of the same name). The 90s were the period of a strategic Neo-Pop Art that unfolded alongside the development of the otaku phenomenon, while the 2000s saw the addition of personal imagery and videos that had become more ubiquitous and easily circulable thanks to social media to the array of Pop motifs.

1.

Graphic design and Pop

In Japan, the "subculture" remained conscious of the "high culture" that came before while seeking to deviate from it. This subculture expanded greatly during a period that began in the late 60s, and was different from the "counterculture" of the 80s that opposed the culture preceding it. There was a tendency for graphic designers to expand the scope of their practice by being influenced by art. Tadanori Yokoo and Shinro Ohtake were greatly inspired by Andy Warhol. These artists discovered anew the possibilities of graphic design at another level, in terms of aesthetics and sociality.

Yokoo was active as a graphic designer starting in the 1960s, creating polished compositions that made deft use of blank space while also drawing on kitsch, vernacular imagery. During the 70s, he produced posters for the likes of the underground theater of Juro Kara, Shuji Terayama, and Tatsumi Hijikata. By the 80s, Yokoo had become one of the central figures in any discussion of Japanese Pop, with his deep connections to Issey Miyake and the formation of YMO. His erotic, irreverent imagery also contained elements of humor and irony that reflected an undercurrent of emotion and his authorial imprint.

Through their "Touristic Art Theory,"[4] formulated together with Hiroshi Nakamura, Tiger Tateishi (who became a manga artist in the late 60s) sought to create a sense of visual shock by fusing surrealism with hyperrealism. This visual shock also manifested itself in the montages of graphic designer Tsunehisa Kimura in the 70s, in the form of allegorical images of urban destruction that also concealed elements of social criticism. For Kimura, montage might be said to be an exercise in simulationism. "By emphasizing the similarities between fiction and reality, my photomontages subjectively reconfigure the situation of our uncertain, autistic era of obstructed visibility by taking a cue from another totality (reality)."[5]

The 80s unfolded in a context where design and high art were seen to be of equal value. Katsuhiko Hibino followed in the footsteps of a style of illustration that represented the links between art and consumer culture — what was known as "Parco culture," orchestrated by the Seibu group. Hibino's collages, which combined the simple, unassuming material of cardboard in a refined, tactile manner, reflected the spirit of the times with their light, frivolous imagery and physicality. The image of a woman at the cutting edge of her times, who supplemented beauty with an almost cyborg strength, was created by Harumi Yamaguchi and Eiko Ishioka as the heroine of this consumer culture. This gave the sensation, "absurd but full of freshness (Kyoko Okazaki),"[6] of being able to put something academic into a shopping bag and take it home with you. While the idea that information was more fascinating than material objects stemmed from a joyous frivolity at a superficial level, it served to reset the hierarchies associated with all manner of existing values.

The manga and anime of the 1990s revealed much about the state of society. Some of the leading manga artists were Katsuhiro Otomo, creator of the *Akira* manga and animated films that portray a dystopian universe, and Kyoko Okazaki, who led the sensibilities of an era with her depictions of the lives of young people with an uncertain future. In terms of the high quality of their concepts and artwork, artists like Otomo and Okazaki might be said to have carved out a position somewhere in between visual art and literature. It was the Neo-Pop movement that directed this sense of existential doubt towards a recovery of one's own identity through art and its motifs. Artists like Takashi Murakami and Makoto Aida strategically deployed traditional Japanese painting techniques and subcultural images as Neo-Pop, offering an ambivalent commentary on politics and consumer society.

An archipelago of six concepts | Yuko Hasegawa

Elsewhere, Kenji Yanobe's work served as a warning against dystopian states.

Murakami is critical of the spirit of Japan in the postwar era and the shifts that society has undergone. He has sought to locate his own identity in manga and anime characters through this process of criticism. Underlying this attempt is an observation and critique of the social phenomenon of otaku. The otakus, who appeared in the second half of the 1970s, engaged in an extreme accumulation of information related to subcultures like anime or sci-fi that were considered "cultures particular to Japan" while also sharpening their critical faculties, to the exclusion of everything that lay outside the orbit of their interests. Although these otaku, with their autistic bent and biased, one-sided pursuits, originally comprised a minority in Japanese society, they emerged as a major force during the 90s. Greedily discovering the objects (worlds) that engaged them in all manner of media ranging from games and the internet to idols, they sought out conscious exchanges along with their desires, and eventually created intense fantasies resembling some sort of hypertrophied narcissism mediated by these objects.

Beginning with Mr. DOB, a kind of Japanized Mickey Mouse character, Murakami created an entire panoply of characters ranging from organisms that transform into amoeba-like forms with countless eyes to smiling cosmoses. These characters, which constitute a new visual language, are little phantasmagoric monsters, equal parts cute and macaber. They spread throughout the world not just through his paintings, but also his designs for Louis Vuitton. Invoking the refined compositional sensibility of the pre-modern Rinpa school of painting, which conveys a profound sense of depth and expansiveness even while it remains two-dimensional, Murakami uses this as a backdrop for his vividly colored characters. This primitive brand of animism that seeks out the soul in all things that inhabit the natural world, as well as pictorial compositions charged with velocity and imbued with multiple, moving perspective points, gave these paintings a dynamism and freshness, just as if they had been put under the spell of Pop. In these paintings, a strange pathological sensibility coexists with a contrasting bottomless, gaudy optimism — a seeming reflection of the complexity of the Japanese reality in the 2000s. In the same manner, Makoto Aida is sharply critical of the state of postwar politics and society. Even as Aida appropriates contemporary imagery, he explored the fundamental origins of sex and life through a mode of expression that tended towards the humorous and grotesque.

This brand of pathological Eros and artistic expression that offers both emotional and visual stimulation is aligned with the reassessment of Yayoi Kusama's work since the 1990s. Kusama covered furniture and the surfaces of boats with floppy phalluses, and blanketed the entire surfaces of bodies and interiors with polka dots. Contaminated by these dots, these objects suddenly take on another kind of life. Viewed up close, these polka dot paintings cause space to expand and contract. Viewers are ushered into a space of infinity: an accumulation of microcosmoses that make up a single entity, none of which are identical to any other. Kusama's vision of "self-obliteration," in which one's own body becomes scattered across the world in the form of polka dots, is also the curse of an exorcism that dispels the uncertainties and anxieties of existence. Works by female artists coming in the wake of Kusama emerged as critiques of patriarchal society and the Japanese surveillance society that were both personal and candid. Tabaimo's works draw on the style of the underground culture of the 70s, conflating both a criticism of surveillance society and the women who are controlled within it, as well as a sense of inward-looking passion and sentiment. Miwa Yanagi fights back against the standards that govern social values stipulating that women must be young and beautiful, sometimes offering us a set of alternative criteria through her sci-fi narratives. Aya Takano articulates a vision of a free spiritual and psychological world that entails a breaking away from this world, including a liberation from Eros.

Behind the cute exterior of their Pop Art are strong messages. In the realm of Japanese contemporary art, it is this Pop Art that has the strongest political charge, and which can tackle issues related to identity and the psychological state of society in various forms.

C Island

Collaboration/Participation/Sharing

The Japanese character, which privileges symbiosis and relationships with others, can be understood in terms of a consistent thread that brings together participatory and collaborative modes of creative expression. In the 1960s, Fluxus encouraged the participation of the public, which was linked to the participatory and collaborative projects that emerged in Japan during the late 90s in response to the relational aesthetics that had become a global movement. In the wake of the Great East Japan Earthquake of 2011, a diverse array of collaborative, socially oriented creative practices by artists and creators unfolded in Japan.

1.

Participatory Art

Fluxus was an international artistic movement that was critical of conventional ideas of authorship (centered on the notion of the author), declaring in no uncertain terms that the involvement of others was necessary to the act of creating an artwork. It had a preference for cheap materials, seeking to reconfigure everyday actions through the implication of an improvised, natural occurrence. Fluxus artists made an effort to open up the consciousness of the audience to the inherent richness of human existence. Japanese artists like Yoko Ono and Mieko Shiomi, each with their own methods, developed elements of affirmation that liberated the imagination of the other, instead of engaging in the anti-Art criticism of European and American artists. Fluxus rejected expressionism and self-expression: it was an attempt to demolish the barriers between the artist and the general public by remaining simple and objective, through the participation and collaboration of the audience. According to Shiomi, the movement was unique for its ludic, game-like aspect, and its jokes and humor.

Yoko Ono produced a conceptual art that sought to make us conscious of the everyday, eliciting the involvement of the audience through a dematerialization of the medium and the use of poetic metaphors. In a sense, her practice consisted of experiments in bringing the act of philosophical inquiry down to the level of the everyday. In this she was greatly influenced by Zen thinking, with its *koan* riddles that leave open the answer to a particular question, and the way in which it viewed daily life itself as a succession of opportunities for the philosophical practice of each moment of one's existence. For Ono, performance was a way of training the gaze of the audience on their own inner selves and encouraging critical thought. It also held the potential to bring about change in society, through actions and behavior that were linked to the act of thinking. Ono's *Instructions*, which she started in 1961, are musical scores made up of words that create artworks when accompanied by certain gestures performed by others. *Mend Piece for John* (1966/1968), which combines fragments of a broken cup with adhesive, is based on the concept of mending and restoration.

Mieko Shiomi's *Events and Games* (1964) is a compilation of sorts of these kinds of instructions to others, akin to a musical score. Like some scientific experiment or sport, Shiomi's instructions are a simple means of eliciting an actual experience from the participant. The circumstances and actions that she chooses, although seemingly simple, have been delicately and thoughtfully considered: there is a sense of expectation of the unknown, of landscapes that we might encounter in actual, real places. The "musicality" of Shiomi stems from the sense of a pliable, gentle co-creation with the environment and the cosmos — orchestrating a melody through various actions in accordance with all-encompassing rhythms and orders, such as gravity or natural forces like the wind and waves. Although Shiomi also works with instructions, there is a certain concrete quality to her work: it is liberated, while maintaining a profound connection to the body, as opposed to the conceptualism of Ono's work that is also influenced by the contemporary art context. In this sense, *Spatial Poem Project* might be said to have prefigured the era of global networks. The gentle conceptualism that places the everyday at the core of our consciousness and methods of eliciting the involvement of the audience have greatly influenced Japanese artists since the 1970s.

2.
Collaboration

During the second half of the 1960s, the term "happening" came into common use to refer to an action or event that exceeded one's expectations, and not just in the realm of art. The Japanese, with their penchant for festivals and events, were predisposed to embrace these happenings, which entailed a sense of spectacle that often functioned to produce a sense of alienation within the everyday. The Play (1967-1999) was a collective of volunteers who attempted to stage happenings that involved the sharing of experiences. It consisted of a fluid lineup of members centering on Keiichi Ikemizu, and solicited participants for each action. While these actions appeared to be innocuous, everyday ideas, they privileged the fact that they were carried out continuously by being anchored in daily experience, akin to the work of a farmer. *Current of Contemporary Art*, where members of The Play traveled down the Yodogawa River on a white, arrow-shaped styrofoam raft, was seen as a happening. Its combination of game-like and surprise elements, however, which permeate the realm of everyday human life and cultivate one's consciousness, was highly aware of itself as a form of art. *Thunder*, on the other hand, was a project where the group built a triangular conical tower at the top of a mountain, attached a lightning rod to it, and waited for the natural phenomenon of thunder to occur. These collaborations, in terms of how they share a sense of loose and languid time, and actions that bring about a displacement of the everyday, can also be found in the work of the artistic collective wah document (2006-). Through workshops, wah document produces "project proposals" based on the wishes of all its members, seeking to share a sense of shock and surprise that deviates from the everyday.

3.
The Sharing of Experiences with Others

Koki Tanaka inherits the spirit of Fluxus and Dada. His methodology consists in staging "haiku-esque" actions in relation to the environment, assembling documentary materials that have caused a transformation as a result of these acts, and exhibiting them as videos or objects. Around the year 2011, in response to the theme of how to share in the experience of others, Tanaka made five pianists working in different idioms such as classical or jazz play the same song, or had several poets or potters work collaboratively on a single piece in experimental constructive performances that he would then film in a documentary manner. The result was one possible answer to the problem of sharing the experience of others, such as the victims of earthquakes and terrorism, and a sense of first-person involvement in these events. By revealing the process of collaborative labor and creation, Tanaka develops in the audience a capacity to imagine the psychological workings of the other. His

An archipelago of six concepts | Yuko Hasegawa

video installations, which also exhibit the results of this collaborative work and the documentation of this labor, are composed with a deftly formalist touch, in the form of a space that generates a magnetic field forged out of empathy.

Ever since the Great East Japan Earthquake, there has been a lively growth in activist and socially engaged art. In particular, the question of what art could do in the disaster zones was repeatedly posed. The video artist Hikaru Fujii shot documentary footage of what artists were doing onsite in the areas affected by the events of March 11, 2011 ("3.11"). According to Fujii, the only thing that artists could do was to transform what had passed into an artwork, each according to his or her own perspective, in order to ensure that these events would not be forgotten. These words evoke the fundamental role of the visual artist: to live an experience, document it, and share emotions and sensibilities. The 3.11 catastrophe also played a catalyzing role in terms of how architects and other creators sought to encourage the spontaneous generation of ideas among participants. Home-for-All was a project led by Toyo Ito, which involved the construction of a building that served as a meeting place by taking into account the feedback from local residents. Another example is Atelier Bow-Wow, which realized innovative, metaphorical proposals through collaboratively produced drawings of the reconstruction plans in the quake-stricken zones.

_____4.
The Borders between Public and Private

The architecture firm SANAA proposes a critical and novel method for the creation of shared spaces. Their concept of a public and private, which link to each other in a soft and gentle rather than fragmentary fashion, seems to have manifested itself in a critical program that seeks to remedy the figure of a hypertrophied self resulting from the affirmation of individual liberties, the attenuation of our relationship to the community and the public, as well as the accompanying sense of responsibility to these constituencies. A light architecture is, in the sense of Gilles Deleuze, nomadic and private. The complexity and sense of presence of SANAA's architecture, which appears light and simple at first glance, are in fact the result of this process of programmatic materialization. This program leads to the construction of an architecture through a performative process, during which the wishes and conditions of the clients, performativity, and the environment are studied and reinterpreted in the form of successive models and plans. This discipline imposed on the users allows them to situate the notion of sharing and coexistence at the center of our consciousness, all the while maintaining a sense of individual space — such is the function of SANAA in terms of eliciting the latent potential of the user. The same can be said of the principle of flexibility that consists in leaving decisions about how something is used to the user. One of SANAA's representative works is the 21st Century Museum of Contemporary Art in Kanazawa, which was built according to a concept that I proposed as museum curator: the transition from the 3 Ms (Man, Money, Materialism) to the 3 Cs (Coexistence, Collective Intelligence, Consciousness), symbolizing the shift from the 20th to the 21st century. Within this circular structure enveloped in transparent glass, uniquely designed exhibition halls have been scattered and dispersed like islands. The design of galleries that communicate visually with common spaces is a critique of modernism. At the same time, this is also one solution to the problem of the "open museum."

All of the works in this third island entail a wide diversity in terms of how they elicit the participation of the other (the spectator), a deft openness that involves giving oneself over to the imagination of the other, flexibility, physicality, and an expressive performativity. These characteristics express themselves at various levels in the form of instructions, collaborative labor, actions, space, and the programming of actions in this space.

D Island

Poetics of Resistance

Kawaii (cute), one of the terms characterizing Japanese visual culture that has gained the most traction both within Japan and abroad, is equally linked to the criticism of Japanese contemporary art as anti-social. This fourth island will seek to make a careful study and exploration of the different connotations — small, vulnerable, infantile, pure, innocent, poetic — attached to the notion of *kawaii*, thereby revealing the unique brand of politics that underlines this mode of expression. This politics consists not of directly political messages, but rather allegories and metaphors that emanate from a surrealist, fantastic, naive, or poetic universe. One of the roots of this sensibility can be traced to the poetic surrealism of Harue Koga, a painter who was influenced by the European avant-garde of the 1920s. The expressions that issue forth from subjects treated by artists like Yoshitomo Nara starting in the 1990s also draw on this politics, which functions as a kind of poetic resistance. Going further, it also denotes an original Japanese conceptualism that can be seen in the realms of anime, architecture, and fashion.

With his lone child and animal characters — symbols of immaturity or innocence — depicted like icons against plain backgrounds, Yoshitomo Nara represents this form of criticism, even of resistance, against reality, with *kawaii* as a backdrop. His adorable children who refuse to become adults stare glumly at us, as a protest against the absurdity of the world. The vulnerability of childhood, joined to its paradoxical strength, also functions as an icon or amulet that keeps evil or demons at bay. This paradox can also be seen in Harue Koga, who sought to pursue both intellectualism and poetry while also being influenced by the avant-garde. Koga, who was both the son of a Buddhist priest and a poet, produced paintings that Yasunari

Kawabata saw as "resonating with the chanting of a childhood impregnated with Buddhism." Here was a vision of a void that was resigned to reality, as well as an affirmation of the joy of life that transcended this void, found in his paintings of children. The painting *Sea* (1929) illustrates the internal conflict of the artist between these two extremes. This montage, combining a diverse range of modern motifs — an airship, a factory, a woman in a bathing suit — that seem very surrealist at first glance, are in fact suffused with a thoroughly realist spirit that scrutinizes the times.

This resistance can also be interiorized. As a means of resisting the ambiguous, floating everyday of the 2000s, a period of uncertainty where reality cannot be seized, Zon Ito combines memory and reverie in a fluid fashion, seeking to give them a fixed form through the physical, handcrafted method of embroidery. In other words, he makes unstable sensations tangible in a critical manner, which, in his own words, "express an invisible, interior space." The architect Junya Ishigami, who conceives of architecture not as a "box" that encloses the human, but as the very environment that surrounds us, enlarges this notion to a point where it surpasses reality. For Ishigami, architectural creation is at the service of the "production of space" (Henri Lefebvre): he subjects the entire environment to a fluctuating relationship in which all things interact with each other. His installation *Balloon* (2007) is a one-ton silver structure on the same scale as a four-storey building measuring sixteen meters tall that floats softly in midair due to the helium gas inside it. This floating, slowly rotating "architecture" modifies the spatial consciousness of visitors, serving as a humorous critique of the notion of architecture itself.

Vernacular and primitive elements are a source of pure poetry. Koji Nakazono's violently meshed images capture the feeling of a clear and present crisis, containing within them a pure "voice" (poetry) that senses and responds to it. Nakazono depicts the sense of rupture and disconnection with reality of the cloud generation, which has grown up in an environment of digital information and the Internet, and their anxiety about an uncertain future, in the form of an ecology of strange, cute, and caricatured tribes living in the forest. The primitive rituals and behaviors, the images that seem to desire to merge with the forests and lakes, and the ghostly figures that cover the pictorial surface in multiple layers can be read as an allegory of a dark ecology. The problem of American military bases still persists in Okinawa today. The work *You-I You-I* by Yuken Teruya, an artist originally from Okinawa, where the issue of American military bases is more current than ever before, is a kimono created through the traditional *bingata* technique of resist-dyeing. The vibrant flower and tree patterns on this kimono transform halfway into fighter planes and parachutes. The result is a quiet but hard-edged lyricism with local motifs. Fuyuki Yamakawa learned the fundamental and primitive poetry of sound through his training in *khoomii*, a traditional Mongolian art of throat singing. By layering the recorded voice of his father, who was a newscaster, onto his own, Yamakawa also superimposes a personal space-time onto the global situation over a period of thirty years. Resonating within the space of the gallery is a kind of dissonance that combines the voice of a newscaster reporting about the war and that of an innocent child.

In Japan, it is the entertainers or comedians like Beat Takeshi (Takeshi Kitano) who often stage the most acerbic, irony-ridden, and unerringly accurate political or socially critical performances. Chim↑Pom's performances are at once comical and journalistic. On display here is the video work *Super Rat*, where we see members of Chim↑Pom running around Shibuya next to huge taxidermied rats, in an orgy of trying to capture the surviving rats, who seem to be sneering at the alleged clean-up of the city. Even with their elevated level of social consciousness, evinced by their actions that are committed to places like Hiroshima and the 3.11 quake-stricken zones, Chim↑Pom also create new narratives that exert an influence on the notion of community or society through the medium of entertainment. Shimabuku and Tsuyoshi Ozawa cause a displacement of the everyday, or dissociate themselves from it completely through the act of travelling or intervening into a particular situation, thereby bringing a new and refreshing point of view to life. Their "powerless looseness" in fact conceals a strong, vigorous critique.

E Island
Soft, Floating Subjectivity/Private Documentary

The unique notion of the private subject in Japan that originates from the literary genre of the I-novel (*shishosetsu*, a kind of autobiographical novel from the early 20th century), while existing at the level of the intimate, also attains a kind of universal dimension, thanks to a powerful centripetal force and a specific mode of interior contemplation. The mental climate of this country, where the demarcation between interior and exterior, individual and society, and self and other is fluid, tends to weaken "expressions" of the self and annihilate the distance from the self, which is necessary for the process of relativization. If there seems to be a large number of photographers and cinematographers among Japanese artists, this is undoubtedly because the camera automatically confers a distance that allows them, by subjectively becoming one with it, to project emotions and sensations while simultaneously facilitating a process of "objectification" that captures this in a mechanical way. Their subjectivity, while centripetal, seems to have a floating center that oscillates endlessly. An unbroken line links successive movements since Daido Moriyama, who, at the end of the 1960s, questioned the notion of documentary photography and promoted a personal photography through a shift from "objective recording" to "subjective memory." This was followed by the 1990s of Takashi Homma, who highlighted the reality of his subjects through a neutral gaze trained on personal, everyday scenes. The 2000s saw the emergence of Rinko Kawauchi and a cosmology that was sensitive to life, drawn from minuscule fragments of the everyday, before finally leading to the current tendency towards personal documentary in the wake of 3.11.

In Japan, even if one is continuously exposed to uncertainty, these works present an "I" that refuses to be assimilated into the group, as well as a documentation of private life. The formation of a self-consciousness, reconstructed after the war, reached a peak and an important benchmark in 1968, when Takuma Nakahira and Daido Moriyama, creators of the magazine *Provoke* that gave birth to the movement of the same name, declared that they would abandon realism. This group of photographers, who became one with their cameras, suppressed all symbolic meaning associated with what lay before their eyes. They developed an aesthetic known as *are, bure, boke* — *are* referring to a rough, granular texture, *bure* the contours of the subject within a frame that was abruptly tilted, and *boke* the state of being out of focus. The images that they took were a precise document of a period plagued by uncertainty and anxiety, which they confronted with their own corporeality and sense of tactile sensation. With no connection to the artistic or informative value of their subjects, the private photographer par excellence (Moriyama) roamed the streets, propelled by some interior force, "taking photos that were ultimately directed at the self, never in the service of some apparent objective." Starting in the 60s and 70s, photography books assumed a major significance in terms of the formats that their own artworks could take. Photographs were not considered in terms of individual pieces, but rather as part of a graphic ensemble: they were ideally suited to expressing the "private" memories and worldview of the photographer. The photo books of Takuma Nakahira are an expression of a dynamic psychological landscape, even as they are riddled with uncertainty. Here, a sense of an intimately private experience and time unfolds: individual memory in the context of one's own identity, as well as society and history.

The term "private photography" also calls to mind the sort of photography that captures the sensation of life and death inherent in the subject in a raw, unvarnished manner, reminiscent of the pornography of Nobuyoshi Araki. Araki began to take these consummately intimate photos as a reaction against the profusion of imagery in a consumer society, while he was working for a major advertising agency. The apparent lightness and impact of Araki's work, which continuously revealed everything from his own everyday existence to the world of prostitution, sex, and bondage from an extremely intimate perspective, distinguished itself as a kind of ontological narrative. Araki himself states that he had abandoned both "criticism" and "expression" at the time. "The act of pressing the shutter is to kill the model, to put it in a state of apparent death. To show the photo is to bring it back to life at one stroke." Araki keeps pressing the shutter as if he were breathing, in order to create a link: he shoots as if he were "activating" the events and people that surround him through his own body. The majority of the women who serve as his subjects feel a close empathy with him and generously offer up their time, thereby creating a relationship of mutual communication that is never voyeuristic. It is precisely the profundity of this relationship to the other that makes Araki's photos not merely "images," but rather organisms of a sort that brim with vitality.

After the collapse of the bubble economy in the 1990s, the ontological question of the confrontation of the self against the world evolved towards a more homogeneous and equal relationship between the two. The photographs of Takashi Homma were transparent and life-sized in scale: they captured the "new world" of the suburbs that had been abandoned by history, as well as the expressionless faces of the children who grew up there in a neutral, unaffected manner, demonstrating a personal point of view that permeated the world. Despite their transparency, Homma's photos also possess a certain opacity that stems from their troubled, ambiguous atmosphere. In his photo book *Tokyo Suburbia*, Homma illustrates the suburban phenomenon as one that is ahistorical, devoid of all context or meaning. The flatness unique to Japan, which has neither marked class difference nor racial conflict, renders these places perfectly devoid of meaning. Through the indecipherable eyes on the expressionless faces of these children born and raised in the suburbs, it seems as if they understand everything about us, while simultaneously rejecting all our attempts to understand them — exactly how we would imagine aliens to be. Homma's photographs, however, earnestly depict them in all their presence, as living, human beings. These deep-focus, brightly lit photos of suburban landscapes that resemble sets, give the impression of "how extremely complex reality is, and how it gives birth to strange things." For Homma, nothing is absolute. His neutral gaze, detached from any specific ideology, is supported by a powerfully critical mind that seeks to eviscerate the reality before his eyes of all meaning. This is why his photos allow themselves to remain open to the free interpretation of the viewer.

The 90s were also a period of experimentation where female photographers sought to construct an ahistorical perspective directed at reality through frank and candid exchanges with their subjects — a tendency that was linked to a sense of spiritual survival. Examples of artists who worked in this mode are Yurie Nagashima, who shot nudes of her own family members as well as herself, and Tomoko Yoneda, who "personalized" sites of historical significance with her own private perspective in order to link them to the present. Continuing in this vein, Rinko Kawauchi began to publish, starting in the 2000s, many photo books containing photos brimming with an interior energy that expressed a sense of the cosmology of life in minuscule, everyday fragments. Her book *Illuminance*, which focused on the compelling personal relationship that she had with light, begins with an eclipse. Amid a sense of vague symbolism, which avoids any specificity with regard to either people or places, Kawauchi makes visible through a chain of photographic images the passage of time, and flows of light. Within this rhythm, she "allows us to feel a distance that does not think of itself in terms of time, and even a sense of excitement, fear, and solemnity that comes from ancient times."[7] Kawauchi captures "instants of beauty" that anyone can feel, even in an era of social media, and posts them on Instagram, thereby sharing a sensibility that exists outside of language. Her works constantly evoke these moments of joy in the viewer. By intentionally producing images that resemble those of advertising — the instantaneous splashing of water spilled onto flowers, for example — Kawauchi dismantles the clichés of this sort of commercial photography, while also restoring the joy of perception contaminated by an information-saturated environment to its original settings, as it were. The essence of these images lies in how they are pure documents that have not been processed in any way. Kawauchi evinces a vague sense of awe at the size and uncertainty of the world around us, and the tension of having no choice but to "be" there enhances the resolution of these "documents." In this way, her works are connected to a sensation of extraordinary distance, and of sublimation.

The 3.11 quake confronted photographers once again with the question of what it means to document or archive something. Naoya Hatakeyama, who lost his family in the disaster, depicts scenery from the quake-stricken regions as "amputated landscapes" while maintaining a certain romantic, apocalyptic style that is unique to him. Lieko Shiga, who lived together with the inhabitants of a village as a community photographer before the disaster, creates performative montages structured by multiple exposures that encompass the before and after of the catastrophe. These images are strongly rooted in the local, where she projects the emotions and state of mind of people onto scenes that lie somewhere between the everyday and the extraordinary, which are also a reflection of her own psychological state. As it is impossible to convey an objective sense of the truth of reality, these artists seek to describe their mental states in the broad sense of a self-documentary. This is nothing other than an act of "remembering" to ensure that one does not forget this particular event from their own perspective.

The director Tetsuaki Matsue shows the acts and behavior of individuals on screen, from a point of view that is radically subjective. The technique of self-documentary permits him to highlight certain truths by creating a fictitious setting that comes from his own view of reality. "No matter how negative the situation may be, the act of filming it makes it positive" (Matsue). His film *Tokyo Drifter*, with Kenta Maeno in the lead role, is filmed by night in Tokyo, a city plunged into darkness as a result of efforts to save energy and the population's self-imposed restraint on its own consumption. The figure of Maeno, drifting throughout a darkened Tokyo on a bike while singing, is focused not on the reality of the afflicted zones, but rather the question of what kind of memory of the quake he can inscribe in the here and now.

Relationships between Materials, and Reductionism

The Japanese have a direct relationship to material objects (*mono*), seeing them just as they are. By doing away with authorial intention or representation, making these objects speak, and constructing a relationship between them, these objects are reduced to their own essence. The fact that Zen met with an extreme level of reductionism in Japan after having passed through India and China is perhaps the result of a tendency towards an existentialism dependent on both reality and the power of abstraction. This sixth island will attempt to demonstrate this fact, through Mono-ha and a diverse range of Minimalist expressions. Notions of time and space are intimately linked with the relational theory of things. While the concept of *ma* is specific and unique to Japan, it is fused to and integrated with notions of time and space. Space is perceived through the events that occur within it: in turn, this space can only be understood in terms of time.

Like Arte Povera, the Mono-ha of the 1970s took its cue from the contemporary tendency to move away from the subject and towards the material, and the external world. Mono-ha also represented a re-questioning of subject-centrism and notions of perception. The aesthetics associated with *ma* exercised a profound influence on works that sought to give a visual or material form to time. Hitoshi Nomura and Hiroshi Sugimoto, for instance, expressed the profundity and intensity of their perception through Minimalist techniques such as difference and repetition. The *Date Paintings* of On Kawara and digital counters of Tatsuo Miyajima highlight the simultaneity of time and its constant change, as well as the Buddhist vision of life and death. Ryoji Ikeda reduces a wide range of elements to digital signals in order to reconstruct the relationships between them, converting big data into a different kind of space-time. For many artists, reduction is a powerful tool for elevating themes of time, space, and the cosmos to a metaphysical level.

Each Mono-ha artist adopted particular approaches and techniques to verify the relationships between objects and the external world. Kishio Suga arranges raw, minimally processed materials, ties them together, or induces a transformation in them with his own hands, revealing the mutual interdependence and pre-existing relationships between things while establishing an intimate relationship to the body. Suga's work is rooted in both Buddhist philosophy and the ecological theory of perception of James Gibson. In his early works, Koji Enokura projected his own body onto the objective world, expressing the relationship between objects and exterior space by allowing oil stains to infiltrate raw canvas, thereby creating border zones of "infiltration."

Hitoshi Nomura and Hiroshi Sugimoto are emblematic artists who, as a reaction against the consumption of images and the increasing shallowness of our perception, seek to move towards a more metaphorical dimension through a mode of observation where the subject has been removed. Nomura uses fixed-point observation photography to trace the movements of the moon and put them into frames that include five lines printed on them in advance, like a musical score. The incidental disparities that vary from one frame to another "subjectivize" the movements of celestial bodies that are an astronomical necessity. Sugimoto, for his part, produces anonymous images divided into black and white parts by shooting long exposures of the maritime horizon in different times and places — an act that reveals the world, instead of defining it. Life is born of the ocean: beginning with this foundational metaphor, Sugimoto seeks to understand this ocean that represents both an originary landscape as well as an infinite future.

Observation and contemplation bring us a more clairvoyant understanding of time and space. Kawara produced his *Date Paintings* as a neutral, indifferent act, through a sort of interior contemplation akin to the observation of time. The fixed observation of time as *chronos* and the consciousness of its coexistence with an existential time — *kairos* — is made possible by the Buddhist state of renunciation, which consists in living each moment with death as a given premise: in other words, to perceive eternity in the moment. It is precisely this conception of time that allows the spectator to become conscious of a simultaneity, an existential synchronicity with these painted dates, and to "relive" this time. The chain reactions of the digits (excluding "0") in Tatsuo Miyajima's flickering digital counters offer us a spatial demonstration of an Oriental notion of time that recurs in a cyclical manner while changing constantly. Change, relationality, and perpetual movement are the presiding factors in a succession of present moments of life, while an infinite number of births and deaths repeat themselves endlessly.

Ryoji Ikeda, for his part, treats different material elements that have been reduced to a minimum as equivalent, arranging them in another space-time. Influenced by the concept of the infinite, he combines diverse elements in order to observe the relationships that emerge between them. *Datamatics* is premised on the idea of a void, or nothingness: it brings into being a cloud of pure stimuli that plays on randomness, intensity, and perception, thereby promoting a fusion between materiality and information. In Kohei Nawa's *Force*, silicon oil possesses a semi-solid materiality, cascading vertically downwards like water without either splashing or making a sound. Placed at the end of the *Japanorama* exhibition, *Force* unites and symbolizes the various elements that unfold over the six islands, thanks to its bizarre materiality that throws our body and perception into disarray, the minimalism of its structure, and its level of abstraction that remains open to many interpretations. *Force* was the torrent of black rain that fell after the atomic bomb fell on Hiroshima, an appropriation of the modernism of Barnett Newman's zip (vertical line), as well as a digital barcode coding a complex program.

Translated from Japanese by Darryl Jingwen Wee

—

Notes

[1] Dark ecology is an environmental concept by the environmental philosopher Timothy Morton. Humans are connected to non-human organisms, and that which surrounds us. We are unable to make judgments about the danger associated with the things around us, even as we might think them hideous, or frightening. Dark ecology advocates a state of intimate coexistence with the "strange stranger" that cannot be pinned down. This bizarre state of coexistence, interwoven with organic matter and bodies that is reminiscent of Tetsumi Kudo's radioactive contamination, also has a connection to contemporary environmental concepts.

[2] Craig Owens, *The Allegorical Impulse: Toward a Theory of Postmodernism*, translated into Japanese by Jun Shindo, Genron 1.3, Genron Inc., 2015-2016.

[3] From a promotional flyer for the S/S 1997 collection of Comme des Garçons.

[4] The *Kanko Geijutsu Kenkyujo* was formed in 1964 by Hiroshi Nakamura and Tiger Tateishi, and was active for about two years until 1966. In contrast to the anti-art and anti-painting trends of the time, Nakamura and Tateishi deliberately stuck to the two-dimensional expressive activity of painting, and pursued various activities centered on the visual "expression" of "seeing" and its intensity, including exhibitions, street performances, TV appearances, and so on.

[5] Tsunehisa Kimura, "The Similarity between Fiction and Reality," *Graphication*, vol. 10 issue 2, 1976, p. 8

[6] Kyoko Okazaki, *Girls' Life on the Battlefield*, Heibonsha, 2015, p. 53 (first appeared in *Bungei*, December 1994, Kawade Shobo Shinsha).

[7] David Chandler, "Weightless Light," *Rinko Kawauchi: Illuminance*, Foil, 2011, p. 152.

Appendix

Yuko Hasegawa

When former Centre Pompidou-Metz director Emma Lavigne asked me to plan this exhibition back in 2015, she told me that the French were interested in Japanese culture, but that two stereotypes dominated: "Zen" and "kawaii." Lavigne wanted me to showcase the diversity of Japanese art and culture that went far beyond these terms. The work of showcasing one's own culture in a different cultural sphere is often a prime opportunity to re-evaluate this culture in a relative light. When trying to extract the key concepts that distinguish contemporary Japanese art, my references were the concepts that often appear in Japanese exhibitions and contemporary art theories from Europe and America — strange bodies, Pop, hyper-subjectivity, symbiosis and coexistence, for example. Using the gaze of the other as a mirror, six concepts (themes) emerged, which were then organized into an "archipelago": a multi-directional constellation that facilitated a process of mutual intervention. I filled this constellation with a diverse array of artistic expressions including fashion, architecture, manga, and music that overflowed from the goblet of these guiding concepts, and extended themselves to the very limit. Even if this exceeds the comprehension of audiences, leaving them confused and almost drowned, the concept of "Pop" will always be on hand to grab onto as a kind of safety buoy.

Even while it is physical and sensuous, this archipelago-like state has also become something to be examined "on its own terms" (Sarah Moroz). The restlessness of these works that "occasionally plays havoc with your mind" (Valérie Duponchelle) can be traced to a certain Japanese peculiarity, a history that has turned this country into an experimental site for nuclear power and capitalist economy, and the distinctiveness of its dense, richly fermented culture stemming from its position as an island nation. The section that attracted the most questions from the exhibition guides at the museum was the one on the thinking that underlies "Politics as Resistance = Kawaii." I still recall speaking about how there was a different intention of resistance behind each artwork, while entrusting the rest to their imagination of the visitors. There were also many among the 100,000 visitors who had come to see the exhibition more than once. Particularly memorable were the remarks of one visitor, who apparently "came again in order to verify what I didn't understand."

Appended below is the article by Sarah Moroz that made the front page of the *New York Times*, as well as Duponchelle's review in *Le Figaro*. I hope readers will find these selected reports of the exhibition useful.

Japaneseart beyond the usual clichés

Sarah Moroz

"Japanorama" picks up where an important 1986 exhibition at the Pompidou Center in Paris, "Avant-Garde Arts of Japan 1910-1970," left off. That show presented some important Japanese artists abroad for the first time — but it examined their work as influenced by, and even dependent on, Western art traditions.

(…)

The subtitle of "Japanorama" is "New Vision on Art Since 1970," the year that Japan began to reassert its own cultural identity, spurred by the new confidence it found at Expo '70 in Osaka. The show is a "discovery of what was overlooked," the curator, Yuko Hasegawa, said. While Japan wrestled with complicated issues of modernization and heritage, its culture was understood in the West through clichéd binaries: The ascetic Zen of a rock garden on one hand, the gleeful kitsch of Hello Kitty on the other.

The exhibition corrects this reductive caricature, examining the way the push and pull between tradition and technology, individual and collective, have shaped the culture in unique ways. For European audiences, what's new about this "New Vision" is examining contemporary Japanese art on its own terms.

(…)

How to prevent flattening cultural context while encouraging foreign audiences to embrace the unfamiliar? Ms. Hasegawa tackles that question in "Japanorama." Having previously presented Japanese contemporary art in Brazil, Britain and Germany, she "looked very carefully at the past 10-15 years: what was organized, what kind of Japanese contemporary art has been collected in public institutions in Europe." She continued: "I want to bring awareness to context behind what people misunderstand, to the social commentary behind the works."

Ms. Hasegawa's vast and thoughtful synopsis encompasses six themes (called "archipelagos") that bridge art, architecture, video, fashion and music. She porously connects movements and multimedia across two floors, with a mise-en-scène conceived by the Tokyo architects SANAA.

(…)

The first section, "Strange Object/Post-Human Body," confronts visitors with "Electric Dress," a multicolored cluster of lights, created in 1956 by Atsuko Tanaka, that prefigures today's evolving relationship between the physical and the digital. The piece resonates with Comme des Garçons garments on display, which present an alternative approach to Western ideas of beauty and body image.

Transfigurations unfurl throughout this section: Ms. Hasegawa notes "traumatic ideas about the atomic bomb and pollution-activated mutation" in two "very weird, very critical" late-1960s cocoon pods by Tetsumi Kudo. New technology informs the work of the '80s collective Dumb Type, the techno-pop musical outfit Yellow Magic Orchestra and the programmers and artists behind Rhizomatiks. Rhizomatiks contributes a visualization of Bitcoin's blockchain system rejigged according to live transactions, in a digital ballet that shows a forward-looking evolution of Japanese creativity.

Within the Pop Art sphere, Ms. Hasegawa has highlighted works with a strong conceptual background and Japanese specificity. She wishes to undercut the way in which Japanese pop culture is often understood as sunny or silly: The graphic kitsch is, in fact, inherently critical, she says. "It's vernacular —but also very sophisticated," she added. Work by the artist Takashi Murakami in this vein is perhaps the most well known, but it is also the most misunderstood. The painted smileys of his "Cosmos" are not just bright and fun — the composition owes everything to 18th-century Edo paintings. His lesser- known "Polyrhythm Red" canvas, adorned with Tamiya soldier figurines, reflects, Ms. Hasegawa said, "Japanese culture becoming childish," and a malaise about violence and vulnerability.

The exhibition also overturns the seeming naïveté of "kawaii," Japan's signature brand of cute, to reveal assertions of sociopolitical frustration. (…)

The exhibition concludes with a section on "Materiality and Minimalism," highlighting examples such as Hiroshi Sugimoto's calm photographs of horizon lines and Ryoji Ikeda's trancelike work based on numerical data. "It's a landing," Ms. Hasegawa said of the exhibition's finale, to "look at something sublime." (…)

The New York Times –International Edition,
Friday, November 3, 2017.

Le Centre Pompidou-Metz rend hommage à l'art japonais
Valérie Duponchelle

Il fallait un bon guide pour introduire le visiteur dans ce Japanorama, vaste kaléidoscope sur la création japonaise contemporaine, de 1970 à nos jours.

Le Centre Pompidou-Metz, qui se met entièrement aux couleurs du Japon cet hiver, a choisi une femme de tête, Yuko Hasegawa, directrice artistique du Museum of Contemporary Art de Tokyo (MOT) et fondatrice du 21st Century Museum of Contemporary Art à Kanazawa. Petit format et volonté de fer, cette intellectuelle avait ébloui les visiteurs de la Biennale de Sharjah au printemps 2013 en transformant une figure imposée - entre censure implicite aux Émirats arabes unis et liberté folle des artistes - en une démonstration sensible, poétique, pleine de sens. Lui revient la tâche de présenter l'Archipel à l'Occident sans tomber dans l'exotisme, les stéréotypes et les contresens.

Comme un long passage de gué

L'artiste allemand Carsten Höller, qui avait mis en scène la collection d'art contemporain japonais de Jean Pigozzi et l'avait confrontée à la scène africaine dans un Japan Congo pionnier au Magasin, à Grenoble, au printemps 2011, avait insisté sur le bouillonnement des formes et des idées, sans donner de clé de lecture. On en sortait intrigué, sans comprendre vraiment ce mouvement ectoplasmique qui naviguait du mignon aux ténèbres, du «kawaii» au butô.

Rien de tel ici, où la scénographie signée SANAA (Prix Pritzker 2010 et agence star de l'architecture japonaise à l'œuvre, du Louvre-Lens à La Samaritaine) met visuellement de l'ordre dans cette odyssée culturelle composée comme une suite d'îlots.
Rompu aux exercices de style, le Centre Pompidou-Metz, que dirige avec foi et pédagogie Emma Lavigne, n'a pas oublié que avait déblayé le terrain en 1986 avec Le Japon des avant-gardes, 1910-1970.

Ce JAPANORAMA qui en est la suite chronologique en a gardé à la fois l'esprit maison - cet art de composer une exposition structurée et claire - et les accents joyeux de fête foraine qu'implique son titre (jusqu'aux costumes déstructurés de Comme des Garçons, exposés ici en «statements» sur une civilisation, ses crites, ses obsessions, ses blessures et ses élans).

Cette leçon de choses venue de l'autre bout du monde entraîne le public de pierre blanche en pierre blanche, comme un long passage de gué, jusqu'à la magique Infinity Mirror Room Fireflies on the Water, 2000, de Yayoi Kusama, 88 ans, star absolue de l'art japonais.

On se souvient du succès de ces installations cosmiques à Beaubourg en 2011 lors de la première rétrospective française consacrée à «la reine des pois». Le Broad Museum de Los Angeles le sait si bien qu'il a limité à trente secondes le temps des selfies et des Instagram dans son petit bout de paradis lumineux.

« Il s'agit d'un État-nation insulaire, marqué par une tradition culturelle de plus de deux mille ans. Le Japon fut parmi les premiers pays d'Asie à se moderniser. » Yuko Hasegawa

«Par certains aspects, le Japon est un pays hautement singulier, prévient Yuko Hasegawa. Il s'agit d'un État-nation insulaire, marqué par une tradition culturelle de plus de deux mille ans. Le Japon fut parmi les premiers pays d'Asie à se moderniser à la fin du XIXe siècle, écrivant sa propre histoire en échappant à la colonisation culturelle, jusqu'à conserver sa langue.»

L'année 1970, point de départ de ce Japanorama , est celle de l'Exposition universelle d'Osaka, Expo '70 , «moment d'apogée du modernisme japonais», et de la 10e Biennale de Tokyo, Biennale '70 - Entre l'homme et la matière , qui accueille nombre d'artistes conceptuels internationaux.

Ce moment est, dit-elle, «le tournant où le pays commence à affirmer son identité culturelle en tant que nation, période de transition où le Japon tente de se libérer de "l'ordre de l'après-guerre", autrement dit de l'influence culturelle occidentale». À Tokyo, dans les années 1980, tant que dure la bulle spéculative, boom technologique et glorification d'une culture japonaise futuriste se mêlent aux souvenirs accablants de la bombe H et des ténèbres qu'elle a ouvertes (la section Japan-ness, consacrée à l'architecture, s'ouvre sur l'énorme photographie, Re-Ruined Hiroshima, 1968, où l'architecte Arata Isozaki redessine en noir l'utopie dans les décombres).

Œuvres parfois dérangeantes

La violence du monde se cache souvent sous des aspects inoffensifs comme des mangas, traditionnels comme l'art du kimono ou du paravent (le néo-pop de Takashi Murakami mêle dans son paravent d'argent, Cosmos, 1998, technique picturale et imagerie traditionnelles et sous-cultures japonaises).

Les artistes traduisent tous les changements de la société dans leurs œuvres, métaphoriques, énigmatiques, parfois très dérangeantes. Le corps

Le Centre Pompidou-Metz rend hommage à l'art japonais | Valérie Duponchelle «post-humain» en est souvent le messager, voire «l'objet étrange», comme en témoignent dès 1959 Denkifuku (Robe électrique) de Tanaka Atsuko, constituée de 86 ampoules couleur, en 1967 Votre portrait chrysalide dans le coconde Tetsumi Kudo ou, en 1996, les vidéos bizarrement belles de Mariko Mori (Miko No Inori).

L'angoisse est vite de retour, du séisme de Kobe le 17 janvier 1995 à l'attaque au gaz sarin par une secte dans le métro de Tokyo, le 20 mars 1995. La dernière œuvre est à ce titre spectaculaire: Force, 2015, de Kohei Nawa, est une pluie noire perpétuelle, code-barres d'un futur menacé par l'homme.

Le Figaro,

November 28, 2017.

© VALERIE DUPONCHELLE

japanorama

1970-2017
galerie 3

20 octobre 2017 –
5 mars 2018

objet étrange - corps post-humain

cultures pop et néo-pop

JAPANORAMA
NEW VISION ON ART SINCE 1970

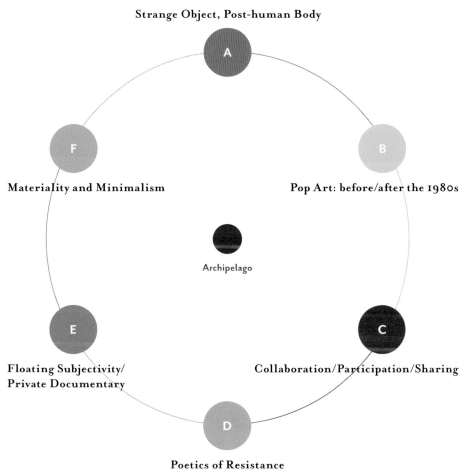

Strange Object, Post-human Body

A

F

Materiality and Minimalism

B

Pop Art: before/after the 1980s

Archipelago

E

Floating Subjectivity/
Private Documentary

C

Collaboration/Participation/Sharing

D

Poetics of Resistance

PLAN GALERIE 3

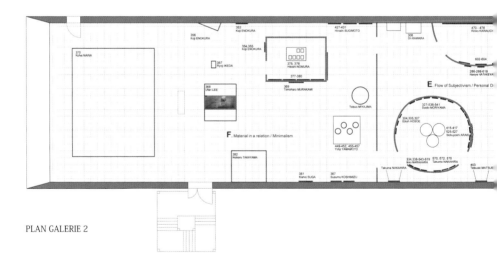

PLAN GALERIE 2

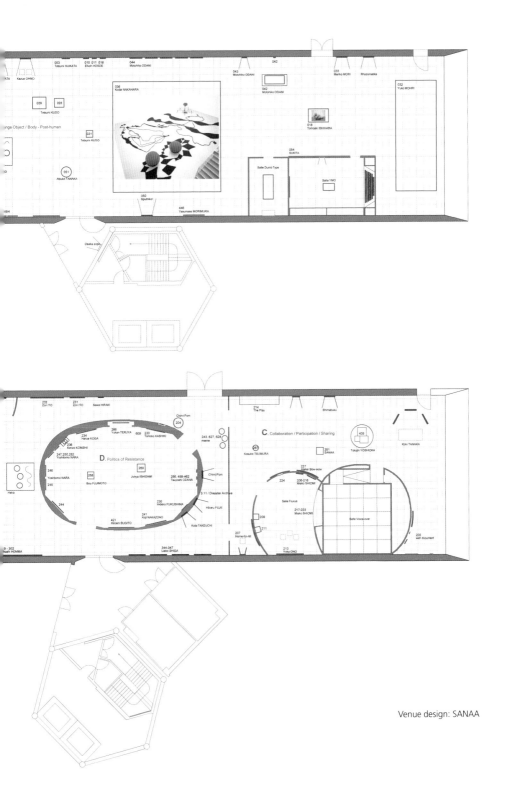

Strange Object, Post-human Body

Genpei AKASEGAWA
Wind, 1963/1985

Comme des Garçons
Comme des Garçons, 1982

Genpei AKASEGAWA (1937-2014)

He was born Katsuhiko Akasegawa. He dropped out of Musashino Art School (now Musashino Art University) and began displaying his work at Nippon Independent and Yomiuri Independent from 1957. In 1960, he went to Tokyo and started as an avant-garde artist, being involved with 'the Neo-Dadaism Organizers' that included Shusaku Arakawa, Ushio Shinohara, and Masunobu Yoshimura among many others. He formed 'Hi-Red Center' with Jiro Takamatsu and Natsuyuki Nakanishi in 1963, and performed many 'Happenings' over the next year. Around the same time, he produced 'Wrapping Art' that wraps the everyday objects in the paper, and began to use copies of 1,000-yen note bills in his work. Most prominent is the 'Model 1,000-Yen Note' series when it became a problem that caused Akasegawa to be indicted for creating imitations of banknotes in 1964. The trial began in 1966, and this '1,000-Yen Note Trial' got attention from both the mass media and the art world. In the court, art critics including Shuzo Takiguchi took the stand in defense, and a variety of avant-garde artworks appeared as evidence. Nevertheless, Akasegawa was found guilty and finally lost the battle in 1970. After that, he branched out

into various fields, for example, cartoons and 'parody journalism'. He also made his debut as a writer in 1978, used the pen name Katsuhiko Otsuji from 1979, and received the Akutagawa Prize in 1981. In 1982, he started the project 'Thomasson', the observation of 'useless but funny roadside oddities' that he had been interested in from the past. In the 1990s, he continued to create original works, such as photographs using Leica, and his bestseller *Rojinryoku* (The Power of the Old). He died in 2014 just before his retrospective exhibition at Chiba City Museum of Art. (K. L.)

Rei KAWAKUBO (1942-)

Rei Kawakubo, born in 1942 in Tokyo, has been pushing anti-fashion as an avant-garde stylist since 1980. After obtaining a degree in philosophy from Keio University, she went into fashion and created her brand "Comme des Garçons" in 1969. Kawakubo belongs to the same generation as other important Japanese stylists such as Kenzo Takada, Issey Miyake, and Yoji Yamamoto, called the "New Wave of Japanese Designers", who developed and grew their creative work in Paris.

Her 1982 prêt-à-porter collection of "Hole Sweater" (a series

Shozo SHIMAMOTO
Work (Holes), c.1950

of black sweaters with many holes) deeply upset the fashion world. Through the unique use of black, which was criticized for being crow-like, she created a new interpretation of feminine beauty differing completely from conventional western standards.

In 1997, Kawakubo presented "Body Meets Dress, Dress Meets Body", in which she succeeded in diverging from a body image based on the western standard of feminine beauty. The dress was stuffed with a number of lumps and bumps on completely unusual parts of the body: on the back, the shoulders, the hips, transforming female body into a strange sculpture. Playing an important role in the history of fashion, she has a strong influence on the next generation of stylists through her extraordinary and provocative forms. (M. O.)

Shozo SHIMAMOTO (1928-2013)

Born in 1928 in Osaka, Shozo Shimamoto is one of founding members of Gutai Association ("Concrete"), a Japanese avant-gardist artist group founded in 1954 in Ashiya. Shimamoto contributed actively to the education and encouragement of young artists through his personal art association AU (Art Unidentified) created in 1980.

As Shimamoto's book title says "Art is about surprising people" (1994), throughout his life as an artist, he continued to surprise people with his extraordinary artistic output. In 1950, Shimamoto created "The Holes" leading him to be noticed by Jiro Yoshihara, his mentor, as well as the international media. This picture was born from an accident in the shortage of materials for his work after the war when he accidentally tore a canvas that was made from a mixture of flour and newspaper and was not yet dry. Thus, in Shimamoto's art, chance or randomness frequently play a fundamental role. In "Action painting", one of his most famous projects, suspended by a crane at thirty meters high, Shimamoto threw bottles filled with colorful ink which would explode over a piece of white fabric laid out across the ground. Collaboration or participation are also essential to his work. As "Head Art" and "Mail Art" asked the collaboration of many participants, "Nyotaku," was a project where hundreds of women created an imprint with their naked bodies. Shocking the artworld of the time, Shimamoto genuinely sought to develop a new path of Japanese avant-garde. (M. O.)

Atsuko TANAKA
Denkifuku (Robe électrique), 1956/1999

Minoru HIRATA
Hi Red Center's Cleaning Event (officially known as Be Clean! and Campaign to Promote Cleanliness and Order in the Metropolitan Area), 1964/2017

Atsuko TANAKA (1932-2005)

Artist. After dropping out of the Kyoto Municipal College of Art (now the Kyoto City University of Arts) in 1951, Tanaka studied at the Art Institute of Osaka Municipal Museum of Art (now the Osaka City Museum of Fine Arts). It was here that she met Akira Kanayama, who would later become her husband, and encourage her to develop an interest in abstract painting. In 1952, she joined the avant-garde art group Zero-kai (Zero Society) together with Kanayama, Kazuo Shiraga, Saburo Murakami, before becoming a member of the Gutai Art Association led by Jiro Yoshihara from 1955 to 1965.

Beginning with her calendar paintings featuring dates drawn on cloth, Tanaka's interest centered on the format of the tableau. She metaphorically transformed immaterial elements into works of art by stretching pink cloth thirty centimeters above the ground and making it flutter in the wind, for example, or by placing bells on the floor and creating a sound "painting" within the space as they rang in sequence. Tanaka was one of the prominently conceptual artists within the Gutai group. Unlike Yoko Ono and Yayoi Kusama, who moved to the United States, Tanaka was based in Japan. Her reputation, however, has been growing internationally since the 2000s.

Electric Dress, the work on display at this exhibition, was first shown at the 2nd Gutai Art Exhibition (1956). It was made up of about 100 tubes painted with 9 different colors of synthetic enamel paint and about 80 light bulbs, joined together in a shape that could be worn by a person. When Tanaka first wore it, she was mortified by the irregular flickering of the lights: she felt how electrical energy became light and experienced the sensation of becoming connected to it in an instant. Throughout her life and career, Tanaka would continue to depict this experience of connection through vividly colored synthetic enamel paintings featuring forms inspired by light bulbs, tubes, and electrical cords. (Y. H.)

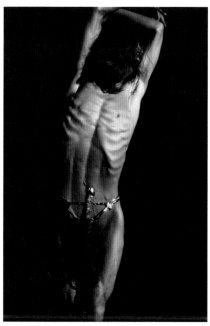

Tatsumi HIJIKATA
Tatsumi Hijikata and Japanese People : Rebellion of the Body, 1968

Kazuo OHNO
Admiring La Argentina (1977, the first performance), 2017

Eikoh HOSOE
"Kamaitachi" #17, 1965/c.2010

Yasumasa MORIMURA
A Requiem: Theater of Creativity. Self Portrait as Marcel Duchamp
(Based on the photo by Julian Wasser), 2010

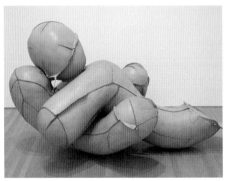

Tomoaki ISHIHARA
I.S.M. (H), 1989

Mariko MORI
Link of the Moon (Miko no Inori), 1996

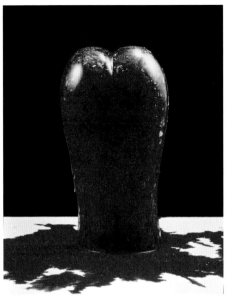

Yukio NAKAGAWA
Flowery Priestess, 1973

Tetsumi KUDO
Homage to the Young Generation - The Cocoon Opens,
1968

Natsuyuki NAKANISHI
Cloths Pegs Assert Churning Action, 1963

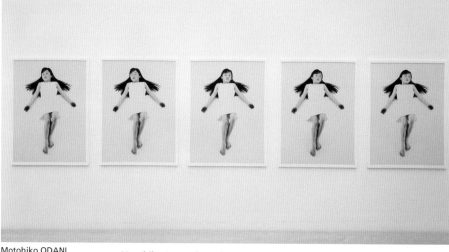

Motohiko ODANI
Phantom-Limb, 1997

Motohiko ODANI (1972-)

Sculptor and artist. Odani studied sculpture at both the Department of Fine Arts and graduate school of the Tokyo University of the Arts. Using a variety of techniques and materials, Odani has explored the nature of sculpture in an age of virtual ambiguity. As suggested by the word "phantom," one of the recurring themes in his work, he is interested in the ambiguous middle ground that lies between existence and non-existence, awakening and semi-awakening, and the human and non-human. Odani seeks to express the shifts in the physical body, perception, consciousness, and materiality that arise therein by interpreting the notion of "sculpture as media" in an expanded sense and deconstructing it — a critical sublation of traditional Japanese Buddhist sculpture and modern sculpture. His works, such as dresses woven from hair, animals wearing restraints, and machine/human hybrid figures, evoke an empathy for and continuity with physical sensations and mental states, such as pain and fear, as well as deformed beings.

Phantom Limb, the work on display at this exhibition, expresses the in-between state of a girl who seems to have lost her (severed) hands. Awakening and semi-awakening, child and adult, floating and groundedness, loss and presence: the title is taken from the psychiatric term "phantom limb," which describes a lost appendage that still feels pain. *Dress*, made of woven human hair, is a deft articulation of sculpture as skin, and the fetishism of matter. *Rompers* is a video that might also be called a tactile "sculptural image" fashioned from intense images and colors, reminiscent of David Lynch. Depicted here is a dark fantasy of a girl as a mutant chameleon-like being that catches insects. (Y. H.)

Sputniko!
Menstruation Machine – Takashi's Take, 2010

A   Strange Object, Post-human Body

Kodai NAKAHARA
Viridian Adaptor + Kodai's Morpho II, 1989

Kodai NAKAHARA (1961-)

Born in 1961 in Okayama, Kodai Nakahara graduated in sculpture from Kyoto City University of Arts and now teaches plastic arts at the university as a professor. His work has shown his transdisciplinary ability to cross drawing, video, performance and installation art, altering the conventional types of sculpture established in the "academic" art field. What characterizes Nakahara's work is an activist and stoic attitude towards the pursuit of new artistic expressions. He modifies sculpture by mixing it with another medium or substituting it by another process. He has always put into question the ontology of mediums in art. In the 1990s, Nakahara used different toys and industrial materials such as LEGO blocks,

plastic models and figurines in his work.

In 2010, he lost most of his work in a fire he fell victim to. Since then, he has made reproductions of these works, calling them "Jikomoho (Imitation of the self)". Thinking of this accident not simply as a tragedy but as a challenge to overcome, he creates projects for recovering, reconstructing and rethinking the lost works, or repairs severely damaged works in order to conserve them, all while honoring the trauma they sustained. His way of thinking about the states of objects (whether a copy or an original) explains his choice to use *ready-made* materials.

The work "Viridian Adopter + Kodai's Morpho" (1989), was inspired by the influence of Mono-ha, an artistic movement of the 1960s and 1907s, and sought to fuse natural and industrial materials in a sculpture that spanned spatial-temporal boundaries. This work eludes interpretation as sculpture in the traditional sense, instead proposing a new approach to the artistic form. (M. O.)

Dumb Type
pH, 1990

Dumb Type (1984-)

Dumb Type is a multi-media performance artist group mainly formed by students in Kyoto City University of Arts in 1984 and became a collective of artists of diverse specializations of film, painting, architecture, design, computer programming, music etc. They are also known as a new type of decentralized artist group with no hierarchal structure that the individual members such as Shiro Takatani or Ryoji Ikeda are also very active independently.

With their characteristics of cross-genre multiplex performance and installation, Dumb Type has significantly been challenging various existing borders within different bodies of sexuality, gender and race of contemporary society. In the beginning of their activity, they were sharply critical of the bubble economy of Japan in the 80s when temptation and despair coexisted through experiments of body in rapidly growing consumerism. They chose to perform "dumb (rejecting speech)," instead of adopting traditional theatrical style and the scenography is elaborately set up as an machinery and informational system that function almost autonomously. Dumb Type was a pioneer, expressing the post-human viewpoint conceived by a new interaction between living body and digital technology as a new standardized matrix of space and time with their attitude to resist any kind of systematic borders in our contemporary society.

In one of the most well known performances, "S/N" (1994), the centripetal figure of the group, Teiji Furuhashi came out that he is HIV positive. From its production process, this performance was significantly sensational and controversial as it critically approached discriminations existing in many aspects of our society through direct messages. In 1995, Furuhashi passed away due to sepsis by AIDS, however, the group has actively presented several sophisticated performances such as "OR" (1997), "memorandum" (1999) and "Voyage" (2002) since then. (S. K.)

Yuko MOHRI
Parade, 2011-2017

A   Strange Object, Post-human Body

Rhizomatiks
Perfume, at Cannes Lions International Festival of Creativity

YMO
Solid State Survivor, 1979

Katsuhiro OTOMO
AKIRA, 1982-90

Rhizomatiks (2006-)

Rhizomatiks is a corporation and a collective of various digital experts, such as hard/software engineers, graphic/web designers, planners, sound artists, and video artists. They have always challenged to expand the scope of possibility of the cutting-edge technologies in inter-disciplinary fields between media art, industry, and business. Rhizomatiks is named after the word "rhizome" famous for a Delleuzian concept, meaning a subterranean stem that produces a complex network of nutrition-rich roots. As their range of creation expands into advertisement, museum, stage theatre projects, and educational settings, they established three new divisions in 2016: Research, Architecture and Design. The Research department led by Daito Manabe and Motoi Ishibashi, two of the founders of Rhizomatiks, have collaborated with external artists and scientists in order to explore the undeveloped area and challenge potentiality of co-existence of machine and human beings in a physical space and time. They seek expression created by seriously sophisticated liaison of the phenomenon, body, programming and computer itself. For instance, Rhizomatiks Research started to work in collaboration with the dance company ELEVENPLAY from 2011 to produce works using mechanical learning technologies for developing resonance of the performing body and other technologies such as drones, robot arms, AR, and VR. This collaboration evolved into the performance in the closing ceremony of Rio de Janeiro Olympic games 2016. Their own installation works that have criticality toward invisible but existing system in our life were exhibited in some exhibitions; *Chains* (2016), which made visible dynamic up and down in bit-coin trades; and *Traders* (2013), which dealt with First Section of the Tokyo Stock Exchange and AI's influence there. (J. U.)

Pop Art: before/after the 1980s

Keiichi TANAAMI
untitled_collagebook03_07, 1973

Yuichi YOKOYAMA
Color Engineering, 2004

Installation view of
Tadanori YOKOO

Tadanori YOKOO
Motorcycle, 1966/2002

Tsunehisa KIMURA
The City Welcomes a Bracing Morning, 1978

Tsunehisa KIMURA (1928-2008)

He graduated from Osaka City Kogei School (now Osaka City Kogei High School). In the 1950s, he mainly designed for posters and newspaper advertisements in Osaka. During this time, he also formed a design group 'A Club' with Kazumasa Nagai, Toshihiro Katayama, and Ikko Tanaka, and they were called 'The Young Big Four'. Kimura moved to Tokyo in 1960 and got involved in the establishment of the Japan Design Center with these people, but decided to become an independent artist in 1964. He also participated in making pictograms for Tokyo Olympics that were held in the same year. In 1966, he displayed his works at the group exhibition 'Persona' with 11 others who were deemed as the second generation of postwar designers. He became an assistant professor (later visiting professor) at Tokyo Zokei University in 1968. At that time, he began to use photo-montage techniques and became the pioneer of photomontage in Japan, while indicating social satire. He shifted to a color montage from monochrome around 1975, and all the works featured in this exhibition are colored ones. Kimura did not take photos himself, but copied existing images and recomposed them for his photomontage works. Many of them represent a scene of a metropolis being destroyed. Kimura called them 'modern *Jigoku-e* (painting of hell)', and said it was based on people's deep-rooted faith of hell and real experience of war. The background itself is typical, an imaginary landscape of the city. But it symbolizes postwar Tokyo in its rapid economic development and also may be interpreted as it shows premonition of catastrophe. Kimura was active not only as a designer but also as a critic of several magazines, for example, he had a discussion with Jean Baudrillard when he visited Japan in 1981. (K. L.)

TABAIMO
Haunted House, 2003

Hiroshi NAKAMURA
Circular Train A (Telescope Train), 1968

Tiger TATEISHI
The Alamo Sphinx, 1966

Shinro OHTAKE
Scrapbook #68, 2014-2016

Shinro OHTAKE (1955-)

He was born in Tokyo and moved to Uwa-jima Island in Ehime Prefecture 1988. Ohtake graduated from Musashino Art University, Tokyo in 1980. In his university, he went to the UK in 1977. While deepening engagement with young artists who would be active later in different fields of art, music and design, Ohtake began to compile his own "scrapbooks" that has been central to his artistic practice. It shows chaotic but intense power in his habitual practices to collect and glue everything on street stimulating him; for instance, scattered posters, tags, photos, currencies, newspapers, tickets and other mass-produced printed matters.

With massive accumulation of the praxis and materials, the found objects turn to be a sculptural work in a form of book, including their time and memory the artist seals off with coats of wax, stain, and varnish, plastic or fiberglass. In addition, things that do not have material substance like light and sound on street can be composed of his art works. Indeed, sound and noise play an important role in his composition. The artist says "There generates tranquility when ultra-accumulation exceeds a certain amount of mass". Through different media, he shows energetic "con-struction" of them in the way of gluing anything by his unstoppable impulse, rather than the contemporary art one in which an artwork is "composed" under a concept that leads to the final form. (J. U.)

Harumi YAMAGUCHI (1941-)

She graduated from Tokyo University of the Arts with a degree in oil painting. She became interested in commercial art when she was in the fourth year of university, having been deeply impressed by an exhibition of JAAC (Japan Advertising Artists Club). She was especially interested in the advertisement for department stores, so she started working for the publicity department of the Seibu Department Store, and was in charge of illustration for the advertisement. Yamaguchi became a freelance illustrator from 1967 and participated in the advertisement for the PARCO department store with its opening in 1969. The dominant feature of the advertisement was that it didn't focus on the products but the image, especially the image of strong, independent women. At first, the posters by Yamaguchi were flat illustrations, but since 1973 they transformed into super-realistic art using the air-brush technique, and it continued until 1985. All the works featured in this exhibition are of this era. These erotic, strong, and dignified female figures were called 'Harumi Gals' and symbolized PARCO. Sociologist Chizuko Ueno commented on 'Harumi Gals' as "too much and over the top", "like cyborg", "drag queen by women who play women". Later, Yamaguchi left air-brush technique and released 'Noyōni (like)' series from 1988 to 1997, which were posters inspired by portraits of famous women of the twentieth century. In this series, she attempted to change the brushwork of each poster. She also worked for brand advertising and book illustration in this era. Although most of her works had been presented at commercial spaces, from the 2000s, her works have become to be exhibited in the museums or galleries, and her solo exhibition is being held continuously until now. (K. L.)

Harumi YAMAGUCHI
Suspender Swimsuit, 1983

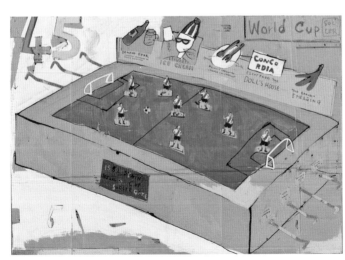

Katsuhiko HIBINO
PRESENT SOCCER, 1982

Miwa YANAGI (1967-)

Yanagi graduated from Kyoto City University of Arts. She was first known for a series of computer-composed photographs, called *Elevator Girl*, created from 1994 to 1999. The series was composed of young women figures in elevator costume with emotionless face making machinery postures in the unrealistic places created by computer based on a particular place. With the cutting-edge technique at the time, what the series ironically depicted was a social impasse caused by Japan's rapid economic growth, its machinic system of production and prevailing masculine discipline in the society. Developing from the *Elevator Girl* series, the theme of the gender role of women in Japanese society has been central to her artistic practices. Yanagi widened her scope by the series *My Grandmothers* from 1999. This series was produced through interviews with girls aged between about 14 and 20. She asked them to imagine what they will be or what they dream of being 50 years later. If the answer stimulates her, Yanagi drew pictures of the images of the elder woman, and finally turned it into a photographic work that was juxtaposed with sentences that the aged figure was supposed to remark. Each vision created through imagination of the artist and interviewed girls turned the other way around the Japanese strong norm that the young, the better, especially for women. Instead, it demonstrated various ways to live and strength grown through aging process in female life-cycle. (J. U.)

Miwa YANAGI
My Grandmothers: YUKA, 2000

Kenji YANOBE (1965-)

Yanobe studied sculpture at Kyoto City University of Arts and received a Master of Arts degree from the university in 1991. He was fascinated by the Osaka Expo in 1970, whose theme was "Progress and Harmony for Mankind". Further, Japanese comics and animated films in which machinery technology and characters appear so attracted him in his childhood that he wished to become an eccentric scientist figure inventing some machine to help people. Accordingly, his sculptural work, *Tanking Machine* (1990), a machine in which a person could sink his/her body in physiological saline and mediate even though the outside world would be unsafe, was created. Successively, Yanobe created, with his distinctive "delusion", lots of large-scale machinic sculptural works that one can ride and manipulate, incorporating the theme of "survival". However, as confronting a mood of fin de siècle in Japan due to the Tokyo Subway Sarin Attack and the Hanshin earthquake in 1995, he began to be unsatisfied with the works that could protect only the master of invention. In 1997, he conducted *Atom Suit Project* (1997), in which he visited Chernobyl, where the horrible damage caused by nuclear power plant accident still remained. It was this time to pave his way to reality with the world of "delusion". Since then, he has created mechanical and figurative sculptural works, shifting to the theme of "revival", including *Sun Child* project (2011-) conducted after the Great East Japan Earthquake. (J. U.)

Kenji YANOBE
Atom Suit Project: The World Fair in Osaka 1, 1998

Teppei KANEUJI
White Discharge, 2012

Makoto AIDA
No One Knows the Title (War Picture Returns), 1996

Makoto AIDA (1965-)

Artist. Graduated from the department of painting at Tokyo University of the Arts and also completed graduate studies at the same institution. Working mainly with painting, Aida also uses various media such as video, sculpture, and performance to present critical perspectives on the Japanese art system, history, and society.

The motifs found in Aida's works are diverse. Spanning *bishojo* (the figure of the nubile young female), *ero-guro* (a grotesque brand of eroticism), violence, war, and politics, they shuttle freely between the modern and pre-modern, and the boundaries that separate West and East. His unique approach is reminiscent of that of an I-novel, while his critical edge is wrapped up in irony and humor. Articulated through the contrast between his graphic quality and fantastical imagery, drawn from the lineage of Edo-era *ukiyo-e* woodblock prints and paintings, these qualities imbue Aida with a strong sense of a "master painter" who

reflects the times. In addition to his practice as an individual artist, he is also active as a member of The Group 1965, formed along with other artists born in the same year, the puppet theater Gekidan Shiki, headed by Hiroko Okada, as well as in various other activities including authoring novels and manga.

In *No One Knows the Title (War Picture Returns)*, a vinyl tablecloth is affixed to an old four-sided folding screen. These cheap materials are then drawn over with enamel paint. During World War II, painters were made to produce "war pictures" to boost morale, and Aida's *War Picture Returns* series is an attempt to reconsider this genre in a critical light. *A Picture of an Air Raid on New York City (War Picture Returns)*, one of the more well-known pieces in this series, is based on the composition of the 16th century painted folding screens *Scenes in and around the Capital*. The cityscape of Kyoto is replaced by that of Manhattan, while the mother-of-pearl clouds are replaced by Zero fighters. In *No One Knows the Title*, the composition features the Parthenon joined to the Atomic Bomb Dome in Hiroshima, thereby questioning the meaning of ruins and historical monuments. (Y. H.)

Takashi MURAKAMI (1962-)

Takashi Murakami, born in 1962 in Tokyo, is one of the most famous Japanese artists in the international art scene and represents artists of newer generations who are deeply influenced by Otaku culture (geek). Though Murakami studied Nihonga, Japanese style paintings, at Tokyo University of the Arts, his dream was to become a manga artist. In 1995, after having finished his doctoral studies, Murakami founded Hiropon Factory, a production studio, as well as Kaikai Kiki Corporation, a company gathering a group of artists sharing the same cultural characteristics, in order to support young artists. Since 2011, he also organizes "Geisai", a series of art festivals that opens doors for creative young artists.

"Superflat" is a notion invented by Murakami in order to identify a group of artists sharing strong influences from manga culture or a bi-dimensional figurative style (lacking perspective) which characterizes popular Japanese art (or neo-pop) and in which he made references to Ukiyo-e (Japanese woodblock prints developed during the Edo period). In the exhibition "Super Flat" which took place in Tokyo in 2000, Murakami presented different forms of works like manga, animation, and figurines. He has also displayed his capacity as a manager and a businessman. The collaboration with Louis Vuitton and other brands allowed him to make a name for himself not simply as an artist but also as a multifaceted person.

In 2010, a retrospective exhibition "Murakami Versailles", presented in Château de Versailles, caused a controversy and certain works were severely criticized, especially his installation in the Hall of Mirrors where visitors discovered a series of "pop-style" sculptures such as "Flower Matango" and "Miss Ko2" that seemed completely out of place. The controversy contributed to ensuring his international reputation. (M. O.)

Takashi MURAKAMI
Cosmos, 1998

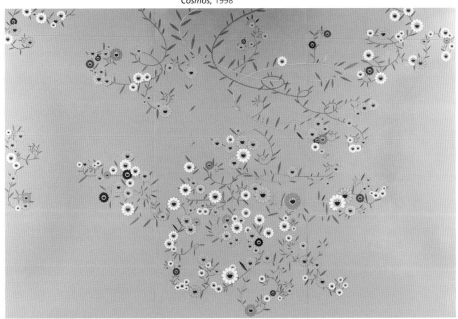

Yayoi KUSAMA (1929-)

Kusama is an internationally well-known visual avant-garde artist whose works range from drawing, painting, sculpture, installation, poem, novels and other various media. She often chooses polka-dots and nets as her motifs that she has been seeing in her hallucinations since her early childhood. She moved to New York in 1957 with the support from Georgia O'Keeffe. Her highly unique form of expression of infinite multiplication of dots and nets had a strong impact to the leading art scene in New York at the time. Her style also highly influenced significant figures of minimalism or pop in American contemporary art history in 1960s such as Donald Judd, Frank Stella and Andy Warhol. During her stay in New York, she was also an important leading female artist of the radical performances, "happenings". The performances included nude-demonstration with body painted polka-dots in order to resist gender gap and androcentrism or to promote anti-war movement in the time of Vietnam War.

She returned to Japan in 1973 and consistently kept producing works while she used psychiatric hospital as base although she was not well received from the prevailing conservative culture in Japan, as "happenings" were too radical. However, in 1993, she participated in 45th Venice Biennial, representing Japanese Pavilion and she turned to be recognized as a respected queen of the avangt-garde. In this period, she also began to be internationally reevaluated, however, including her unique concepts of "self-obliteration", "accumulation" or "repetition", that challenge to overcome her obsession, her works cross even beyond the major artistic contexts of abstract expressionism, minimalism, pop or post-minimalism. In her installation, Fireflies on the Water (2000), audiences can physically experiences the process of "self-obliteration" through the seemingly endless space carefully created by light bulbs, mirrors and water. Through her works, the audiences are also able to trace KUSAMA's ultimate vitality to express 'infinity' that is often complemented or substituted by "Love" in her philosophical concept.

Her solo exhibitions have been held in numerous worldwide locations. In 2011 – 2012, her largest Europe and North America retrospective tour was held at Museo Naçional Centro De Arte Reina Sofia, Madrid (2011), Centre Pompidou, Paris (2011-2012), the Tate Modern, London (2012) and Whitney Museum of American Art, New York (2012). (S. K.)

Yayoi KUSAMA
Fireflies on the Water, 2000

Yayoi DEKI
Mimichin, 1998

Aya TAKANO
Milk of tender love, 2003

ANREALAGE
Ensemble from 2011 A/W Collection "LOW", 2011

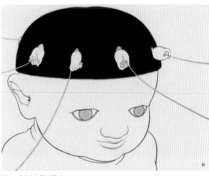

Kumi MACHIDA
Visitor, 2004

Taro IZUMI
Cannot see the shadow of the rainbow, 2015

Izumi KATO
Untitled, 2010

Haruka KOJIN
Relectwo, 2008/2017

Kyoko OKAZAKI (1963-)

Okazaki is a Tokyo-based, Japanese manga artist. She made her debut by contributing illustrations and writings to magazines in 1983 while still a student at Atomi Junior College.

Okazaki's choice to have, as her lead characters, girls who are facing the vicissitudes of the times and living in unstable conditions, possibly reflects the atmosphere in Japan from the late 1980s to the 1990s – a time when Okazaki was most active. This time was marked by a great change in Japanese society and the country's urban landscapes due to the bubble economy and its consequences.

Helter Skelter is a representative work of Okazaki. It was serialized in 1995-1996, published independently in 2003, and made into a movie by the photographer and director, Mika Ninagawa, in 2012. The main character, Lilico, is a popular model who undergoes an overall plastic surgery to realize her beauty ideal but is then gradually ruined by the haunting emptiness coming from the way people treat her – by never looking beyond her beautiful surface – and the physical aftereffects of numerous surgeries.

Okazaki is not only a manga artist. Her interests range widely and include fashion, music, movies, literature, and contemporary art. In her works. Thus, through Okazaki's works, we gain access to the culture she was exposed to while producing her works. In 1994, contemporary artist, Takashi Murakami, held Okazaki's first exhibition in his private gallery.

When Okazaki debuted in the 1980s, the genre of Shojo Manga (comics for girls) was not yet established, and thus Okazaki and her contemporaries worked to shape and further this genre. Meanwhile, the following generation, who grew up being inspired by Okazaki, made their debuts and became popular, so that now, such artists as Moyoko Anno, who worked as an assistant to Okazaki, work in the front lines of the industry.

In 1996, Okazaki had a traffic accident and stopped producing her work because she was in rehabilitation. In 2015, a large retrospective exhibition of Okazaki's works was held in Setagaya Literary Museum, Tokyo. (A. K.)

Kyoko OKAZAKI
River's edge, 1993-94

Mika NINAGAWA
Tokyo Douchu, 2017

C

Collaboration/Participation/Sharing

"Home-for-All"

"Home-for-All" in Kumamoto

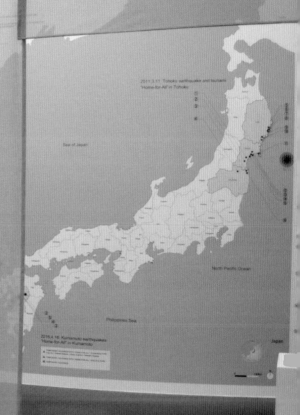

2011.3.11 Tohoku earthquaker and tsunami
"Home-for-All" in Tohoku

Sea of Japan

North Pacific Ocean

Philippines Sea

2016.4.16 Kumamoto earthquakes
"Home-for-All" in Kumamoto

Japan

Yoko ONO
Eyeblink (Fluxfilm n°9)(1966), Mend Piece for John (1968), Grapefruits (1964)

Kosuke TSUMURA
Coat "Final Home", c. 1994

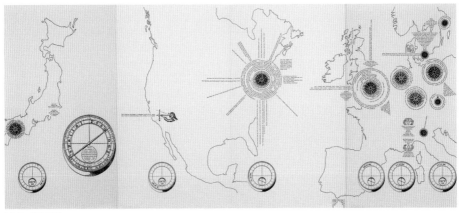

Mieko SHIOMI
Spatial Poem N°2, 1965

Mieko SHIOMI (1938-)

She was born Chieko Shiomi. Trained in music from childhood, she identifies herself as a composer, while her intermedia works cross the lines between music, visual art, poem, and performance. Her artistic career started from 'Group Ongaku (Group Music)', an avant-garde music group she founded when she was studying musicology at Tokyo University of Arts in 1960. Group Ongaku composed and performed improvisational music and musique concrète. Since then, many of her works attempted to create a new form of music, for example, a visualization of music/sound (*Endless Box*), or a combination of music and natural elements (*Water Music*). In 1964, she flew to the US to join Fluxus, having been invited by George Maciunas. After she came back to Japan in 1965, more of her works adopted the form of event, such as the 'direction event' that used the mail system to make people participate in it from all over the world (*Spatial Poem*). In the late 1960s, with the birth of term 'intermedia', Shiomi started releasing intermedia works using technology. However, it can be said that she had consistently created combined media art before then. Although her career became less active from the 1970s, she returned to create/reinterpret her own works from the 1990s. Shiomi's works do not only combine media but concentrate more on converting one medium to another or representing one theme by various media. For example, often in her works, the wind turns to sound, the music turns to object, and one work turns to visual art, performance, or video and others. She calls her own works 'transmedia' in recent years, because of these features. (K. L.)

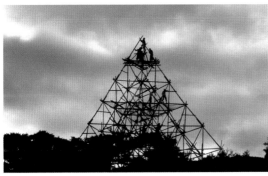

THE PLAY
THUNDER, 1977-1986

Shimabuku
The Chance to Recover Our Humanity, 1995 Suma Kobe, 1995

Shimabuku (1969-)

Shimabuku or Michihiro Shimabuku has travelled the world since the early 1990s, creating a number of installations and performances about the lifestyles and cultures of the people who live there and new ways of communication. His poetic and humorous projects have attracted international attention, as they consider how we should live our lives through croiss-disciplinary expressions not bound by the existing art framework.

In addition to travel, the relationship with animals is also an important part of Shimabuku's expression. Many animals have appeared in his work, including owl, life-saving dog, deer and turtle. In particular, his film "Then, I decided to give a tour of Tokyo to the octopus from Akashi" (2000), in which he brings an octopus from Akashi to Tokyo by bullet train, show it around Tokyo, and then return it to the see, is a representative work on the subject of travel itself. The work, "Catching Octopus with self-made ceramic pots", is a unique idea that raise the question of the relationship between food and the environment.

The project "Ningensei Kaifuku no Chance (The opportunity to recover humanity)" is a work in which he hung a sign on the roof of a collapsed friend's house, against the backdrop of the loss over time of the compassion of people that was so striking in the emergency situation immediately after the Great Hanshin-Awaji Earthquake. Shimabuku continues to shake the boundaries of artistic disciplines through his diverse means of expression and collaborations with artists from other disciplines. (M. O.)

Koki TANAKA (1975-)

Tanaka received MA from Tokyo University of the Arts in 2005 and spent four years in Los Angeles from 2008. In his earlier career, he shed the light on the simple everyday acts that otherwise would be overlooked; movements of ordinary objects and relationships between behaviors of those living in a modern society and found objects on street. Since the Great East Japan Earthquake on March 11 in 2011, a major part of his work has dealt with participatory projects; for instance, a few of professional hairdressers gather and try to cut one's hair at once. For each project, he assembles individuals with various backgrounds; for example, in the haircut project, the participants are composed of various nationalities and have different experiences of years and styles at their job occasion. As Tanaka describes, the thematic question his art asks is about "[h]ow can share, or take possession of, the experience of events?" His works investigate not only aesthetics and forms of art works created through collaborative processes, but also how people collaborate with each other when put in an unusual situation. What the artist wants to reveal is another rule from the prevailing social and neo-liberal structure that "even if a haircut turns out wrong, hair grows, then you can go get it cut again. If a performance does not go well, play the piece again". (J. U.)

Koki TANAKA
A pottery produced by 5 potters at once (silent attempt)(2013), A Piano Played by Five Pianists at Once (First Attempt)(2012), A behavioral statement (or an unconscious protest)(2013)

in Shiga in 1980, graduated from Bukkyo University. Their activities, based on communication and exchange with participants and residents, aim to invite the experience of sympathy towards others through collective acts.

Wah document participates in collective exhibitions both in Japan and in foreign countries: wah lab (2008, Museum of contemporary art of Tokyo), a project for The Echigo-Tsumari Art Triennale 2007 (Nigata), Home Ground Football (2010, Rotterdam), Tight rope walking (2011, Kyoto). (M. O.)

Wah document (2006-)

Wah document is an artist duo formed in 2006 for the purpose of exploring diverse participative and collaborative activities with local people. Wah document is composed of: Minamigawa Kenji, born in Osaka in 1979, graduated from Tokyo University of Arts, and Hirofumi Masui, born

wah document
wah27 "Bath on the ground", 2008

Tokujin YOSHIOKA
Honey-pop, 2001

Kazuhiko HACHIYA
M-02 [Möwe, replica of plane of Nausica, Hayao Miyazaki's Film], version of 2016

SANAA(Kazuyo Sejima and Ryue Nishizawa)
21st Century Museum of Contemporary Art, Kanazawa, 2004

Kumamoto Artpolis Tohoku Support Group (Toyo ITO,
Hideki KATSURA, Kaoru SUEHIRO, Masashi SOGABE)
Home-for-All, Sendai, Miyagi, 2011

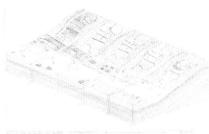

Atelier Bow-Wow+Kaijima Lab, University of Tsukuba
Momonoura Village Public Drawing, 2017

Home-for-All (*Minna no Ie*, 2011-)

"Home-for-All" is a project initiated by Toyo Ito, Kazuyo Sejima, and Riken Yamamoto, togetger with a younger generation of architects, out of the "Kishin-no-Kai", a group of five architects set up immediately after the Great East Japan Earthquake stuck on 11 March 2011. To begin with, sixteen "Home-for-All"s have been built across Tohoku in order to make the lives of those who lost their homes in the disaster as vibrant as possible, despite the difficult circumstances. These "Home-for-All"s were built at the sites of temporary housing complexes, and near shopping street to create a place for local residents to get together, and playgrounds for local children and a base for those seeking to rebuild their farming and fishing industries.

The first "Home-for-All" in Miyagino-ku was completed in Sendai City with the support of Kumamoto Prefecture and, using this experience, two "Home-for-All"s were built in the aftermath of the floods in Kumamoto in July 2012. After the Kumamoto earthquake in April 2016, more than 120 "Home-for-All"s were built in wood under the leadership of the prefectural governor and with public funding (some from foundations and private donors).

With the passage of time since the disasters, the consolidation of temporary housing and local disaster prevention plans have progressed, and some of the "Home-for-All"s have had to be relocated of demolished. There are also "Home-for-All"s that have been reborn as meeting places for people who have moved out of temporary housing in new areas, and this has the potential to go beyond the role of simply supporting the affected areas, referring to the future of public facilities and society. (M. O.)

Poetics of Resistance

Yoshitomo NARA
In the White Room II, 1995

Harue KOGA
Sea, 1929

Harue KOGA (1895-1933)

Koga is a painter and poet, whose father was a Buddhist priest of Zenpukuji. Aspiring to be a painter, he had repeatedly visited Tokyo, but his inherently weak constitution had often bothered him. He eventually got serious neuralgia in the spring of 1932 and died at 38 the following year.

Koga had tried every style of art in that time quickly, the same as Japanese artists who had enthusiastically imported Western art trends. He had participated in the artist group "Action" (1922-1924) pursuing his interest in the rising trend of avant-gardism in both art and literature. After that, he created cubistic style paintings and *doga* (fancy drawings for children) watercolors, influenced by André Lhote and Paul Klee through reproductions. He deepened his original thought from the acquaintance with people such as a painter Seiji Togo who had studied futurism in Italy and a formalist poet Kyushichi Takenaka who was

proposing "scientific surrealism". Although Koga was one of the artistic supremacists, in the latter half of the 1920's he could no longer avoid thinking about the relationship between art and social reality in response to the upsurge of the proletarian art movement.

In this situation, "The Sea" (1929) was created. This painting is widely accepted as the beginning of surrealism in Japan, but Koga's surrealism is different from the French one for his consciousness and intellectualism. Modern motifs such as factories, airships and a woman in swimsuits were intendedly extracted from science magazines and postcards at the time. His montage was neither for exploring nonsense connection of things, nor honoring the modern technology and culture. Koga combined consciously these fragmental images of contemporary social reality in order to rock the reality to its foundation. (Y. S.)

D   **Poetics of Resistance**

Yoshitomo NARA
Sayon, 2006

Yoshitomo NARA (1959-)

Nara is broadly known for his paintings, drawings, and sculptures depict innocent children and animals. He had lived in Aomori until entering in the Aichi Prefectural University of Fine Arts and Music, from which he received his M.F.A. in 1987. He had studied in Germany from 1988, and backed to Japan in 2000. He emerged as Neo-Pop artist in 90's and soon became popular among widespread fans. He started working on ceramics from 2007. He fell into a slump when the 2011 Tohoku earthquake and tsunami struck Japan, but resumed after creating big bronze sculptures with clay. He has continued creation in varied medium including installation and photography.

To analyze his reduced lines and colors, many critics had often referred to manga and anime as the most influential subculture then in Japan. The simplicity of his depiction, however, was abstraction came from an urge to purify the subject and his message, that was obtained during his study in Germany. For this, something in common with early Italian renaissance painters can be pointed. The 90's also saw an increasing attention on subjectivity of weak person for feminism and post-colonialism movement at that time. In this context, Nara's persistent representation of "kawaii" children was reinterpreted by Midori Matsui, a Japanese critic, as a resistant statement of "Micro-Pop". In fact, he cultivated his rebellious spirit with the punk rock music through his adolescence in 70's, through which he closely felt helplessness of the failures of 60's student activism, hippie movement, and Vietnam War. A lot of references to punk lyrics can be found in many of titles and sentences in his drawings. Among varied activities of Nara, drawing takes notable position because emotional energy is directly expressed on it in contrast to his paintings finished with highly controlled, minute attention. (Y. S.)

Yuken TERUYA (1973-)

Teruya is a visual artist who often utilizes ordinary objects and tools which are familiar with our daily life such as paper bags. He coverts original usage of these materials to aesthetical artworks with micro-political messages towards contemporary social issues. He graduated from Tama Art University in 1996 and completed MFA in School of Visual Arts, New York in 2001. He is originally from Okinawa, the southwest region of Japan and through his artworks he often approaches various complex problems of society, culture and environment in Okinawa.

His work entitled *You-I You-I* (2002/2007) is a kimono of Bingata, a traditional dyeing technique in Okinawa. Within its garment's patterns, viewers can find U.S. paratroopers and jet fighters aesthetically harmonized with local flowers and butterflies. It is a micro-political comment - with the beautiful language of Okinawa's traditional color sensation - on the social and environmental issues lying in between local residents and the U.S. military base that has been settled for many decades through the occupation by U.S. after the Second World War.

His other well-known series Notice - Forest (1999-) - cutting a silhouette of tree in one side of a paper bags of famous high brands or fast food companies and bending it inward- shows ultimate simplicity and sophisticated technique of cut-out that derive diverse interpretation and sensation from viewers. This series strongly has a political connotation towards consumerism ignited by the global capitalism by metaphorically and visually returning the paper as material back to what it used to be: trees and forests. Although his works contain critical sharpness to the current global and local affairs, they never remain at simple justification or indicate a clear border between good and bad. He crosses over the dichotomy of society and nature and his micro-politics and aesthetics are blended in a complex manner through his ingenious simplicity.

He has participated into various solo and group exhibitions all over the world such as Yuken Teruya: On Okinawa, COLLECTIONS FROM THE PAST AND THE FUTURE at Humboldt-Lab-Dahlem, Berlin (2014-2015) and Who interprets the world? at 21th Century Museum of Contemporary Art, Kanazawa (2015). (S. K.)

Hideko FUKUSHIMA
Wings, 1950

Yuken TERUYA
You-I You-I, 2002

Koji NAKAZONO
Untitled, 2012

Koji NAKAZONO (1989-2015)

Nakazono is a painter who mainly uses oil on canvas and crayon on wooden panel and is known as prolific young artist. He received BA degree in oil painting of Tokyo University of the Arts in 2012 and had his first solo exhibition at Tomio Koyama Gallery, Tokyo in 2013. In his paitings, multiple layers are accumulated and these stratified images of outlined portraits and background motifs create complex pictorial spaces that are partially humorous and ghostly floating primitive appearance.

His style of paintings is free from an orthodox framework of painting methods. He often utilizes his own fingers and sometimes elbows as well as unique materials such as tissue papers to blur his motifs in between figurative and abstract or to scrape deep monochrome or colorful layers. However, the works also show certain level of precise technique of composition although his process of painting was highly improvisational.

He explains that what is painted "inside" of the painting is not very important but it is more important for him to paint many works and create what he calls "outer edge" as it is impossible to see and touch the "inside" of his paintings. With this artistic notion of "outer edge", visual scenery of his paintings flourish and when assembled together as well as each individual painting is incredibly varied and beautiful.

He is also known for his free and adventurous personality and habitat. He often walks up alone to mountains or to bays in the midnight and come back in the early morning. Unfortunately, at the age of 25 in the summer of 2015, he went to swim in Seto Island Sea in the west part of Japan and never return alive. (S. K.)

Tomoko KASHIKI
Shadow Play, 2009

Zon ITO (1971-)

Ito is mainly known for canvased embroidered textiles. He graduated from Kyoto City University of Arts in 1996. He made his debut with embroidery work in 2000, and the following year he had a high profile at "Yokohama Triennale 2001". After that he has participated in numerous exhibitions both in Japan and abroad. The wide variety of mediums he uses cover animation, installation, drawing, paper-cut, clay and so on.

He started painting as an art student in the 1990s when problems of painting like a dichotomy between concrete and abstract had already been dissolved. In this situation, the method of embroidery was selected from the following point of view: you can create something flat, which has no order in strength of expression or content, by an embroidery progressing little by little with pile of small decisions without wavering in nuances that may be produced in case of drawing. He wanted to avoid uncertain nuances compelling him to judge the occasional effects each time he strokes, because it inevitably makes outdated order of subjects in a picture. At first motives often chosen had been everyday objects, such as insects in empty lots and creatures of neighboring rivers. As his career progresses, depicted image has changed via mutually overlapping motifs in which the hierarchy disappeared, to highly abstracted and structured image inspired from the pattern of threads formed on the back side of an embroidery. Paradoxically, he succeeds at generating an ambient mood that can't be reduced to the structure of work as a result of the methodology that had been sophisticated into a well-controlled scheme making all seams, images and production acts equivalent. (Y. S.)

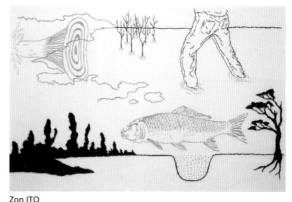

Zon ITO
Traveling in The Shallows, 2000

Sou FUJIMOTO
Residential treatment center for emotionally disturbed children, 2004-2006

Mame Kurogouchi
Personal Memory 2014AW, 2014

Hiroshi SUGITO
connecting man no.2, 2006

Junya ISHIGAMI (1974-)

Ishigami is a Japanese architect who has an innovative voice even in contemporary art world. He acquired his master's degree in architecture and planning at Tokyo National University of Fine Arts and Music (now Tokyo University of Arts) in 2000, and worked at SANAA for 4 years, before establishing his own firm in 2004. He showed at the 11th and 12th Venice Architecture Biennale and won the Golden Lion for Best Project in latter, 2010. He is the youngest ever recipient of the Architectural Institute of Japan Prize, the most authentic prize in Japan, for the Kanagawa Institute of Technology KAIT Workshop in 2009. In 2019, he was chosen to be a Serpentine pavilion architect, and built a huge canopy roof made of 61 tons of slates that was supported by 106 superfine airy pillars.

A number of Ishigami's projects share fantastic imagination and realistic simulation to realize unprecedented vision of space. One of his early work was "table" (2005) consisting of only four legs and one aluminum top board 9.5meters long and 3mm thick. To support the own weight and stand flatly, it required a curve of roughly one and a half revolution in the material itself, and minutely calculated arrangement of ornaments on the top of table. The appearance of the miracle scaled table standing conveyed a strange feeling like there was no gravity, and just a water surface floating.

The "balloon" (2007) is an indescribable structure something between sculpture, balloon, and building. The massive 13 x 6 x 13 meter rectangular, made of aluminum foil 0.2 mm thick and weighing about 1 ton, was literary floating in the large atrium of the Museum of Contemporary Art, Tokyo. It would faintly and slowly swell, deflate and sway as if it were a breathing creature. This overwhelming phenomenon came true by delicately balanced design of helium gas and all the details of parts.

Ishigami's works are apparently impossible but actually they always are designed on physical and environmental conditions, so he can create airy, organic structure from inorganic materials. Beyond a traditional idea of architecture in harmony with nature, his extending approach can be described as architecture as nature itself. (Y. S.)

Tsuyoshi OZAWA
Jizoing: Panmunjon, July 2, 1992, 1992

Junya ISHIGAMI
Documentation of Balloon, 2007

Fuyuki YAMAKAWA (1973-)

Yamakawa is artist and Khoomei singer who creates improvised musical performances and installations. He was born in London because of his father's job and grew up in US and Japan. After graduating the Tama Art University Masters of Fine Art in 1999, he started experimental body performance. He also deepened his consciousness on social problems with various projects such as the series in Oshima, which is to work on the dignity of life, continuing elaborate study on the history of leprosy there. He has performed at many different places throughout the world.

His cross-disciplinary performance activates a human body as a musical instrument by organizing a stage with electronic devices to create physical resonance as a whole system. In many cases, he amplifies a sound of his heart-beat with a microphone and a base-speaker, triggering musical flickers of light-bulbs with the tempo and velocity of the beats, which he can control at will, so the room becomes his extended body rumbling like a living thing. Meanwhile, he makes another sound in various ways, such as playing an electric guitar, knocking his own skull connected to bone conduction mic, or singing in a Khoomei style throat vocalism which utters unique double-tone vocal.

The "Voice-over" (2006) is one of his installation work, which consists of five tube televisions and cassette tapes that recorded his father's voice, a famous announcer who died of cancer of the throat in 1988 when Yamakawa was in the Middle School. The installation in darkroom evokes audience's memories with videos and sounds mashed up of a huge collection of his father's image and voice recorded in a varied situation such as news broadcasting, family conversation, and speaking teaching, which are deeply connected to Yamakawa's personal history but also represent public memory of mass-media. Through the mediated vibration of his father's lost voice, Yamakawa recollects and raises awareness on the body incarnated with the inheritance from his flesh and blood who had performed as an announcer. (Y. S.)

Fuyuki YAMAKAWA
The Voice-Over, 1997-2008

Chim↑Pom
SUPER RAT (DIORAMA), 2008

Chim↑Pom (2005-)

Chim↑Pom is an art collective formed by Ellie, Yasutaka Hayashi, Motomu Inaoka, Toshinori Mizuno, Masataka Okada and Ryuta Ushiro in 2005. They first came together in a studio of the Japanese artist, Makoto Aida.

Their early works were mostly inspired by the street cultures of Tokyo. They have produced a wide range of works by using the media of video, installation and performance. Chim↑Pom's pieces are always imbued with black humor and social critique, aimed at the contemporary Japanese society. In Chim↑Pom's well-known piece, "Super Rat" (2006-), they caught "super rats" (rats that evolved to fit the current society and are therefore likely to have certain traits to protect them from the next onslaught of poisons). Chim↑Pom caught the super rats in Shibuya, which is a city in Tokyo mainly visited by young people, and preserved these rats using taxidermy. Chim↑Pom colored them in yellow to resemble a famous Jap-

anese character Pikachu of the Pokémon series.

When commenting on this work, Ryuta Ushiro said "I had sympathy for these super rats because they have a strange coexistence with humans, but I captured each rat in an insect net I bought at Shibuya's huge discount store named Don Quixote".

In 2011, after the Tohoku earthquake, Chim↑Pom went to Fukushima, the location of the Fukushima Daiichi Nuclear Disaster. They broke into the exclusion zone and tried to approach the nuclear power plant to capture its condition by filming it and taking photographs. Through this, they showed the audience how they interact with reality. Soon after, they held an exhibition titled "Real Times" (2011) at the Mujin-to Production Gallery. Since then, this nuclear disaster became their main subject.

In 2016, together with Kenji Kubota (curator), Jason Waite (curator), Chim↑Pom curated a group exhibition titled "Don't Follow the Wind", exploring the unusual idea of using the exclusion zone as a venue for an exhibition. Numerous other well-known artists, such as Ai Weiwei, Trevor Paglen and Taryn Simon, also took part in the project. (A. K.)

E

Floating Subjectivity/Private Documentary

Takashi Homma (1962-)

Born in 1962, Takashi Homma lives and works in Tokyo. He began working for a publishing company during his studies at Ninon University College of Art, and later joined the staff of London-based fashion and culture magazine "i-D" in 1991-1992. He is a guest professor at Tokyo Zokei University since 2010. Since the 1990s, he takes pictures of landscapes of suburban Tokyo, called "new town", or other quarters of Tokyo. The resulting photo book *Tokyo Suburbia* (1998) earned him the Kimura Ihei Award, one of the most prestigious awards for photographers.

To describe his work, Takashi Homma uses the term Genfukei – an internal image or a landscape based on primitive experiences. Having grown up in a suburb of Tokyo where most residents inhabit modern apartment buildings, and multiple large new department store chains coexist along outdated commercial streets, Homma was attracted by the contrast of contemporary urbanism and the ability of photography to fix these ephemeral, always changing landscapes, into a material form. During Tokyo's urban development years, the image of his "Tokyo suburbia" became a primitive landscape shared by a large number of a population. The photography of Homma, showing different quarters of Tokyo such as *Shonan International Village*, evoques a strong generational and regional nostalgia.

The series "Tokyo and my Daughter" (2006) leads us to reconsider the essence of photography: the significance of assigning a title to an image, reality memorialized by the image. This series lets us observe a little girl, "my daughter" as she grows up. This is not a family photo album but a provocative work of art. The little girl is not his own daughter, as the work invites us to question reality and what we see. (M. O.)

Installation view of Takashi HOMMA

Takashi HOMMA
Boy 1, Keio Tama Center, Tokyo, 1998

On KAWARA
Nov.5, 1988 (1988), *DEC 18, 1992 "TODAY" Series No.46* (1992)

On KAWARA (1932-2014)

On Kawara was an internationally acclaimed artist who exerted a profound influence on other conceptual artists through his symbolic representations that sought to repress the subjective emotions of the artist or creator. After beginning his artistic career in Tokyo in 1951, he moved to New York in 1965.

Kawara turns "time" into numerical symbol. His *Date Paintings* express the synchronicity of time, while his book *One Million Years* sought to articulate a certain concept of time, or "timeliness," that transcends the scale of individual time. *One Million Years* is a typewritten sequence of the names of the one million years between 998,031 BC and 1969 AD, with 500 years inscribed on each page of the book. During his itinerant period, during which he started in the US and wandered through Central and South America and Europe, Kawara sent postcards and telegrams to friends and acquaintances as a form of mail art. The message "I am still alive" found in his telegrams alludes to a certain Buddhist attitude that regards death as a normal, readily apparent condition.

In the work on display, which comes from Kawara's *Date Paintings, 1966-2013* series, the date of its production is inscribed in white typography in the center of a canvas that has been painted in monochrome acrylic. Kawara imposed a rule on himself which stipulated that any particular work was to be completed the day it was started: if this could not be achieved, the work was to be destroyed. This series was inspired by the artist's practice of making a note of the date in the local language whenever he traveled abroad. After completing each *Date Painting*, Kawara would pack the work together with a newspaper from the day of its creation, storing the time and events associated with that particular day together with his painting. These *Date Paintings*, which encapsulate dates and the shifts in the objective situations around us within a format of difference and repetition across elements that have been reduced to a minimum, are a universal expression of the relationship between an individual existence (part) and the world (whole).

Kawara never appeared at any of his own openings during his lifetime, and maintained a consistent attitude of anonymity regarding his own status as an artist. He died while preparing for his first retrospective exhibition, *Silence*, at the Guggenheim Museum in New York in 2015, which was held after his death. (Y. H.)

Takuma NAKAHIRA (1938-2015)

Nakahira is a photographer who made an achievement also as a photo critic. After graduating from Tokyo University of Foreign Studies with a degree in Spanish, he launched his career as an editor of the general magazine *Gendai no Me* (*Contemporary Eye*). In 1968, he and coteries published the three-issue journal *Provoke* which was subtitled "provocative material for thought". In early 70's he published self-critical discourses one after another, and fall into a slump as a photographer. In 1977 he was stricken with memory loss and partial aphasia, but not long after resumed his activities. He continued to create and show new and previous work in solo and group exhibitions until his death in 2015.

Nakahira was certain of that the essence of photograph is recording, and was strongly critical of art photography as image of self-expression. He wasn't interested in art any further than as a socially structured concept. His early rough and blurred work

was influenced by William Klein, but he was well equipped as critic to create by himself a discourse to support his work as an objective methodology of sight. This sharpness made his work unique in quality. When he participated in the 7th Biennale de Paris in 1971, he carried out the project entitled "Circulation: Date, Place, Event" that was guerrilla-like exhibition in which he did in a single day from photographing each moment he spent to displaying developed photos, and reiterated it day by day. It was a complete implementation of the way that he had dreamt at the time, to thoroughly abolish lyricism and generate almost automatically lawless juxtaposition of photos in real time. Many of them had been torn down in places by themselves or someone's mischief but he thought it as a part of his work to be presented as it was. A radical actuality that he had shown here is continuing to vibrate the backbone of contemporary photography. (Y. S.)

Ikko NARAHARA
Domains, Garden of Scilence, 1958/1977

Takuma NAKAHIRA
For a Language to Come, 1970

Takuma NAKAHIRA
Untitled, 2005

Daido MORIYAMA
provoke no.2, 1968/2017

Diado MORIYAMA (1938-)

Moriyama first trained in graphic design before working as a professional photographer. His sense of collage of images in a city was raised in this term. After an assistant under Takeji Iwamiya in Osaka, and Eikoh Hosoe in Tokyo, he started his career as an independent photographer in 1964, publishing his first book *Nippon Gekijo Shashincho* (Japan Theater Photo Album) in 1968 and joining the avant-garde movement Provoke in 1968-69. In provoke no.2, although his street snaps were his es-

sential style, influenced by William Klein's photographic series of New York, Moriyama captured intimate atmosphere in a room between lovers, powerfully charged with eroticism that can be seen too in his street shots. He had marked a significant turning point on the photographic and art world both in Japan and in the West, with his distinctive style of *"are, bure, boke"* (rough, blurred and out-of-focus) and of quick snapshots without looking in the viewfinder. This technique culminated in his controversial work, *Shashin yo Sayounara* (Farewell Photography) published in 1972; the series contained images that were so out-of-focus and unrecognizable that almost all of them would normally be discarded. With his style of snapshots, he has taken thousands of photos of the city Shinjuku, where he has, from the beginning of his career, been really attracted. What he captures shows a shadow of the city that appears in a moment with uncanny and intense form. (J. U.)

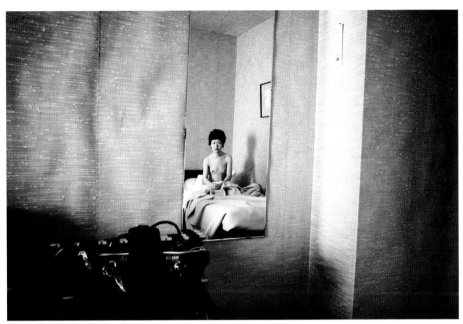

Nobuyoshi ARAKI
Sentimental Journey, 1971/2012

Nobuyoshi ARAKI (1940-)

Araki studied film and photography at Chiba University's Department of Photography, Painting and Engineering. Even in his bachelor course, he got many awards from Japanese photo journals and his photobook *Satchin* earned him the prestigious Taiyo Award in 1964. After his graduation, he started to work at the advertising agency Dentsu in 1963 until 1972. At Dentsu he met his wife Yoko, who was Araki's most important subject from their first meeting to even after her death in 1990: his most famous photobook published in 1971, *Senchimentaru na tabi* (*Sentimental Journey*), a photographic and private record of their honeymoon; one year later she passed away, Araki in 1991 created a second *Sentimental Journey* series, *Fuyu no Tabi* (*Winter Journey*), documenting their social gatherings, life at home and, sadly, his wife's final days. With this set of photobooks, Araki's style was recognized with the word "*Shi Shyashin*" (*private photography*): he approaches both objects and human subjects with his intimate and private gaze. The result of his approach demonstrates the relationship beyond between subject and object. The photographer is no longer in objective position but forced to change during the production. He calls this proess of production "sex". Araki is also known for the large number of his books such as still-life projects, nudes and portraiture. A theme of Eros and Thanatos (sex and death) is always central to his interest and appears in many forms; female genitalia, women's bodies in Japanese bondage, zoomed-up flowers and foods, and even Tokyo street scenes. (J. U.)

Naoya HATAKEYAMA
Rikuzentakata / 2011.5.1 Yonesaki-cho, 2011/2015

Hikaru FUJII
Documentary about Fukushima, 2011

Finger Pointing Worker
Pointing at Fukuichi Live Cam, 2011

Lieko SHIGA
RASEN KAIGAN, 2008-

Lieko SHIGA (1980-)

Shiga graduated in 2004 from Chelsea College of Art and Design's Department of Fine Art New Media, London. Raised in the middle class, she felt that her life was a sham and unreal due to the convenience and automation of daily life. "My photographs render everything into reality: they are a way of bringing something back to life," she remarks. According to her desire to find reality in her mind, Shiga always depicts dreamscapes by putting objects and human subjects in seemingly chaotic and surrealistic position that evokes unrealistic but intense emotion. In addition to mysterious relation among the objects in her composition, she also manages streaks of striking light and primitive energy to produce her dream-like images. Encountering Miyagi Prefecture during her residency for the exhibition *Re: search* held in Sendai Mediatheque in 2006, she found Kitakama, a small coastal village in Miyagi, where she could feel the most reality. In 2008, she moved there and began working as the village's official photographer who records festivals, other official events and oral history, while creating her art works. This move was remarkable for Shiga, and *Rasen Kaigan* (*Spiral Coast*) series (2008-) was created in concert with the local residents. The village was severely affected by tsunami in 2011, and the artist herself was one of the victims. However, what this series reflects is beyond those documenting local life before and after the tsunami. Instead, the result of her engagement with the fundamental question towards her own production appears: How and what can the photos show out of the realm of visibility? (J. U.)

HATRA
HATRA AW 2011 "ASYMMETRY HOODIE", 2011

HATRA
HATRA AW2012 "VT-MYNA", 2012
HATRA AW2011 "WAVE PANTS", 2011

Tetsuaki MATSUE
Tokyo Drifter, 2011

Rinko KAWAUCHI (1972-)

Kawauchi is a photographer who shoots through intimate and private gazes of everyday life. She graduated from Seian Women's College (now Seian University of Arts and Design) in 1993 and made a memorable debut in domestic and international photographic scene by simultaneously releasing a series of three photographic books of *Utatane*, *Hanabi* and *Hanako* in 2001 and she was awarded prestigious 27th Kimura Ihei Award - one of the most influential and significant photographic award in Japan - for *UTATANE* and *HANABI* in 2002.

Her works unfold the scent of "death", which consistently remains in our daily life, or in reverse, it shows some sense of "life" that is momentarily peeped through "death" as a flash of light. Thus, subjects of her photography are chosen from very diverse scenery which we glimpse in somewhere in our real ordinary life – little flowers and giant stem of a tree, insects, familiar pets, vast nature, micro city landscape, little girls, dead birds and so on.

She composes sequence of photographic books and exhibitions with highly delicate manner and that enables her sensual world of photography to generate beautiful, poetic and emotional but unexpected atmosphere. Series of *Illuminance* (2011) was the first photographic book to be published outside of Japan. This series is comprised of shots captured from 15 years of her private life experience. It is extremely intimate as well as almost autobiographical, but still anonymous. This ambiguity makes audience uneasy to completely grasp the sensibility that potentially exists from microcosms to macrocosms. Regardless of visibility for human eyes, this series shows gradation of light that fragments our continuous flow of consciousness and unconsciousness, and it leads viewers to remain at various layers of uncertainty of our daily reality. *Illuminance* took an exhibition form in Gallery at Hermès, New York (2011), Tokyo Metropolitan Museum of Photography, Tokyo (2012), and other locations. (S. K.)

Rinko KAWAUCHI
Untitled from Illuminance, 2007

Hiraki SAWA
Spotter, 2003

F

Materiality and Minimalism

Ryoji IKEDA
the transcendental (τ)
[n°1-2d], 2017

Noboru TAKAYAMA
Underground Zoo (Part), 1969/2003

LEE Ufan (1936-)

Lee was born in Korea and educated about painting at Seoul National University, but he moved to Japan and studied philosophy in Nihon University. At the end of 1960s, he has come to be recognized as one of the founding artists of "Mono-ha" (literally translated as "School of Things") movement, as well as a theorist of modern art. Mono-ha is a Japanese avant-garde art movement around 1970, whose artists used raw materials such as wood, stone and steel to make their sculptures.

All of Lee's sculptures are named *Relatum*, which is a philosophical term signifying objects or events which have a certain relation. A notion of relation between objects or human and object is the center of his philosophy of art and Lee called it "encounter." He focused on what we see in the bare existence and aimed at a kind of lived experience that the viewer would encounter things "as it is." Lee criticizes the method of modern Western art in his works although it might

LEE Ufan
Relatum (Formerly Phenomena and Perception B),
1968/2017

Susumu KOSHIMIZU
Relief '80-8, 1980

have been pointed out the similarity with minimalism. In fact, it is considered that he has combined his artistic practice with modern Western metaphysics and traditional Asian philosophy, such as Taoism. He has also produced paintings since 1960s, such as series of *From Line* and *From Point* (1972-1984), with mineral pigment and glue on canvas. In his paintings, the drawn forms are minimal and abstract to signify an interest of the artist about East Asian aesthetics, similar to his sculptures.

Lee's works and theory of art attracted attention in Japan and consequently he began to be known internationally, including in Korea, Europe and the U.S. In 2010, designed by Tadao Ando, Lee Ufan Museum, which is his first personal museum, opened at Naoshima, Japan. After that, in 2015, Space Lee Ufan also opened at Busan Museum of Art in Korea. (R. K.)

Hiroshi SUGIMOTO
Mediterranean Sea, La Galère from the series of Ten Seascape (1989), *Mirtoan Sea, Sounion
I from the series of Ten Seascape* (1990), , *North Sea, Berriedale from the series of Ten
Seascape*(1990)*Sea of Okhotsk, Hokkaido from the series of Ten Seascape* (1989)

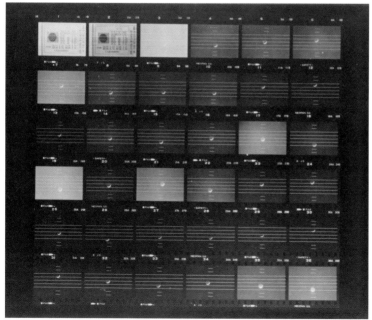

Hitoshi NOMURA
'moon' score
1979.1.1, 1980

F   **Materiality and Minimalism**

Yohji YAMAMOTO
Women's jacket, 1990/1991

Tomoharu MURAKAMI
Untitled, 1981

Tatsuo MIYAJIMA
Moon in the ground no.2, 2015

Ryoji IKEDA (1966-)

Ikeda is an electronic composer and a visual artist who experiments minimal features of computer- based sound and light as fundamentally reduced combination of units for human perception. He highly emphasizes on mathematical precision and mathematical aesthetics in his creation process and makes a synthesized live -performance or installation of sound and light through extremely elaborated mathematical and physical notions.

While he worked as a musical producer, he met a multi-media performance group "Dumb Type" and was extremely influenced by their cross disciplinary artistic expressions. Through creative production experience with Dumb Type, he began to compose his own music and started his artistic career with his first album 1000 fragments in 1995.

Around 2000, while he consistently developed techno-minimal music and experimenting units of sound especially through series of matrix (2000-), he also started experimenting use of light in his installation, mainly represented by his project spectra (2001-). Questioning very essential components of sound and reducing them into minimized scientific signals and physical impulses resulted an unclear distinction between sound and light. Through this realization, he started synthesized concerts of sound and light such as formula (2000-), and eventually he assumed the most minimalized informational units as "data" which resulted his project datamatics (2006-).

The work, data.scan (2009) - part of the project datamatics - is an audiovisual installation which presents a relationship of sets of data from meta-scientific human body and astronomical universe through image shown from horizontal monitor-based equipment with sound. It shows mapping of our body and universe both reduced into scale-less random units as "data".

His exhibition has been held worldwide including +/- [the infinite between 0 and 1] at Museum of Contemporary Art Tokyo (2008), supersymmetry at le lieu unique, Nantes (2014), micro | macro at ZKM centre for Art and Media, Karlsruhe (2015) and other various major locations all over the world. (S. K.)

Ryoji IKEDA
data.tron, 2007

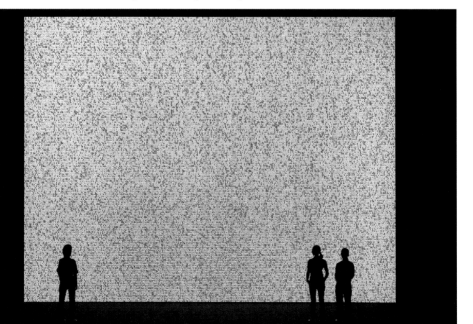

Koji ENOKURA (1942-1995)

Enokura is considered to be an important artist of the 1970s and often introduced as one of the "Mono-ha" artists, for his varied works focusing on stains and blotches, or in more abstract term, erosion and intervention. His concern was a threshold of perception in that things perceive each other. Especially he emphasized interaction between his physical body and a surrounding environment, with critical feeling about an informatization and mediatisation. This theme had been explored in not only the works itself using daily unstructured materials like oil, grease, paper, soil, mortar, leather, etc., but also experimental projects that vitalize not-institutionalized places such as the Space Totsuka in 1970 which was held at the vacant lot near his friend Noboru Takayama's apartment, and "Points exhibition" in 1973 using the garden of Enokura's own home.

Enokura entered Tokyo University of the Arts and tried surrealistic paintings at first but began to face the material from when he realized that oil paints are a colored sticky substance rather than a medium for drawing. In 1970, he installed the *Place* in which he paved the floor with a lot of papers and dipped them in oil, at 'Tokyo Biennale '70 Between Man and matter' curated by Yusuke Nakahara, a Japanese art critic, who surveyed 'When Attitudes Become Form' one year before. In the following year he participated in the section called "interventions" of the 7th Biennale de Paris and received the highest scholarship award for the *Wall* that was a wall built with blocks and mortar between the trees at the Parc Floral. Around this time, he created many photographs entitled *Symptom* problematizing a sense of the tactile. In the 1990s, he resumed the work of photography, *STORY & MEMORY*, combining two photos which contains old and new ones to give not only conceptual but also lyrical suggestions. (Y. S.)

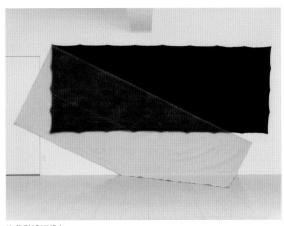

Koji ENOKURA
Untitled, 1980

Tadashi KAWAMATA
Tree Huts in Place Vendome, 2013

Kishio SUGA
Law of Peripheral Units, 1997/2017

Kishio SUGA (1944-)

Artist. Kishio Suga studied modernism and
theories of deconstruction under Yoshishige
Saito at Tama Art University. He was a core
member of the Mono-ha school of art that
emerged around 1968. The Mono-ha artists
questioned theories of art making centered
on Western artists and emphasized the
ontology of things ("*mono*"), allowing these
mono (materials) to speak for themselves,
instead of reflecting the intentions of their
creators.

Suga basically establishes new relationships
between materials without altering or
modifying them, by splitting, cutting, tear-
ing, or tying them together with his own
hands. He produces encounters between
natural and industrial materials such as
stone, wood, earth, paper, concrete, metal,
glass, rope, and wire. Suga sublates the inter-
dependent existences of objects within a
space based on the concept of *hōchi* (which
roughly corresponds to "release/abandon-
ment"), turning the resultant scenes —
which he calls "situations" — into works of
art. Influenced by James Gibson's notion
of "direct perception," in which the per-
ceiver identifies objects that already have a
structure within the environment, Suga has
developed what he calls "activations" — the
act of activating spaces by installing objects
and replacing them — since 1974. These
activations demonstrate the "temporality"
(Achille Bonito Oliva) in Mono-ha's pursuit
of ontology.

Law of Surroundings (Shuiritsu), the work on
display at this exhibition, consists of pipes
that make up the upper portion of a grid-
like structure installed at the entrance to the
space, joined by ropes to stones that have
been placed on the floor. The ropes are intri-
cately interlaced, and various spaces emerge
between the slender pillars one after another
within our field of vision as we circle around
the work. (Y. H.)

Kohei NAWA (1975-)

Received his doctoral from Fine Art Sculpture at Kyoto City University of Arts with his thesis "Sensibility and Skin" in 2003. Having the unique concept of "CELL" in 2000, Nawa has transformed materials into different forms of expression. For instance, his *PixCell* series, which is a word that integrates "pixel", which demonstrates digital image resolution, and the biological "cell", makes visible current sensibility with which we feel more reality in a virtual image than real one. A part of *PixCell* series, *PRISM* (2002-) is a sculptural embodiment of motifs collected through the internet. Prism sheets covering a cell holding the object makes various images appear and disappear according to the actual perspective of the viewer. Through this process, the subject which should remain in the box (cell) loses its sense of realness, lingers as a virtual image, and its meaning and symbolic aspects are disappearing as its perception and its physical sense of distance are unified. Then, instead of material or symbolic meaning that usually help to connect with a viewer, the materiality and reality in the contemporary society appear through "skin" which is not touchable but able to contact. *Force* (2016-) is an installation work that provides a visualization of the force of gravity via black silicone oil. This strange liquid creates viscous spots on the celling, streams constantly under the influence of gravity, forms a black pool on the floor and makes muddy marks like rain drops. Inventing the new interface of solids and liquids, it provides a unclassifiable physical impulse for our paralyzed "skin" with the new intensity of materiality. (J. U.)

Kohei NAWA
Force, 2015

Japanese culture since 1970:
A cinematic panorama in a letter

—

Yasuo Kobayashi

Imagine receiving a letter from a friend in Japan, an old friend. A letter in which he says he's decided that the only way to talk to you, a foreigner, about Japanese culture from 1970 to the present day, to discuss its essence (assuming there is a such a thing), is to do so in the manner of a silent movie, cinematographically, moreover by serving himself as the narrator and interpreter, in old-style Japanese *benshi* fashion. To explain the vast spread of all things cultural in Japan over half a century from a benchmark of objectivity would be impossible. Plus, he says, the period of time over which that culture unfolded overlapping as it does with the time he has been alive, in other words, also, to some extent, the unfolding of his own life, perhaps the most honest approach would be to try to describe the cultural landscape as he physically sensed it, from a fractal point of view somewhere between the first and third person, no matter how personal a perspective this might be.

In 1970, your friend was twenty years old. That's right, half a century on from when he first adopted his pet saying, Paul Nizan's "I was twenty, I won't let anyone say those are the best years of your life." He had grown up in the intense, violent, literally hellish "season" referred to by the term "postwar," spanning the years 1945 to 1970, only to find that this storm had abruptly abated, came to an end, leaving him, like many others, facing a sudden void in the space-time of history. A severing, a turning point, nothingness.

Yet at the same time, for someone of twenty, still naked and unencumbered with nothing to lose or protect, this also marked the arrival of a new "season." And let us be clear, this was also a season of new knowledge arriving from where else but, France. Obviously, even in the "postwar" period up to 1970, the cultural axis had been formed by the existentialism of Sartre, coupled with Marxism. When in France however, the nexus of violent, struggle-oriented existence fell from favor, and a new intellectual understanding made itself apparent, one that instead decentralized subjective centrality, it wasn't long before in Japan too that "knowledge" – in the form of structuralism, linguistics, semiotics, Lacanian psychoanalysis, rhetoric, post-structuralism, deconstructionist philosophy, Deleuzian philosophy, postmodern cultural theory, etc. etc. – was introduced, and began, little by little, deliberately or otherwise, to offer new cultural frameworks. Since the age of twenty your friend had been an introducer, an interpreter, and a critical practitioner of the current of "new knowledge" bundled in Japan under "20th century French philosophy."

Which is why, having thus spent so many years as a kind of "ferryman" he says he would like to try telling you, who dwell in French culture, about Japanese culture from 1970 onward – culture not without its French aspects – based on his own bodily sensation of having lived through it. Key here are the words "body" (*shintai*) and "sensation." He has already, elsewhere, discussed postwar Japanese culture from 1945 to 1970 with a focus on "the flesh" (*nikutai*).[1] Here, instead of this term shot through with violence and carnality, he chooses the more neutral "body," a largely phenomenological designation. In very symbolic or economic terms, the perverse suicide (on November 25, 1970) of the author Yukio Mishima marked the demise of the dynamic "postwar" "flesh" and its replacement by the neutral, quotidian, sensate "body." And that was the phase shift of cultural severing your friend sensed. How the cultural landscape that virtually anonymous "body" walked amid panned out from that point, is the cinematographic version of events he will offer you here.

To begin with he will explain, "This 'movie' consists broadly of two parts. In simple terms, Part 1 covers from 1970 to 1990. Strictly speaking, 1989, the year the 'Showa' era became 'Heisei' would be just as acceptable, or 1990, which marked the bursting of Japan's economic bubble. As you are well aware, 1989 saw the fall of the Berlin Wall, and an end to the global order of the Cold War. This was also the year of Tiananmen Square. During this period, the whole structure of the world was shaken up, and Japan changed too. Part 2 should then extend from 1991 to 2011 perhaps. In Japan these were the 'lost years' of economic stagnation that came to a tragic close with the 2011 Tohoku earthquake. The subsequent six years are still our 'present,' and to gain insight into this culture-in-progress and tell someone else about it is not yet possible. Those years will simply serve as an incomplete coda to the blank in our 'movie.'"

Thus at long last, a title appears on screen before you.

1.

Towards space, followed by fantasy (1970–1990)

Projected behind this title is an urban landscape, or more accurately, images of a city being shaped, incrementally, yet swiftly. To give just a few indicators in the setting of the capital, Tokyo, this period saw the construction, in rapid succession, of a series of high-rises starting with the Kasumigaseki Building (156m) in 1968, followed by the World Trade Center Building (163m) in 1970, the Keio Plaza Hotel (179m) in 1971, Shinjuku Sumitomo Building (210m) and Shinjuku Mitsui Building (225m) in 1974, and Sunshine 60 (240m) in 1978, reorganizing the Tokyo cityscape – which up to then had retained a distinctly "postwar" air – into a totally new urban space, thus transforming the reality of the city. Woven into this was a transformation not only vertically, in the form of high-rise buildings, but horizontally too, in the large-scale development of suburbs such as Tama New Town. *Building a New Japan: A Plan for Remodeling the Japanese Archipelago* was the manifesto of Kakuei Tanaka, who became prime minister in 1972, and indeed, the Japanese archipelago would be drawn into a maniacal maelstrom of spatial modification in the form of a reconfiguring of its cities. So if there was a main actor dominating the screen during this period, it would have been the city, the constantly proliferating urban space itself.

Your friend continues, "Actually, the phrase *kukan e* (towards space) is the title of a book, a collection of architectural essays published by architect Arata Isozaki in 1971. Be careful though not to mistake the intended meaning as 'spaces for living.' Rather, to leave meaning up in the air, stop time, and borrow the words of Isozaki, it is a phrase that advocates 'severing the continuity of history.' That is, rather than optimistically lauding the formation of new cities of the future, it is a phrase that declares the cities of the future to be inherently desolate. In other words, the new, what could perhaps be described as postmodern, cities emerging here and now overlap with Isozaki's memories of the desolation brought about by firebombing, the ruins he ran about in 'with childish innocence.' Creation is already a vestige. A deviation. If, in the previous era, it was asserted that the strength of the 'flesh,' or 'time' of violence would inherit history, and create it, one could say that in this era, there was a switch from this aesthetic (pathognomy) of the strength of the subject, to an aesthetic of 'deviations' and vestiges in which different multiple temporalities coexist. So though rather sudden of me, I should like to translate the maxim of 'towards space' as the *différance* of Isozaki's contemporary Jacques Derrida, or rather, if I may be so bold, my version, 'towards *diffé-errance*.' Meaning, during this period, rather than differentiating itself by impulsive motion as in the previous era, the subject crosses various borders running through space, discovers different worlds, senses those very 'deviations,' and attempts to live them."

Thus one ostinato for this period was clearly the discovery of other cultures, in particular non-Western cultures. Moreover these "other cultures" included the "discovery" of the forgotten foundational culture, and popular culture, of "Japan." Japanese culture itself was recognized and recreated anew as an "other culture." An example of this is fashion designer Issey Miyake, who abandoned Parisian haute couture to return to Japan and "discover" the workwear of tradesmen in the streets and traditional garb of ordinary people in the provinces, and establish his own originality, and titled a book on his early work *East Meets West* (1978); thus the "cultural anthropological gaze" that encountered and engaged in dialogue with other cultures, including "Japan," replacing the rather urgent ideological/political gaze of the previous era, formed a major cultural axis. Furthermore – though of course Japan also had a long tradition of ethnological studies by figures such as Kunio Yanagita and Shinobu Orikuchi – this shift does, first and foremost, seem to have been under the influence of French cultural anthropology as typified by Levi-

Strauss, among others. Precisely for that reason, if we were to insist on selecting one "intellectual" from the many to represent the era in Japan, if in the previous "postwar" era it was political philosopher Masao Maruyama, then perhaps it should be cultural anthropologist, and incidentally, friend of Arata Isozaki, Masao Yamaguchi. In the 1970s, Yamaguchi turned his gaze on the complementary relationship between the cultural "center" and "fringes," theorizing that subjects that move and mediate between the two have the status of "tricksters." In 1975 he published *Doke no minzokugaku* (Folkloristics of the trickster) therein while referencing various cultures around the world, discussed a trickster culture that fosters celebratory spaces for eros and laughter while insouciantly violating boundaries, that also served as a lesson in how to be a subject after the disappointment of political radicalism.

The fact is that during this period many Japanese intellectuals experienced encounters with cultures all over the globe, from Bali to Mexico, Hawaii to Africa, their gaze focused on the search for an alternative "universality" itself manifesting only as specificity; one fundamentally different to the concentration on playing catch-up with "Western culture" that had hitherto dominated Japan's modernization. Moreover, that gaze was directed, first and foremost, at Japanese culture itself, leading to a rediscovery of that culture. The fruits of that rediscovery were in turn disseminated to the world, for instance at the 1978 "Festival d'automne" in Paris, for which Arata Isozaki organized the exhibition "Ma: Space-Time in Japan." There, a survey of Japanese culture was presented under the basic concept of "ma," that is to say, "*zure*" (deviation, gap, or slippage).

It is important to remember though that this anthropological "trickster" gaze was simultaneously a gaze that "saw" a world beyond reality, or strictly speaking, an imaginative world "beneath" reality, that is, fantasy.

According to our letter-writer, "The mood during this period was fundamentally one of euphoria, yet cognizant of the fact that 'beneath' reality lie desolation, disappointment, death, like a cavity. This kind of 'void' can erupt at any time as fantasy, via a small 'chink' or 'moment' in reality. 'There is no war here, but we can see scenes from a war taking place over the sea as a mirage.' Or, 'Beneath the ground of this reality of ours, extend the labyrinthine streets of the "the end of the world."'" Thus fantasy and reality complement and intersect with one another.[2] Between them, I, who can no longer believe in any kind of ultimate 'solution' am destined to wander, endlessly. It is only looking back now I feel deeply that herein may lie some kind of new morals. That is to say, morals that take onboard the chaos of coexisting with the 'end of the world' as predicted by Alexandre Kojève. In terms of cultural phenomena, this seems to have manifested clearly in the fault line symbolized by Hayao Miyazaki's fantasy *Nausicaä of the Valley of the Wind* (1984) and Haruki Murakami's *Hard-Boiled Wonderland and the End of the World* (1985). No doubt one could cite any number of things, such as the intellectual phenomenon dubbed 'new academism,' but by the mid '80s, it would be fair to say a new form of culture starts to become quite apparent."

Thus before we knew it, on our screen, the real urban landscape had been replaced for example by the image of 16-year-old Nausicaä riding a winged Möwe (a kind of light flying machine) over the poisonous fungi forest known as the "Sea of Corruption" in the *Nausicaä of the Valley of the Wind* animated film. The "brightness" of the innocent infans floating above the "end of the world": this is what symbolized this period.

<hr>

2.

Scenes on the social frontline, and catastrophe (1991–2011)

Yet things that by right ought to have been fantasy, keep rearing their heads as reality. This is the drama in the second half of our cinematic guide. 1991 marked the disintegration of an era of stable growth that had characterized the Japanese economy since 1973, plunging the country into an extended low-growth period dubbed the "lost decades." To this were added terrorism, earthquakes and their accompanying natural disasters and accidents. Our screen now shows not animated movies but images from a string of real tragedies: burning townscapes after the Hanshin Earthquake of 1995, and also in 1995, people collapsing in multiple Tokyo subway stations, victims of sarin gas released by a religious cult. Finally culminating in images of the tsunami sweeping away all in its path, and the destroyed reactor at Fukushima, following the Tohoku quake (2011).

Our self-appointed narrator continues, "As you can see, it's just one catastrophic image after another, but do note this doesn't mean these years were utterly shrouded in gloom. Looking back from where we are now, it was a period of dramatic change in the nature of culture as a whole. Moreover not one peculiar to Japan, but a cultural transformation on an international scale – globalization – connected to the IT revolution.

"In barely twenty years, the whole of capitalist-based human culture underwent a major shift. Though not entirely without the kind of optimistic 'brightness' brought by technological progress, at the same time such change also had the effect of hollowing out and dismantling the existing culture and social frameworks from the inside. In light of this, the question of how to redefine and reconfigure 'being human' is an urgent one for everyone on the planet. Yet it is less a matter of there being a single universal answer, as the only likely option being to venture answers in each instance, accompanied by their execution, in specific, singular settings. In that sense, Japanese culture during this period was not governed by any single 'grand narrative' or 'big idea'; more important by far was practice in individual 'small scenes' within society. That is, boundaries do not only run between the culture of one's own country and those of others, but all over society: in the streets, in communities, families, workplaces, systems, human relationships. All sorts of discrimination – on the basis of gender, disability, nationality, poverty – run through all sorts of settings. Actually making an issue of, rendering visible, and expressing the boundaries running between the self and others, in individually unique, anonymous settings was perhaps a requirement of this era, as opposed to any 'language of ideas' encapsulated in a single proper noun."

If this is the case, one might venture that this age was one not so much of sociology as an academic discipline, as of sociology in the form of "small praxes" on the social frontline. Even in international terms, Japan is experiencing a conspicuous aging of its population, coupled with an overall population decline. Thus people are concentrated in the major cities, the flip side being rapid depopulation in more rural areas. The question of how to sustain local communities is an extremely pressing, critical one for Japanese society, compounded by the urgent challenge of reviving localities devastated by earthquakes and other large-scale natural disasters. But no two localities are the same, each being different in every respect, including natural and historical conditions. There is no general, no universal course of action; it is necessary to engage in very complex praxes intertwining politics, economics, social and cultural aspects, in response to the unique qualities of each location.

Note – and this does not apply only to Japan – that this complex issue is precisely what artistic practice can address. In other words, art goes beyond personal expression to become praxis that while crossing the various boundaries running through individual settings within society, activates those settings and connects them to others. Art thus contributes to the revival of social bonds. And for its part, is also transformed. And when art activity such as this is organized in a specific locality as an art festival such as a biennial or triennial, it also addresses the social issue of promoting that locality. Only a few examples can be given here, such as the Yokohama Triennale launched in 1999, the Echigo-Tsumari Art Triennale launched in 2000, and Setouchi Triennale, run since 2010, but the opening up of what is also a celebratory setting between art and society is not just some feelgood story from the provinces, but a development that speaks more powerfully than anything of the direction of culture during this era.

Your friend concludes, "On the one hand, a gaping hole has been torn in the fabric of our reality by an apocalyptic catastrophe. On the other, remarkable progress in digital technologies has resulted in the growing infiltration of a virtual, game-like, fantasy-filled world into every facet of culture. It seems that while our bodies too, oscillate between these two "ends," i.e. real catastrophe and fantasy game, still, in these islands on the edge of the world (or at least the vast Eurasian continent), we are developing 'small praxes' in an effort to connect heaven and earth in our sensations. Meaning 'small praxes' that are trying to reconstruct and reproduce human reality, starting on the smallest possible scale, that of our own bodily sensations. We never doubt however that this diminutive quality in itself is connected to the true vastness of the world. Therein we find hope. Not hope for me, of course, or us.

Hope for others, the kind that Benjamin meant when he stated, reading Goethe's *Effective Affinities*, that 'Only for the sake of the hopeless, are we given hope.' In the scene in which we find ourselves, practicing, between catastrophe and fantasy, not some 'overarching logic' but 'small hopes' that are true to our senses, even if that means being 'tricksters,' perhaps that was in fact the best culture of this era."

Thus the movie reel of this letter from your Japanese acquaintance finishes by speaking, even after all that has occurred, of "hope." Now, half a century on from 1970, his letter expresses a wish that the many "small praxes" pursued following the discovery and belief that in the Japanese archipelago, the sensations of a single body are connected directly to the sensations of the world, make their way to you as tiny rays of hope.

Translated from Japanese by Pamela Miki Associates

Notes

[1] The author gave four lectures on the theme of postwar Japanese culture in 2012 at the Collège de France in Paris. The research began there continued and was published in 2016 as *Opera sengo bunkaron I: Nikutai no kuraki unmei 1945–1970 (Miraisha)*. As the title indicates, this discussed culture up to the year 1970, however observations on culture after 1970 continued until the end of 2019 in the form of a series in a magazine. These were collected and published in May 2020 as *Opera sengo bunkaron II: Nichijo hijo, meikyu no jidai 1970–1995*.

[2] This refers not only to Haruki Murakami's *Hard-Boiled Wonderland and the End of the World* (1985), but also Ryu Murakami's *War Begins Beyond the Sea* (1977).

The 3.11 earthquake and social media

—

Yoshitaka Mōri

1.

A shift from mass media to social media?

The Tohoku earthquake of 2011, commonly referred to in Japan by the shorthand "3.11," was a crucial moment for Japan in the sense that most people began to recognize the genuine usefulness of social media sites such as Twitter, Facebook and Ustream. By 2011, the development of internet digital technology and mobile terminals including smartphones and tablets had encouraged the widespread use of social media among younger people in particular. By 2011, 75.2 percent of Japanese were using social media services (Facebook and mixi), 54.8 percent blogs, and 50 percent Twitter.[1] Many however used social media merely for recreation, second to conventional media such as newspapers, magazines and television.

It would however be a mistake to assume that the 3.11 earthquake and arrival of social media alone caused an epistemological rupture, even though these did have a huge impact on the ensuing intellectual debate; the shift from mass media to social media did not only mean a transformation in media conditions, but an entire restructuring of the social, political and cultural conditions by, and reproduced by, the ideological apparatus of the state. Although new digital media play a crucial role in contemporary society, it would be wrong to attribute social changes entirely to the development of media technology; we must be careful to avoid reductionist explanations, including those involving historical causation or technological determinism. Social media is not merely a product of technology but also one of culture, society and even politics.

It may thus be more appropriate to see the sociocultural shift around the 3.11 earthquake as a part of "the long revolution" in culture that has been taking place since the second half of the twentieth century, following the democratic and industrial revolutions.[2] Or perhaps examining experiences in the earthquake and its aftermath inevitably invites us to deal with a new historical consciousness that goes beyond a humanist understanding of history: the awareness that when it comes to making history, natural disaster may in fact be the most powerful actor. It may take far longer than any human life span to solve all the problems with radiation Japan is now facing. Our experiences recorded, collected and accumulated in social media may survive in digital format even after we are gone. There is a need to situate social media and the experience of the 3.11 earthquake not only within a local and contemporary context, but also a more general and historical context.

_____2.

Affective communication

The 3.11 earthquake and its aftermath were, to me, living in the capital, a mixed experience of physical earthquake, and a series of media events. I was alone at home in Tokyo when the earthquake struck the Tohoku area just before three o'clock in the afternoon on March 11, 2011. Continuing for some time, it was the strongest tremor I had ever experienced. From the duration of the shaking, my high-school knowledge told me that the quake had occurred some distance from Tokyo.

Turning on the TV I found it had taken place in the Tohoku area, but could not find any concrete information. I tried to call family and friends but was unable to reach anyone. The internet was not working properly. Turning off the TV, I had started to tidy up fallen books and CDs when a second tremor occurred.

I do not remember exactly what time it was. Turning on the TV again, I was shocked to see a coastal city being washed away by a tsunami. The sight was like something out of a sci-fi film, and I could not believe what was really happening. If the next quake hit Tokyo, I was afraid it might be devastated in the same way; aftershocks were still continuing in the capital. The whole situation was extremely frightening. Family members all walked home because public transportation had shut down completely. My mother, who happened to be shopping in Shibuya, gave up going back to her home and came to our flat nearby. I still could not make contact with my father at their suburban home in the east of Tokyo, due to a power failure in their neighborhood.

In his detailed analysis of TV and media archives following the earthquake on March 11, Mamoru Ito confirmed that it was just after 15:50 when NHK and other TV stations started to broadcast the first footage of the tsunami, shot from a helicopter in the sky over the city of Sendai.[3] This footage showing the tsunami sweeping away cars, bikes, roads, fields and buildings in Sendai was so incredibly shocking that it was repeatedly aired not only in Japan, but around the world. By this time, internet services were slowly being restored, though some social media services still had problems. Social media such as YouTube and Ustream started to disseminate images of the tsunami as well. Soon after, more images of the tsunami in different cities and ports began to be broadcast on TV, while footage flooded onto the internet, TV stations picking up these uploaded images as a part of their program-ming. All the footage was circulated on multiple media including TV, social media and Twitter, some of it translated into different languages and circulated overseas.

Uncertainty, fear and anxiety like I had never experienced drove me to devour TV, websites and social media information. My e-mail server was not yet working properly, meaning I could not send or receive personal e-mail, but other services were functioning relatively well. Information could be shared on the internet.

At 17:37 that day, NHK mentioned the Fukushima nuclear power plant for the first time, very briefly. This was followed by news at 17:40 in more detail about a power failure at the plant due to the tsunami, but suggested there were no concerns about radiation leakage. While at this point, the mass media did not discuss the issue of the Fukushima power plant any further, social media erupted into a loud debate over the risk of an accident at the nuclear plant. Some even started to argue that people should leave Tokyo before the situation got worse.

The chaos in the media ramped up even further the following day. Recovery of the IT infrastructure unleashed a torrent of information, visuals and discussion. It was difficult to leave the house, as the ground was still continuously shaking, public transportation systems still in the process of recovering, and most shops and restaurants closed. Most of us had no choice other than to stay at home and watch TV or check the internet. We were surrounded by overwhelming media images of the disaster.

Digital cameras on every mobile phone and smartphone in the stricken area functioned as thousands of not only social-media eyes, but eyes for television as well; all the TV stations began to use footage captured by social media users, even if the technical quality was not always very good. As a result, those watching television were able to experience through the "eyes" of social media what was actually happening somewhere distant, virtually as it happened. Thus the social media experience became more environmental, rather than merely receptive.

I am not sure to what extent my experience on social media during the first hectic couple of days after the earthquake was shared by others, but what is clear is that I was trying to directly relate to those caught up in the earthquake, tsunami and the nuclear plant incident that followed. What I did definitely share with others was a collective uncertainty, fear and anxiety about the future, as no one knew what would happen next. Maybe social media users were united by fears of catastrophe to come.

We felt like we were sharing a common destiny, as if in a small village. I was reminded of Marshall McLuhan, who in the early 1960s, long before the development of digital media, predicted the arrival of a "global village" in the age of electronic media such as television and the telephone.[4] In his interview with Canadian TV channel CBC in 1960, McLuhan referred to the experience of an earthquake in order to explain this new media environment, suggesting that in the event of a quake, "no matter where we live, [due to the shaking] we all get the message," and going on to say, "today's teenager, the future villager, who feels especially at home with our new gadgets... will bring our tribe even closer together."[5] He argued that villagers acquire a sense of belonging through non-verbal communication: "tribal drums" as a means of affective communication. Following McLuhan's argument, I would argue that images and sound on social media, together with the experience of the earthquake, including the shaking of the ground, and power outages, spawned a new kind of earthquake-village consciousness under a particular set of emergency conditions: a collective, but fragmented and digitalized, sensation in which we live contemporaneously beyond time and space.

We should, of course, maintain a critical viewpoint here: even social media could not supply images in the very early stages of the disaster. In the most heavily damaged areas, social media did not function at all; power supply ceased, preventing access to any kind of IT infrastructure. Mobile phones did not work either, because in the worst-hit areas almost all the relay stations were closed down. It was impossible to represent the experiences of the true victims, even on social media. Their voices were unheard, their figures unseen, at least in the very midst of the disaster.

Naoya Hatakeyama's high-resolution photographs of the Tohoku landscape remind us of one of the dilemmas of media: the complex relationship between memory and record. No media technology can capture all the memories or experiences, especially of victims, but only record what remains, the visible, and the audible. The media never represents what is real, what happens behind the landscape. However, recorded images continue to endlessly produce and reproduce memories. Hatakeyama's works may look very quiet, or silent, but at the same time, behind them we can feel something having happened, still happening and probably going to happen in the future. This creates a shared consciousness even among those who have not experienced the disaster.

Immediately after the earthquake, despite the quake's devastating impact on people, land and economy, one could sense a strange kind of "hope" shared particularly among the younger generation. They believed that this worst of situations might prove a great opportunity to change the world, with some actively participating in reconstruction projects as volunteers, others organizing lifeline communication networks on social media to circulate vital information, others starting to organize new political campaigns, including against nuclear power, and yet others beginning to explore new anti-capitalist ways of life. This may be viewed as an excellent example of the rise of "extraordinary communities in disasters," as brilliantly explained by Rebecca Solnit.[6] The architectural project Home-for-All, initiated by a group of architects including Toyo Ito, Riken Yamamoto and Kazuyo Sejima, may be seen as an example of establishing utopian communities amid a calamity of historical proportions. Challenging the modernist ideology of architecture, the group attempted to build temporary, ephemeral architectural communities where people can live together, share their experiences and help each other. The aim of the project was to build a "home" for those who had lost their homes both physically and psychologically.

Social media as alternative media

The 3.11 earthquake and the ensuing Fukushima nuclear power plant disaster gave a different social role to social media: that of an alternative to mainstream media. Social media began to be used to scrutinize information circulated by mainstream media sources, to analyze the situation from both critical and professional viewpoints, and to deliver information not dealt with by mainstream media. In particular, starting with the series of accidents at the Fukushima power plant on March 12–15 leading to nuclear meltdown, hydrogen-air explosions and the release of radioactive material, while the mainstream media confined itself to delivering only official messages from the government and TEPCO, certain social media platforms started to circulate their own interpretations of what was happening and demanded that the government reveal the truth. Social media thus played a crucial role in mobilizing, organizing and assembling people in the growing movement opposed to nuclear power plants.

In the immediate wake of the nuclear accident, most TV shows reported only official announcements, not engaging in any investigative journalism themselves,[7] instead repeatedly reporting that the nuclear reactors had no problems, and that there was no immediate risk to health even from radiation leaks. Recent investigations however have shown that the government and TEPCO shared information on the risk of meltdowns and radioactive contamination very soon after the accident.

It was, on the contrary, independent journalists that actively disseminated news of the incident at the plant by conducting their own investigations.[8] On March 13, six members of the Japan Visual Journalist Association (JVJA) and the editor of *Days Japan* went to the town of Futaba near the nuclear plant to collect information on the incident. These were journalists who specialized in incidents at nuclear power plants and the health impacts of radiation, and who had been actively engaged in discussions around nuclear energy since the Chernobyl disaster in 1986. They found radiation levels in the area that were too high to be measured using the Geiger counter they carried, filmed this and sent the footage to Tokyo by Skype, where it was immediately uploaded by OurPlanet-TV, a non-profit independent web-based media organization, shocking many people not only in Japan, but around the world.

The Citizen's Nuclear Information Center (CNIC) is a non-profit organization that disseminated information about the accident, and scientific knowledge related to nuclear energy. Since their establishment in Tokyo in 1975, they have conducted a variety of research, providing reliable information, and educating the public. On March 12, they launched their first web-streaming program, in which Masashi Goto, an ex-Toshiba engineer previously involved for many years in nuclear reactor design, in particular, the durability of reactors, suggested from a specialist perspective that it was highly possible the cooling system was malfunctioning and meltdown had already begun.

The CNIC had no previous experience of social media. It was an internet journalist organization established by Yasumi Iwakami in 2010, Independent Web Journal (IWJ), that set up the first program for the CNIC on the 12th. The CNIC acquired social media know-how from IWJ, and soon were producing regular programs by themselves that served as a source of information on the nuclear accident. CNIC spokesperson Masako Sawai later said in a symposium that she had not even watched the Ustream service until March 11, and they had started streaming on social media because they received too many phone inquiries just after the earthquake. This is a good example of how the quake and ensuing events encouraged people to use social media.

The transnational nature of social media was also important, as conventional mass media remained national. Once uploaded, social media information was translated into different languages by anonymous volunteers and disseminated across the globe. Overseas media coverage, specialist analyses and responses, also made their way back into Japan, where they were translated, dubbed, subtitled and circulated. Grassroots organizations like the CNIC functioned as hubs of transnational information networks. In particular, around the issue of the nuclear incident, what Karl Marx would have called "general intellect",[9] was quickly organized and produced with the help of social media on a global scale. Based on knowledge resources and technology, anonymous experts produced common, collective knowledge to solve specific problems.

The 3.11 earthquake and the nuclear power plant accident that followed could be seen as a turning point in the history of social movements in Japan. A series of street rallies and gatherings to oppose nuclear energy were subsequently organized, starting with a demonstration at the temple of Koenji in April 2011, a month after the accident, and followed almost every weekend by demonstrations, workshops and meetings elsewhere. In July 2012, when the government decided to reactivate the Oi nuclear power plant for the first time since all the nuclear power plants in Japan had been shut down for inspections post-quake, about two hundred thousand people gathered to protest in front of the Prime Minister's residence.

This was the largest protest movement since the 1960s opposition to the Treaty of Security between the US and Japan and subsequent student protests, apart from political gatherings in Okinawa. To my mind however, more important than its size is that the anti-nuclear movement in this period had three unique features in terms of the history of Japanese social movements. First, most people took part as individuals, not as members of any association or organization such as a labor union. Second, there were more young participants including university students, and families with children, previously seen as apolitical, than in any previous movement. Third, the anti-nuclear movement of this period adopted a variety of cultural forms as gestures of protest, including rap music, drumming, well-designed banners, placards, posters and T-shirts. These features went on to appear repeatedly in subsequent social movements, from the protest against the state secrets law in 2013, to the protest against the national security legislation of 2015.[10]

Social media played a crucial role here in the dissemination of information, sharing of ideas, political discussion, and in assembling people. The actions of these movements were recorded and uploaded to publicize their activities. Social media created an autonomous cycle to promote social campaigns. Social media is a means of mobilizing people,[11] particularly young people, by directly connecting people to each other without any intermediate groups, and it should also be noted that social media can convey "affection" via image-sound experiences that go beyond merely linear textual logic and political ideology. The process of individuation, not of individualization, in which experiences are able be shared without intermediation, also offers the opportunity to construct new ways of organizing individuals as a digital "public," as classical sociologist Gabriel Tarde once imagined in the age of print media.[12] He argued that those who gathered in public spaces for political reasons were not disorganized individuals without any knowledge, but organized by knowledge from print media such as newspapers and magazines. They could work collectively imitating others, a means of non-verbal affective communication, even though they did not directly know each other.

There have been some, albeit not many, interesting artistic interventions in politics in the age of social media. Kota Takeuchi's video work *Pointing at Fukuichi Live Camera* was one of the most intriguing artworks to emerge after the 3.11 earthquake. It consisted of footage of an anonymous Fukushima nuclear power plant worker, clad in a full-body radiation suit, pointing an accusatory finger for twenty minutes at a 24-hour security camera at the plant. Circulated on the internet, this mysterious video clip ignited conversation: Was it a political action, or art performance? A real plant worker? A terrorist? What was his intention? Speculation continued until an unnamed man revealed that it was part of a performance in homage to American artist Vito Acconci. Viewers were quick to identify the pointing figure as Takeuchi, although he did not make clear whether the worker was himself, and tried to maintain the worker's anonymity. *Pointing at Fukuichi Live Camera* was a critical intervention in both art and the contemporary media system, questioning as it did who watches, who is watched, who controls the media system, and who is controlled. It also critically examines both the physical and psychological distance between Tokyo, a global city that consumes electricity, and Fukushima, that provides it.

The video work *Level 7 feat. 'Myth of Tomorrow'* by artist collective Chim↑Pom was another example of such interventionist art. On April 11, 2011, Taro Okamoto's famous mural installed in Shibuya Station was "bombed" with an additional small painting depicting the exploding Fukushima nuclear power plant. Okamoto's mural was well known as an artwork depicting the historic tragedy of the atomic bombing. This graffiti-styled intervention was initially conducted anonymously and then revealed as part of a Chim ↑ Pom project, in a video work at an exhibition by the collective. Like Takeuchi's performance, their guerrilla performance became a hot topic on social media, spanning art and politics. Such artistic political interventions, often based on anonymity and topicality and guerrilla in style, may be understood as responses to a media environment changing with the development of social media as alternative media.

4.
Conservative politics, chauvinistic nationalism and the far-right

Social media serves not only progressive politics, but reactionary politics too. In fact, examining the general mood of politics in Japan in recent years, it is easy to plot the rise of conservative, nationalist and right-wing power, while liberal, let alone left-wing or socialist blocs have been declining.

In the Diet, the Abe administration has enjoyed a high approval rating since the LDP took back power from the JDP after the earthquake, in 2012. This may be due to support for Abe's economic policy under the banner of Abenomics, not his nationalist policies. But considering that more than 60 percent of people approved the Prime Minister's 2013 visit to Yasukuni Shrine, a controversial Shinto institution that enshrines war criminals and is thus associated with pre-war Japanese imperialism, and that the government's approval rating even increased slightly after his visit, it must be admitted that his right-leaning politics are basically well accepted.

Over the last seven years, the LDP has gained a sizable majority of seats in the Diet through their alliance with New Komeito (NKP), supported by Nichiren-Buddhist based religious movement, Soka Gakkai. On the other hand, the second largest party, the JDP, which partly includes the former Socialist Party, has suffered dramatic losses and is unlikely to recover sufficiently to replace the LDP again in the near future. The Social Democratic Party (SDP) has almost disappeared. Among the liberal or left-wing parties, only the Japan Communist Party (JCP) has made slight gains, probably because it is seen as the only alternative to the existing conservative politics, though it is too small to form a government. While social movements have been active outside the Diet, liberal, socialist and leftist politics are united in facing a serious crisis in conventional representative democracy.

Historically speaking, the LDP has always managed to manipulate the media expertly in various ways, not by directly controlling it, but by organizing hegemonic discourse through consensus with an oligopolistic media industry.[13] Within this tradition, the Abe administration has been the most successful. They also control the internet and social media much better than other parties, by organizing the volunteer group J-NSC (LDP=Jiminto Net Supporter Club).[14] This shows, ironically, that social media is easy to control with sufficient investment of cash and human resources.

Apart from politics in the Diet, the internet space has taken on much more nationalistic, often chauvinistic and even racist tendencies in recent times.[15] The Japanese term *netouyo* or *netto uyoku*, literally meaning "internet right wing," is commonly used in everyday language; most Japanese recognizing that those on the right wing are much more active on the internet than those at the more liberal or left-wing end of the political spectrum. For instance, if you look at the largest bulletin board in Japan, 2channel, nasty, far-right, chauvinistic, racist, sexist and other discriminatory language is well in evidence. And on Japan's successful video-sharing website *Nico Nico Douga*, which allows you to write comments directly on videos, most viewers are supportive of conservatives and rightists.

The extreme case is the ultra-nationalist and far-right political organization, Zainichi Tokken wo Yurusanai Kai or Zaitokukai (Association of citizens against the special privileges of the Zainichi [Korean and other foreign residents in Japan]). Unlike conventional right-wingers, Zaitokukai position themselves as "citizens" or "ordinary people." They form networks on the internet, and organize street rallies and meetings in the same manner as progressive social campaigners. Members make skillful use of video-streaming and video-sharing services as well as social media such as Twitter and Facebook, while at the same time sharing a hatred of the mass media. The mass media, including TV and newspapers, is their enemy, because they believe that the mass media in Japan is controlled by the left and foreigners, especially Korean residents in Japan, and thus does not tell the truth. They feel that they have been marginalized and even repressed by the post-war ideology of democracy. For them, truth is not in the mass media, but hidden in the internet.

It is beyond my scope here to discuss the issue of *netouyo*; suffice to suggest that in Japan, social media probably serves reactionary politics better than it does liberal or progressive, let alone, radical politics.

_____5.

From still-shaking islands

We have been in a strange mood since the earthquake and nuclear power plant accident. The optimistic media slogan "Be one, Japan, *Hitotsu ni naro Nippon*" championed by Fuji Television just after the earthquake, unintentionally reveals that the Japanese people are not, in fact, "one" anymore but fractured, polarizing into two, or even fragmented into many. The rise of ultra-conservative and far-right politics may be understood as a reaction to unease with this state of affairs. The spread of fake news, often characterized by the term "post-truth," is a result of suspicion not only of the mass media, but of existing knowledge production. The time for believing in the stable, single value system long created by the nation-state/mass-media complex is almost over.

Japan is still shaking. Since the earthquake we have realized that the land is not a fixed and stable entity, but fluid and unstable. This is leading to a more fundamental epistemological shift. All the modern values we once believed in are in crisis: progress, science, even democracy. We have to accept that we cannot return to the "good old days" when we were able to naively believe in such promises. The question then becomes, how can we create a new culture, art and life in an age when all that is solid melts into relativism?

Translated from Japanese by Pamela Miki Associates

—

Notes

[1] Ministry of Internal Affairs and Communications, *White Paper 2011: Information and Communications in Japan* (Tokyo: Ministry of Internal Affairs and Communications, Japan, 2011), p. 47-49.

[2] Raymond Williams, *The Long Revolution* (London: Chatto & Windus, 1961).

[3] Mamoru Ito, *Terebi wa genpatsujiko wo dō tsutaeta no ka* (Tokyo: Heibonsha, 2012), p. 263.

[4] Marshall McLuhan, *The Gutenberg Galaxy: The Making of Typographic Man* (Toronto: University of Toronto Press, 1962).

[5] Marshall McLuhan, "Marshall McLuhan on Video: The Global Village (1960)," https://mcluhangalaxy.wordpress.com/2013/06/12/marshall-mcluhans-vision-of-the-global-village-1960/

[6] Rebecca Solnit, *A Paradise Built in Hell: The Extraordinary Communities That Arise in Disaster* (New York: Penguin, 2010).

[7] Ito, *Terebi wa genpatsujiko wo dō tsutaeta no ka*, p. 159.

[8] Yoshitaka Mōri, "*Genpatsu jiko wo meguru social media to journalism*," in *Gakujutsu no doko* (Tokyo: Science Council of Japan, 2013), pp. 26-33.

[9] Karl Marx, "Economic Manuscripts of 1857-58 [*Grundrisse*, conclusion]," in *Marx/Engels, Collected Works*, vol. 29 (New York: International Publishers, 1987), p. 92.

[10] Genichiro Takahashi and SEALDs, *Minshushugitte nanda* (Tokyo: Kawade Shobo Shinsha, 2015).

[11] Daisuke Tsuda, *Doin no kakumei* (Tokyo: Chuko Shinsho, 2012).

[12] Gabriel Tarde, *L'opinion et la foule* (Les Presses universitaires de France, 1901).

[13] Iwao Osaka, *Nihon seiji to media* (Tokyo: Chuko Shinsho, 2014).

[14] Ryosuke Nishida, *Media to Jiminto* (Tokyo: Kadokawa Shinsho, 2015).

[15] Masaaki Ito, *Netto uha no rekishi shakaigaku: Andaagraund Heiseishi 1990-2000 nen* (Seikyu-sha. 2019).

A genealogy of shadow,
or a logic of visual bricolage

—

Keisuke Kitano

Toward the end of the film *Women in the Mirror* directed by Yoshishige Yoshida, there is a scene that causes utter consternation in viewers. A little girl's shadow appears on a shoji screen, attracting the gaze of Mariko Okada, who is kneeling formally on the floor, yet remains motionless with her eyes wide open. Upon seeing that shadow, we imagine the character Okada plays, Ai, muttering to herself that the shadow is that of the daughter she lost, of the granddaughter sitting beside her, and also of the daughter that her granddaughter will likely give birth to in the future.

What I would like to close in on in this brief essay is an aspect of the aesthetics (i.e. ontology) of shadows that lingers in this scene. In order to do this, two methodologies and two historical viewpoints are necessary.

1.

A Genealogy of Shadow

In the animated film *Pom Poko* (1994) by Isao Takahata, there is a scene in which a horde of ghosts and monsters stage a boisterous procession. On viewing this scene, those familiar with Japanese literature might well call to mind certain phrases from Junichiro Tanizaki's essay *In Praise of Shadows*. Because in a short passage dealing with "visible darkness," Tanizaki refers to it as "the darkness in which ghosts and monsters were active."[1] There are superficial differences, including that Tanizaki is talking about darkness indoors whereas Takahata's ghosts and monsters appear out-of-doors, but these are not all that important. Because from the audience's point of view, they are encountering ghosts and monsters running riot in the shadows of a screen in the indoor setting of a movie theater. Tanizaki himself also pays particular attention to the shadows created and substantialized in noh, bunraku and other theatrical spaces.

One might add that Tanizaki detects in the darkness of theaters more than just uniquely Japanese characteristics from the point of view of expressive performance. Rather, his focus is directed at the fact within such darkness there is the flickering of a kind of vital force that is constantly present. The darkness that Tanizaki describes as the "pulse of the night" stirs. (Because of this, for the time being, we need not make a distinction here between what in cognitive psychology are called "cast shadow" and "shading." Because shadows assail us as one.) As to the difference compared to the West, and in particular to America, in the minds and bodies of audiences that perceived a feeling of vitality in shadows, and furthermore perceived it *physically*, Tanizaki formed a critical consciousness of what he called "the magic of shadows." But Tanizaki was not alone in coming to such an understanding.[2]

Perhaps it is something that could also be perceived by gazes from outside Japan. One such observer was Roland Barthes. In his treatise on Japan, Barthes mentions an "animate" quality with regard to the puppets in bunraku, perhaps detecting in these puppets that move around surrounded by darkness a kind of vital energy.[3]

We need to be mindful of the fact that the shadows we are trying to focus on exist as materialized images. The "magic of shadows" emits a force of affect that acts on viewers' minds and bodies. As suggested by Hans Belting, perhaps the distinction between the English words "image" and "picture" is more helpful than the French word "*image*" or the German word "*Bild*."[4] Because whether it is the gold or silver decorations on lacquerware, the puppets in bunraku or the architecture of toilets, what is being exercised is not a representation of shadows in our consciousness but a force of affect mobilizing our minds and bodies. Moreover, it operates in the context of a yearning for something transcendental.

This also applies to the cinema. As correctly pointed by Tanizaki in *In Praise of Shadows*, "[i]n the photographic image itself, to say nothing of the acting and the script," there are differences between Japanese films and Hollywood movies. In other words, the light and shadow emitted by Japanese films are genealogically linked to "the magic of shadows." Let us consider this in more detail.

2.
Visual Bricolage

Let us look at the arrangements underpinning "the magic of shadows."

Firstly, let us recall that when the image-generating device called film alighted on human history, the term "*photographie animé*" was used in France, "animated photography" in the English-speaking world, and "*katsudo shashin*" (literally "action photographs") in Japan.

All mechanically generated images, including film, are none other than images materialized using some kind of technological device. Before a system for representing something can be complete, both in theory and in practice, an image must first be materialized by some mechanical device and presented to viewers. Furthermore, as long as materialized images are materialized *things*, they must comprise various parts. This being the case, in a broad sense, film or mechanically produced images can surely only be generated on the basis of a system of bricolage. In fact, bricolage is at work here on two fronts: not only in the device development, but also the handwork necessary to maximize the effects of the device.

How does this apply to the history of film in Japan?

When cinema was introduced to Japan, projection equipment first took root along the streets lined with show tents in the neighborhood of Asakusa and other amusement areas. The first film to be shot in Japan was *Momijigari* (Maple Leaf Viewing) (1899), which depicts a scene from a kabuki play that was based on a noh play. These circumstances point to extremely close links in Japan between film and theater. Yet, until now, such links have been explained in terms of the "indigenization" of Western media devices in Japan. We need a frame of reference for rethinking this. Because the media devices used in the West were not intrinsic in any sense at all, this essay would argue that media devices in Japan were simply constructed differently, or came into being in different arrangements.[5] The "magic of shadows" was deeply embedded into these arrangements.

3.
Edo Transmedia

Let us now delve more deeply into "the magic of shadows" from this viewpoint.

An illuminating point of reference is a wet plate photograph taken in Niigata Prefecture sometime between the late Edo and early Meiji periods. This photograph, which shows a man sitting on a veranda clutching a woodblock print depicting a kabuki actor with the top edge resting under his chin and the bottom edge held in his right hand, was given the title "Man Holding a Colored Woodblock Print" by the researcher who discovered it.

According to the researcher, at the time, taking photographs of scenes from kabuki plays acted out in the homes of wealthy families was something that was commonly done in the region concerned. This was part of a cultural ecosystem that could be called the "kabuki cultural sphere."[6] To be precise, as the researcher also pointed out, the figure in "Man Holding a Colored Woodblock Print" is mimicking not a woodblock print, but an illustration from Santo Kyoden's illustrated storybook *Hitogokoro kagami no ustushie* (1796).[7] What the illustration depicts is the effect of the *nozoki-karakuri* (a street performance in which spectators watched moving dolls and pictures through a glass window in a box) that were then being imported from overseas and proving extremely popular on the street; that is to say, the fabricated effect of being able to see into the recesses of people's minds. The man in the photograph was emulating a narrative describing this peculiar effect of the *nozoki-karakuri*. What we have here is a transmedia environment in which the physical movements of kabuki, the image of the body in woodblock prints, *nozoki-karakuri*, popular fiction and photographic devices are closely intertwined.

Let me refer to a remark by anthropologist Marcel Mauss, who once observed that the gaits of both female nurses in a hospital in New York and of women strolling through the streets of Paris were affected by the physical movements of film stars on screen.[8] In other words, the body image endogenous in a human being in the age of modern media is first formed in the context of a transmedia ecology. One can also probably say that the image of the body in 19th-century Japan also came about in a transmedia ecological system that included photography. Of greater importance is the fact that in Japan shadows were a materialized image manufactured by bricolage created in such a transmedia environment. The shadow in question here were materialized not via language, but via affect and sensation. In the above-mentioned "Man Holding a Colored Woodblock Print," too, it is affect and sensation that are materialized in the shadow.

4.
Atomic shadows

In this way, one could say that photography and cinematography in Japan in their early stages as modern technologies of visual bricolage had to incorporate into themselves existing strategies concerning shadows.

But one has to be attentive to the difference between *The Woman in the Mirror* and *Pom Poko*, which are far removed from the time when Tanizaki praised shadows. Here let me draw on a perceptive insight by Akira Mizuta Lippit in his book *Atomic Light (Shadow Optics).*[9] Lippet points out that the three media technologies of X-ray, cinema, and psychoanalysis appeared at the end of the nineteenth century in world history, all of them embodying the state of being invisible/visible, and adding that in Japan this redirects the constellation of what might be called a shadow archive. He further argues that the dropping of the atomic bombs also modified this constellation at the most profound level. Thereafter, amid changes in the episteme surrounding shadows, Japanese cinema transformed its ontology, re-charting its aesthetics.

It is well known that atomic light left behind shadows of human minds and bodies in the form of marks on stone steps. Thereafter, shadows, which flickered at the level of sensibility, became entities that adhered indexically to the dropping of the bombs on Hiroshima and Nagasaki.

One could say that since the war, the Japanese have lived their lives surrounded by ghosts materialized as images of shadows. One could further say that they have lived their lives while questioning why their own minds and bodies ended up having to become shadows in a sense. That is to dare say, perhaps their acts as perpetrators in part of the massive killing now labeled World War Two, and their states as victims due to the atomic bombings adhere tightly to each other, being so closely intertwined that they cannot be distinguished.

One can detect this most pointedly in visuals from the 1960s. From around the time of the protests against the ratification of the Treaty of Mutual Cooperation and Security between the United States and Japan in 1960, in Japanese filmmaking there was a sharp intensification of the re-questioning of the self-consciousness of wanting to photograph subjects. The people who took this on most strongly as their own responsibility were the artists who sided with the student movement. Nagisa Oshima made *Cruel Story of Youth* (1960), in which he made extensive use of footage shot with a hand-held camera while crawling on the ground and wandering in the dark of the night, with the intent of being radical. Another example is *Funeral Parade of Roses* directed by Toshio Matsumoto, which dashes through the dimly lit space-time amid the buildings of Tokyo of the same period.

5.
The Sensuality of Shadows

But it also seems that the genealogy of "the magic of shadows" in the history of Japanese photography and cinema has undergone a further transformation since the 1970s. One could say this was the effect of a post-festum atmosphere after the season of political involvement, but at the same time it was also probably due to things American having begun to penetrate deeply into people's lifeworld. Frederic Jameson argues that in the 1970s the movement of capital caused a turnaround in the world system, and that this could be seen in the lens-based expression of various countries.[10] In fact, in 1970, Nagisa Oshima had already perceived that mechanically generated images had rapidly expanded their involvement in the distribution system, increasingly penetrated by capital, and had begun to pass by the minds and bodies of directors, and by artists in general.[11] Is it too much to say that in the 1970s, the magic of shadows was entering a state of dynamism that extended beyond the problems concerning the ethos of a single country?

These observations by Oshima appeared in a publication concerning the photographer Shomei Tomatsu, who, though he was active in a different field, Oshima regarded as his rival of the same period. Having previously devoted his life to the subjects of the occupation and the atomic bombing of Nagasaki, Tomatsu shifted the base of his activities to Okinawa. There he took a series of photographs that attracted public attention, but one in particular speaks of a turning point in the genealogy of the magic of shadows.

In the background of this photograph is the keen awareness Tomatsu showed regarding the return of Okinawa to Japan following American occupation. This included the observation that it was after its return to Japan that the Americanization of Okinawa had completed. This was due to the fact that, despite there having been resistance by Okinawans to preserve their own lifestyles even during the US occupation, the governing mechanism of Japan, where Americanization had already ironically advanced, penetrated every nook and cranny of Okinawan society. Focusing on this, the critic Isao Nakazato astutely notices in this photograph a shadow.[12] The critic Koji Taki, whose writings sparked this idea in Nakazato, also recognizes a shadow there; as sediments, perhaps, of deep historicities that could not be put into words.

It could possibly be argued that this photograph calls to mind Hegel's *The Phenomenology of Spirit*, in which reference is made to Antigone as part of a discussion of the differences between "divine law" and "human law." There appears something divinely empyreal about the shadows that cover the cloud, and in the very contrast with this arguably empyreal appearance, the dimension of human law and the dimension of history appear as invisible shadows. However, it may have been that this empyreal appearance was what would soon be consumed and impregnated amid the clamor of what would be called "postmodernism," which came to the fore in Japan shortly thereafter.

In a world that has been Americanized all over, commercially symbolized and made the subject of consumption, it seems that everything is completely bright and filled with advertising images as simulacra. Nevertheless, in this space-time whose every nook and cranny has been artificially lit up, there have also been artists that have continued in the tradition of Tomatsu, who staked everything on existential speculation, in the form of their own questioning of visuality. One such artist was Daido Moriyama, who persistently chased not subdued light but the effects of shadows on the fragmented existential figures of people living at the same time and tried to accept these with his own body. Shadows also lie in the clothing in the photographs of Miyako Ishiuchi, mobilizing sensory and sensual communications between the clothes and the viewer.

In the work by Yoshishige Yoshida mentioned at the beginning of this essay, perhaps the reason Mariko Okada turns her entire body towards the shoji screen upon which the shadow flickers is because she is trying to embrace, at the moment, the genealogy of "the magic of shadows." And in the evanescent embrace of Okada's body and of the shadow, viewers feel viscerally affected.

The questions of shadows posed in this post-March 11 world are none other than the problems cited in this essay. These are problems that prompt a strategy of transcending politics not by forgetting the body through for instance aestheticizing or philosophizing catastrophe, but rather through evoking sensibilities and sensuality in the physicality of shadows in and for bodies.

Translated from Japanese by Pamela Miki Associates

Notes

[1] All quoted Tanizaki passages are from: Junichiro Tanizaki, *In Praise of Shadows*, trans, Thomas J. Harper and Edward J. Seidensticker (Sedgwick: Leete's Island Books, 1977).

[2] Regarding the formation of a critical consciousness of the Japanese characteristics of the emotional effect of media by Tanizaki and contemporaneous intellectuals, see Keisuke Kitano, "Kobayashi

Hideo and the question of Media," in *Media Theory in Japan*, ed. M. Steinberg and A. Zahlten (Durham: Duke University Press, 2017).

³ Roland Barthes, *Empire of Signs*, trans. Richard Howard (New York: Hill and Wang, 1983).

⁴ Hans Belting, *An Anthropology of Images: Picture, Medium, Body*, trans. Thomas Dunlap, (Princeton: Princeton University Press, 2011).

⁵ In recent years, the fact that Japanese movies, and in particular Japanese animated movies, exist within such logic of visual bricolage has been elucidated by more than a few researchers. Thomas LaMarre, *The Anime Machine: A Media Theory of Animation* (Minneapolis: University of Minnesota Press, 2009).

⁶ Chikako Enomoto, "Early Japanese Stage Photographs: The Imanari Family Photography Collection and 'Kabuki Culture,'" *Eizogaku* 93 (Japan Society of Image Arts and Sciences, 2014), pp. 7-13.

⁷ Chikako Enomoto, "The Culture of Minamiuonuma and the History of Early Japanese Photography as seen in the Photography of the Imanari Family," *Niigata Local Image Archive* 5 (October 2014), Faculty of Humanities, Niigata University.

⁸ Marcel Mauss, *Sociology and Anthropology: Essays by Marcel Mauss*, trans. Ben Brewster (London: Routledge & Kegan Paul, 1973), p. 72.

⁹ Akira Mizuta Lippit, *Atomic Light (Shadow Optics)* (Minneapolis: University of Minnesota Press, 2005).

¹⁰ Fredric Jameson, *The Geopolitical Aesthetic* (BFI, 1992).

¹¹ Nagisa Oshima, *Kaitai to funshutsu* (Haga Shoten, 1970), p. 255.

¹² Isao Nakazato, "*Imeji no gunto to hikari no shigaku,*" *Gendai Shiso Rinji Zokan Tomatsu Shomei*, 2013, p. 165.

Expo '70: A panorama of postwar Japanese art

Manabu Miki

1.

The eve of the expo of the future and unknown

The 1970 World Exposition in Osaka, or Expo '70 as it is commonly known, was Asia's first world exposition, attracting some 64.21 million visitors, a record number at the time, and ranking alongside the 1964 Tokyo Olympics as a national project that symbolized the period of rapid economic growth in which Japan completed its recovery from the devastation of World War Two. It can also be called the largest art event of the postwar era, with avant-garde artists representing such tendencies as Metabolism, contemporary art, contemporary music, experimental film and graphic design mobilized en masse. Expo '70 was unique in the history of world expositions in that it attempted to combine on an unprecedented scale the "future" of cutting edge technology and the "unknown" of avant-garde art.

In postwar Japan, various avant-garde art groups, including Jikken Kobo and Gutai in the 1950s, and the self-professed "anti-art" Neo-Dadaism Organizers, Hi-Red Center and Group Ongaku in the 1960s, were active and a range of cross-disciplinary events were being held.

Following the decision in 1965, the year after the Tokyo Olympics, to stage Expo '70 in Osaka, gradually a large number of avant-garde artists came to be involved. In particular, for those who used state-of-the-art media and for whom opportunities to present their work were limited, the exposition, in which sizeable budgets and audiences were guaranteed, was undoubtedly an attractive opportunity.

However, in the late 1960s, the anti-Vietnam War movement and the student movement were gathering momentum. Nineteen-seventy was also the year in which the Treaty of Mutual Cooperation and Security between the United States and Japan (commonly known as Anpo), to which the students were strongly opposed, was to be automatically extended, and it was thought that Expo '70 was being used to distract people's attention from this. Thus "anti-Expo" movements also attracted a strong following around the country.

In particular, the protests that occurred in Paris in May 1968 had an impact in Japan. There were bitter disputes among artists over the pros and cons of Expo '70 and over avant-garde principles, with an anti-Expo conference involving design and architecture groups taking place in 1968 and an anti-Expo event organized by avant-garde art groups and attended by Zero Jigen (Zero Dimension) among others held the following year. On the industrial front, pollution and other affects on the environment came to be recognized as social issues.

_____ **2.**

A festival combining avant-garde artists and Eastern/Western cultures

The theme of Expo '70 was "Progress and Harmony for Mankind," and while the conflict between culture and the reckless pursuit of science and technology was recognized as an issue, it was anticipated that with the progress of science/technology and culture in the 21st century such social contradictions would be resolved. With this in mind, it was decided that a mock "city of the future" would be created at Expo '70 and an overall impression of progress was sought. The innovative expression of the Metabolist architects, who took "metabolism" as their theme and made frequent use of new construction methods that differed from modernist reinforced concrete construction, and of avant-garde artists met these requirements.

Kenzo Tange, who created the master plan for the Expo site, was appointed producer of the core facility and designed the Festival Plaza with its 30m-high space-frame "The Grand Roof." Meanwhile, Taro Okamoto, a leading figure in the postwar avant-garde art movement, was appointed producer of the Theme Pavilions. Okamoto had created a set of murals for the Tange-designed former Tokyo Metropolitan Government Building, and in 1959 was awarded the International Grand Award for Architectural Painting by the French magazine *L'Architecture d'Aujourd'hui*. As well, as a young man in Paris, he had associated with the Abstraction-Création group, the Surrealists and George Bataille, and had studied ethnology under the tutelage of Marcel Mauss at the Sorbonne. Using as motifs primitive Japanese art in the form of Jomon pottery and mandalas as the "crystallization of Eastern wisdom," Okamoto designed the Tower of the Sun, which at a height of 70m pierced the Grand Roof, making the symbol of Expo '70 a giant sculpture that at first sight seems the antithesis of progress. Mandalas have a hierarchical structure pairing inner and outer universes, so as part of the Theme Pavilions, the Tree of Life, representing the inner universe, was created inside the Tower of the Sun, to form a three-dimensional mandala with a three-tiered structure extending underground, aboveground and into the sky, representing the past (genesis), present (harmony) and future (progress).

In the lake in the middle of the site, Isamu Noguchi created fountains not like those found in Western-style gardens, but fountains inspired by waterfalls in the East, fountains that rotated, and that produced spray. There were twelve such fountains, all bearing names with a space theme. The largest, *Comet*, was 33m high and sprayed water from jet nozzles underneath an aluminum cube. As well, outdoor sculptures were installed in seven sub-plazas, with art critic Yusuke Nakahara, curator of the 10th Tokyo Biennale "Between Man and Matter" in 1970, among those consulted on the selection of the artists, who included Jiro Takamatsu, Tomio Miki and Katsuhiro Yamaguchi, all mid-career artists at the time.

Jiro Yoshihara, founder of the Gutai group, which was already well known internationally, was appointed a member of the Expo's Art Exhibition Committee, and group members held the Gutai Art Festival at the Festival Plaza as well as contributing work to the Expo Museum of Fine Arts and staging an outdoor display of group works and a group exhibition at the entrance to the Midori Pavilion. There were avant-garde performances including people wearing parachutes dropping from the Grand Roof and people clad in silver-colored material moving around with lights trained on them. Centered on the Festival Plaza, which combined the functions of a Western "plaza" and an Eastern "festival," but using the entire site as its stage, one could say this was an attempt by avant-garde artists to stage a "festival" combining past and future, and Eastern and Western cultures.

3.
Avant-garde artists and corporate pavilions

Unlike international art exhibitions, Expo '70 had no overall artistic director. The appointments of the architects and artists in charge of the Japan Association for the 1970 World Exposition-led core facilities were mainly decided by committees of experts. For the corporate pavilions, however, this was left up to each company or organization. Large numbers of avant-garde artists took on the task of projecting an image of the future, with advertising agencies acting as intermediaries in their selection.

In the case of the Textiles Pavilion, an advertising agency commissioned by the Japan Textiles Association asked the internationally acclaimed avant-garde filmmaker Toshio Matsumoto to serve as general director. Matsumoto demanded there be no interference in his selection of the staff or the content of the pavilion, and requested the appointment of Tadanori Yokoo, a graphic designer who had produced posters for underground theater, as design director responsible for the architectural design among other things. In order to realize Matsumoto's vision of a space-time environment on the theme of Eros and Thanatos (Love and Death), Yokoo came up with a design for a dome inside which films would be shown using multi-screen projection and on whose internal walls would be installed multiple relief sculptures of women covered with fluorescent paint. Outside, scaffolding and figures representing construction workers were installed and painted bright red, incorporating into the design an anti-Expo element suggesting construction had been suspended before completion of the pavilion that, contrary to expectations, received critical acclaim. Further examples of corporate pavilions serving as testing grounds for art and technology include E.A.T. member Fujiko Nakaya's creation of the world's first atmospheric fog sculpture at the Pepsi Pavilion and Katsuhiro Yamaguchi's production of the Mitsui Group Pavilion.

————————4·

The demise of avant-garde art and the passing into oblivion of Expo '70

At Expo '70, nuclear power generation was used to supply electricity to the site as the energy source of the city of the future. During the Expo, the first nuclear power plant to be operated by one of Japan's nine private power companies went on line and supplied power to the site on a trial basis. In an effort to mitigate Japan's "nuclear allergy" as the only country to have experienced atomic bombings, Expo '70 became a model for the peaceful use of nuclear power.

However, some artists felt guilty about their roles in Expo '70 on the grounds that they participated in an event tailored to the needs of state policies and corporate advertising. They made no mention of their contributions after the conclusion of the event, nor were they given a place in art history. For this reason, in contrast to the regional Expo boom that continued afterwards, in terms of the history of postwar art, Expo '70, which occurred during a transitional period between the cross-disciplinary avant-garde art of the 1960s and Mono-ha and other reductionist groups of the '70s, was for a long time forgotten.

However, not only Jiro Takamatsu, who influenced Mono-ha, but one of the group's central figures, Nobuo Sekine, showed work at the Expo Museum of Fine Arts as well as participating in the outdoor display at the Mitsui Group Pavilion site, in which sense one can also recognize a continuity of expression. But while the current of avant-garde art reached a peak at Expo '70, it also began to decline as the contradiction of the lack of targets of criticism was laid bare, and following the 1973 oil crisis, people's trust in science and technology and their optimistic view of the future also suddenly waned.

————————5·

The impact on 21st century art

It was from the 2010s onwards when the influence of artists and critics born in the 1960s and influenced by Expo '70 in their youth increased that Expo '70 came to attract attention in the context of the history of Japanese postwar art. A notable example is Kenji Yanobe, who grew up playing at the former site of Expo '70 and for whom the ruins of the city of the future (i.e. "the ruins of the future") were among the most indelible scenes of his childhood. Yanobe went on to create artworks on the theme of survival in a dystopian world, visited Chernobyl following the nuclear accident wearing *Atom Suit*, a radiation-detecting suit he made himself, and has also been active in Fukushima following the Tohoku earthquake and tsunami and the Fukushima Daiichi nuclear disaster.

In the 21st century, the natural environment and society's contradictions have become even more acute, and many aspects of the future depicted at Expo '70 have failed to eventuate. However, due to its wide-ranging cultural influences and advances in digital technology, even artists and critics born after the exposition are now able to grasp paradoxically the attempt to combine the latest technology and avant-garde art at Expo '70 is being looked at again from a new perspective. The innovativeness of analog multi-media expression is being reconsidered afresh.

Translated from Japanese by Pamela Miki Associates

—

Main references

Expo '70 Official Guide. Japan Association for the 1970 World Exposition, 1970.

Japan World Exposition: Invitation to the Theme Pavilions. Japan Association for the 1970 World Exposition, 1970.

Sen'ikan—Sen'i wa ningen seikatsu o yutaka ni suru. Nihon Sen'ikan Kyoryokukai, 1970.

Japan World Exposition, Osaka 1970: Official Photo Album. Commemorative Association for the Japan World Exposition, 1971.

Official Report of the Japan World Exposition, Osaka, 1970. Vol 1-3. Commemorative Association for the Japan World Exposition, 1972.

Sawaragi, Noi. *Sensō to banpaku.* Tokyo: Bijutsu Shuppan-sha, 2005.

Metabolism: The City of the Future—Dreams and Visions of Reconstruction in Postwar Japan. Shinkenchiku-sha, 2011.

Hirano, Akiome. *Ōsaka banpaku—nijūseiki ga yumemita nijūisseiki.* Shogakukan, 2014.

Kuresawa, Takemi and Eto, Mitsunori. *Ōsaka banpaku ga enshutsu shita mirai—zen'ei geijutsu no sōzōryoku to sono jidai.* Seikyusha, 2014.

Ma, Jung-Yeon. *A Critical History of Media Arts in Japan*, Artes Publishing, 2014.

Mono-ha

—

Kenji Kajiya

Born in the late 1960s, Mono-ha is an art movement that reached its apogee in the first half of the 1970s. Its works are known for using natural and artificial materials such as stone, wood, steel, earth, paper and clay in the raw, showing the existence and structure of things. The main protagonists include Nobuo Sekine (1936–2019), Lee Ufan (b. 1936), Kishio Suga (b. 1944), Katsuhiko Narita (1944–92), Susumu Koshimizu (b. 1944), Katsurō Yoshida (1943–99), Kōji Enokura (1942–95), Noboru Takayama (b. 1944) and Noriyuki Haraguchi (b. 1946).

One of the contexts from which Mono-ha emerged is the activities of Jirō Takamatsu (1936-98), an artist who interrogated the very foundation of art. In the early 1960s, Takamatsu attracted attention with works that hypostasized the concepts of point and line. He painted shadows and had them confused with the real ones, or revealed the mechanism of the convention of perspective. What characterized these works is their recourse to "trick" or illusionism, namely techniques that exploited the difference between image and reality. By definition art is inseparable from illusion, for, be it painting or sculpture, art employs its materials to represent something other than itself. Because he saw illusion in the heart of art and examined the issues arising from it, Takamatsu's thinking can be compared to Clement Greenberg's (1909–94) theory of modernism. While the American art critic emphasized the primacy of vision and was led by the reductionism of his own tenet to admire Color-Field Painting for its simple color and composition, Takamatsu, sometimes described "intellectualist," was more interested in the processes of cognition than vision, probing illusionism in a diverse range of media including painting, sculpture and installation.[1] Takamatsu's preoccupation with "trick," then, embodied an alternative modernism in art.

The same concern crops up in the early works of the Mono-ha artists, who knew Takamatsu personally. Sekine worked as his assistant, and Narita, Koshimizu, Yoshida and Suga were in contact with Takamatsu through Tama Art University and the Tokyo Gallery. Suga's *Shadow Working* (1967), conferring three-dimensionality on shadows, recalled Takamatlsu's precedence. Sekine produced *Phase No. 4* (1968), a relief apparently cylindrical but actually half three-dimensional and half two-dimensional, while Lee Ufan created a two-dimensional work that featured a Moebius strip in fluorescent colors (*Fourth Structure A*, 1969). Both pieces were an investigation of the uncertainty of vision via antinomy between two and three dimensions, and as such betrayed Takamatsu's influence. Illusion was also explored by the Shizuoka-based group "Genshoku," which consisted of Shōji Iida (1927–2019), Katsuji Niwa (b. 1931), Morikazu Maeda (1932–2007), Yoshinori Suzuki (1936–2010), Kazushige Koike (1940–2008) and others. The exhibition "Tricks and Vision," held at the Tokyo and Muramatsu Galleries between April and May of 1968, included many works dealing with similar issues. The preoccupation with illusion was thus manifest in the Japanese art of the late 1960s, with Takamatsu at its center.

When the artists soon to be called "Mono-ha" shifted their focus from illusion to the existence and structure of things, thereby founding their own movement, it was Sekine's *Phase—Mother Earth* that provided the decisive stimulus. Consisting of a cylinder of compacted earth 2.2 meters across and 2.6 meters high and a hole in the ground of the identical shape, it was shown first at the Outdoor Sculpture Exhibition held in October of 1968 at the Suma Rikyū Park in Kobe. While the work was seen as a mere *trompe l'oeil*, Lee refuted the description and argued that *Phase—Mother Earth* expressed the "change in the condition of things," precipitating the crystallization of Mono-ha's philosophy.[2]

Not infrequently Mono-ha's works could be taken either as an illusion or a thing. While insisting on the physicality of its material, Sekine's *Phase of Nothingness—Oil Clay* (1969), a vast amount of the namesake material piled up in a gallery, owed much of its effect to the contrast between the clay and the white cube of the exhibition space. According to Lee's own statement, his *Relatum* (formerly *Phenomenon and Perception B*, 1968), originally made a sheet of glass appear as though it had cracked under the weight of a stone block on top of it, both elements sitting on an iron sheet with slits.[3] Similarly, Koshimizu's *Paper* (formerly *Paper 2*, 1969), places an enormous rock in a paper bag, with the contrast between the former's solidity and the latter's fragility yielding an illusionistic effect. These examples suggest that at stake here was not so much abandoning illusionism for the actual existence of things. Rather, these artists replaced difference between illusion and reality, which Takamatsu's "trick" had dramatized, with difference between objects. In that sense, Mono-ha's evolution was a continuous one.

If difference was Mono-ha's concern, it is only logical that the movement put as much emphasis on "relation" as on "existence." In his text "In Search of Encounter" (1970), Mono-ha's *de facto* manifesto, Lee spoke of "encounters" with things that would reveal the world as it is.[4] By contrast, Suga was interested in how an object, unmediated by human subjectivity, can relate to another, and produced works like *Law of Situation* (1971), placing a certain number of stones on a bubble sheet set afloat in a pond to create a condition in which buoyancy and gravity vied with each other.[5]

Enokura engaged in acts like making a spot of oil on a sheet of paper or a piece of cotton cloth, as in *A Stain No. 1* (1975), or sprinkling water over the ground to generate cracks as it dried. It was an attempt to investigate not only various "relations," such as permeation and interaction between different kinds of matter, but also "surface" that embodies those relations.[6] For his part, Noboru Takayama took interest in what lay behind the matter. His "Underground Zoo" series was inspired by the crosstie used on railroad tracks.[7] For the artist this material is what made transportation of people and goods possible during Japan's economic growth, an allusion, then, to the sacrifice made by the countless anonymous workers for the country's prosperity.

Mono-ha critiqued the artist's agency in the production of an artwork. Sekine, who stated that "the best we can do is to brush dust off the surface of things and reveal the world they contain," saw the author as a being whose involvement was reduced to a bare minimum, not much more than that of bringing the object into sharper focus.[8] Mono-ha's was a radical self-critique of the artistic subjectivity.

Mono-ha is loosely related to the contemporaneous movements in Europe and the United States. Parallels have often been drawn with the Italian Arte Povera artists such as Jannis Kounellis (1936–2017) and Giuseppe Penone (b. 1947), or the American Minimalist and Post-Minimalist practitioners such as Robert Morris (1931–2018), Carl Andre (b. 1935), Richard Serra (b. 1938), and Robert Smithson (1938–1973). While these movements did have commonalities, such as the critique of modernism and the straightforward use of natural and artificial materials, the critique of distinction between "art and life" in Arte Povera and the engagement with the spectator's body in Minimalism and Post-Minimalism were not foregrounded in Mono-ha. It is arguably its critique of the artistic subjectivity, the most thorough of its time, that distinguished this movement.

Translated from Japanese by Tsutomu Nakano

—

Notes

[1] Minemura Toshiaki, "On Mono-ha," in *Requiem for the Sun: The Art of Mono-ha* (Los Angeles: Blum & Poe, 2012), 120-123. Originally published as "Mono-ha ni tsuite," *Bijutsu techō*, no. 436 (July 1978): 225-235.

[2] Lee Ufan and Nakahara Yusuke, "Torikkusu ando vijon-ten to Ishiko Junzo no koto," in *Ishiko Junzō to sono nakama tachi: Taidan shū* (Shimizu: Kankyo geijutsu nettowāku niji no bijutsukan, 2002), 70-71.

[3] Oral History Interview with Lee Ufan, conducted by Nakai Yasuyuki and Kajiya Kenji, December 18, 2008, Oral History Archives of Japanese Art (URL: www.oralarthistory.org)

[4] Lee Ufan, "Deai o motomete," *Bijutsu techō*, no. 324 (February 1970): 14-23.

[5] Hasegawa Yuko, "Thoughts on Kishio Suga," in *Suga Kishio: Okareta senzaisei* (Tokyo: HeHe, 2015), 166-167.

[6] Minemura Toshiaki, "What was Mono-ha?," in *Mono-ha* (Tokyo: Kamakura Gallery, 1986), no pagination.

[7] Takayama Noboru, "Makuragi ni suite," *Mono-ha saikō* (Osaka: National Museum of Modern Art, 2005), 120-121.

[8] Ikeda Masuo, Sugai Kumi, Sekine Nobuo, Horiuchi Masakazu, and Tono Yoshiaki, "'Tsukuru' to iu koto, 'Tsukuranai' to iu koto," *Bijutsu techō*, no. 315 (July 1969): 181.

Mono-ha | Kenji Kajiya

Looking at today through the lens of the 1980s

—

Akio Miyazawa

A magazine interview with a Seibu Department Stores senior manager in the mid-1980s made a deep impression on me that has persisted ever since. In it, this individual described the company's management philosophy as selling not things, but information.

By which they meant, to take the example of a plate, for instance, instead of placing value on the plate itself, selling "information" in the form of an image of the sort of lifestyle one might expect to enjoy with that plate on one's table. Having experienced sustained growth in the previous decades, heading into the '80s the Japanese economy soared to even greater heights. Department stores were exploring smart strategies for altering the mindset of the Japanese consumer. So using images of life with a beautifully designed plate on the table to encourage more spending made sense. Deriving from this was a change in the consciousness around "culture"; it could be said that the conspicuous consumption and growth in digital technology that characterized the '80s, quite by accident served to direct people's gaze toward "culture." So the copy written by Shigesato Itoi to advertise Seibu Department Stores symbolized this aspect of the era perfectly.

"*Oishii Seikatsu*" (Delicious life) (1982)

A phrase open to multiple interpretations, Itoi's line is even now spoken of as symbolizing the era. Moreover the visuals for the ads made just as powerful, or perhaps an even more powerful, impression on those on the receiving end. Having the words "*Oishii Seikatsu*" rendered in brush on paper like a piece of New Year's calligraphy, then placing that paper in the hands of Woody Allen, proved hugely significant in this regard. Thus the mission of Seibu Department Stores and the Saison Group to sell information rather than goods had quite an influence on a certain class of people, the mood also rippling out to those further down the economic ladder in the "middle class" that was so often talked about at the time, and below.

Thus spread the lifestyle of the information society, in which a single plate could change your life.

It bears repeating that during the '80s, every Japanese could sense the booming economy at a personal level. Which is why American sociologist Ezra Vogel's *Japan as Number One* (1979) was such a hit in Japan, with over 700,000 copies sold. Vogel's book analyzed Japan's economic growth since the 1960s, focusing on and lauding the innate qualities of the Japanese as a people, though later the extent to which it over-egged things here would be revealed. At the time though, the notion of "Japan as number one" dominated, and a certain class of individuals, buoyed by Vogel's paean, carried on consuming "information" without ever doubting that this was how life should be.

On the other hand, these fortunates were also in constant fear of social breakdown, and simultaneously captivated by noisier, vulgar visions of the world as a form of beauty. Which is why they were so drawn to the desolate city, the dark side of affluence, in Ridley Scott's post-nuclear-apocalypse *Blade Runner* (1982). The picture painted by the chaotic, corrupted world of Scott's film could hardly be more different to that of "*Oishii Seikatsu.*" On a visit to Japan, Ridley Scott apparently walked around Kabukicho in Shinjuku, sensing a singular energy in this dubious neighborhood with its all-pervasive adult entertainment offerings and garish signs. Those impressions bore fruit in the world of *Blade Runner*. Faced with realism of this stripe, the idea that by consuming information you too could enjoy *la dolce vita*, is exposed as very fragile indeed.

Which is to say, someone went and broke the plate.

Meaning there were those who noted the fragile nature of a sophisticated information society that claimed to sell information rather than objects. It was a realization that came to many simultaneously. In 1990, a youth-oriented magazine ran a special feature titled "The Subcul Armageddon," and in this instant the term "subculture" (*sabukaruchaa*) hitherto generally used in Japan changed to "subcul" (*sabukaru*), which from then on became common parlance. This was no mere abbreviation, but a phenomenon that changed the meaning. What was the significance of this? "Subculture" displayed an awareness of the "high culture" preceding it, and an intention to deviate from that, while "counter-culture" literally ran counter to the preceding culture.

Yet in "subcul" lies no such way of thinking or feeling.

"Subcul" existed with no connection at all to any preceding cultural phenomenon. Take for example the existence of the "otaku." Up to a certain point in history, the "otaku" had been an object of rejection; in fact otaku themselves were reticent when it came to discussing their awkward obsessions, fearful of scorn. This led to the emergence of "otaku culture," a solidarity among individuals of similar inclinations that positioned them in total opposition to the culture spawned by Saison. Otaku now had no qualms about their inclinations. A tendency to be perfectly comfortable saying they liked what they liked – whether that be anime, Comiket, or whatever – emerged from the '90s onward. This was reflected in a change in the rendition of "otaku" in Japanese from hiragana to katakana, this change in how the term was written in turn changing the meaning, to something cooler and more acceptable.

Perhaps what manga artist Kyoko Okazaki depicted were various aspects of the "*Oishii Seikatsu.*" In *Tokyo Girls Bravo* she presented a humorous portrayal of the brittleness and possibilities of the '80s by showing the lives of young girls during these years, but the slightly later *River's Edge*, in contrast, captures the mood of the '90s more seriously. Comparing the two, one sees in the fashions adopted by the protagonists, an archetypal shift in the times. Sakae Kaneda of *Tokyo Girls Bravo* in her stylish label and vintage imported gear simply oozes "*Oishii Seikatsu*," while Haruna Wakagusa of *River's Edge* in jeans and flannel shirt calls to mind Kurt Cobain of Nirvana, the indy band that released its first album in 1989 and for a short time afterward came to symbolize the era.

So how did otaku fare heading into the '90s? Taking an interest in the hope of finding out, in a sense means thinking about Takashi Murakami. I cannot help feeling that, whether one likes it or not, Murakami's output spawned a fresh new way to express the sensibilities of otaku in a different context. Thinking about it anew, expression originating in otaku sensibilities constitutes a splendid critique of the otaku, which is why when Murakami exhibited his work at the celebration of figurines known as the Wonder Festival, otaku recognized it as something different to themselves. Doubtless this was not conscious on the part of the artist. Without even him noticing, he had offered a critique. However, by losing much of their criticality, Murakami's works would become acknowledged as a new form of expression. What the creative endeavors of Kyoko Okazaki and Takashi Murakami bore witness to was on the one hand, "the end of '80s things" and on the other, the meteoric rise of otaku culture. We are no longer talking simply of some trend or phenomenon in social customs, but a change between the '80s and '90s in the "view of the body" underlying Japanese subculture. That is to say, just like Haruna Wakagusa sporting her flannel shirt in *River's Edge*, the '90s sight of high school students sprawled on the ground in front of convenience stores slurping cup ramen would have been unthinkable in the "*Oishii Seikatsu*" atmosphere of the '80s, and in otaku standing on their own feet and standing up for themselves, one senses a definitive shift from the hiragana "*otaku*." All this is linked to the demise of the bubble economy. The environment around the body changed. The "*Oishii Seikatsu*" body that would do anything, for instance, to garb itself in fashions by famous designers, disappeared. The body constructed by images in which not things but information are sold, and revels in it, is nowhere to be found.

In a conversation with Akira Asada in the 1990s, Kyoko Okazaki affirmed the potential of the 1980s. One factor behind the widespread discourse rejecting the '80s was the economic decline in Japan in the '90s. But does this mean one cannot discuss the aspects of that period that should be affirmed? No doubt this is why Kyoko Okazaki stated there was potential beyond "*Oishii Seikatsu*." A view I support; not out of nostalgia, but because the decade of the '80s offers hints for reconsidering the present. And because I am sick and tired of the chaotic, mean vision of the world that has gradually spread since the '90s.

Translated from Japanese by Pamela Miki Associates

Post-Provoke and Post-Conpora: Understanding Japanese photography since the 1970s
—

Minoru Shimizu

Modernism in photography entails believing in the existence of a world as it is. This is a world unsullied (undifferentiated) by ordinary concepts and values, an "outside world" as seen from the public in general. It is often described as "natural," "childlike," "undifferentiated," "peculiarly feminine," "supple" or "constantly eluding rational thought." In other words, the modern "outside world" pertains to the discourse of adult males. On the one hand there is the existing, ossified social system of men, while on the other there is the undifferentiated, rich chaos of women, children and the amodern, and photography entails casting the former loose among the latter. Photography ought to expose existence as it is, and accordingly it must be selfless, random, transparent and natural.

From the late 1960s through the 1970s, the medium of photography went through a particular dislocation. These modern beliefs waned. During this period, coinciding with the advent of the information and media society, "as it is" and "natural" were plundered by capital as the most powerful catch phrases. The days, the "natural," "pure" and "real" "outside world" was nothing but another name for a new product. At this same time in Japan, in response to this dislocation, artists engaged in various forms of expression between the twilight of modernist photography and the coming post-modernist photography. However, it was not until the 1980s at the earliest that Japan, having been defeated in the war, became an affluent country with an established information/media environment, as a result of which there was a time difference with the rest of the world. In understanding Japanese photography since the 1970s, it must not be forgotten that it began as premature post-modern photography isolated from a still immature Japanese society, or in other words that the expression of Japanese photographers preceded social reality.

A mediatized society is a society coping with the stress of being entangled in a complex network of media and not being able to escape it. Representation loses all direct ties to the reality it was supposed to represent and is deemed untrustworthy, while amid the torrent of media an attitude of securing a minimum bridgehead and rethinking everything on this basis arises. Based on this, it is possible to educe common directions among the artists from this period. These are 1) criticism of representation, 2) ordinariness and individuality, 3) a longing for directness, and 4) verification of media. Within the "various forms of expression" of these artists there are two broad currents: "the last modernists" (1 and 3 above) and "Conpora" (2 and 4).

The last modernists

In a world in which the circulation of capital has engulfed the "outside world," what are modernists to do when they understand that the world "as it is" can no longer be captured in photographs, that this itself is the great lie of the present that has been transformed into advertising and that such "lying photography" (Nobuyoshi Araki) is unbearable, yet still do not abandon their faith?

a. Reality as negativity: The real "world as it is" must manifest itself not simply realistically but above all negatively at the boundaries of criticism. One arrives at the manifestation of the world as it is by thoroughly negating false representation. "*Are-bure-boke*" (grainy, blurry, out of focus) was one such method of negation (no representation, no meaning, no expression). Just as strong light blinds us, the manifestation of the real world burns up photographs. The less we understand what is in a photograph, the closer that photograph is to "reality." This type is perhaps best represented by the Provoke photographers, in particular Takuma Nakahira and Daido Moriyama in the early 1970s.

b. Theatrical type: In order not to sully the existence of the world "as it is," or in other words not to make photographs tell lies, the photographer purposely takes photographs that make us aware that "this is a lie." Representative of this theatrical type is Nobuyoshi Araki. The prolongation of modernism by Araki brought to the Japanese photography world of the 1990s a peculiar anachronism (see d below).

c. Absorption in landscapes devoid of people: In order to preserve the purity of the world "as it is," the photographer vaporizes from the photographs all impure semantic content. These restrained landscape photographs devoid of people, which also have similarities with works from around the same period showcased at the "New Topographics" exhibition (1975), preserve the "world as it is" as a pure vacuum. Representative of this absorptive type is Hiroshi Sugimoto.

d. "Girlie photos": The *hetauma* (at first glance poor, but on closer examination skillful) photographs taken by young "natural" women photographers in the 1990s capturing here and now "real moments" in everyday life were photographic nostalgia recalling the distant dreams of the last modernist (male) generation, or perhaps simulacra of modernist photography. Representative of this type are Hiromix and Hanayo.

Conpora

"Conpora" is a generic term for the first generation of post-modern photography in Japan that arose under the influence of the "Contemporary Photographers: Toward a Social Landscape" exhibition held at George Eastman House in Rochester, New York, in 1966. If Provoke chose a path of radically exhausting modernist photography, then Conpora was photographic expression that deconstructed the premise of this ("the world as it is") and in doing so resonated strongly with contemporary art of the same period.

a. The original Conpora: Shigeo Gocho, one of the leading Conpora photographers, took photographs of *Self and Others* as they went about their *Days* (2 and 4 above; both being titles of photo collections by Gocho). This term itself disappeared in the mid-1970s, and with Gocho's premature death (1983) this tendency comes to an end temporarily.

b. Theatrical type: In the 1970s and 80s, a type of photography that exaggerated a Provoke-like concept (arriving at reality) emerged from among the generation of photographers that succeeded Moriyama, Nakahira and Araki. The early works of Keizo Kitajima, who was typical of the post-Provoke generation, are reminiscent of the kind of expression seen at Provoke's CAMP (a leading independent gallery of this period).

c. "Concept photos": Works mainly by artistic photographers who developed a kind of meta-photography based on the principles and history of photography in the 1980s while also having a connection with conceptual art. There has been a noticeable re-evaluation in recent years of photographs by the likes of Jiro Takamatsu, Kiyoji Otsuji and Masafumi Maita.

d. Digital pictorialism: In the 1980s, Japan belatedly joined the ranks of the information and media societies and modernism in photography came to be questioned again as it is now. Also during this period, not only was there a re-evaluation of the history of pictorialism in Japan, which had been neglected under the shadow of realism, but the first examples of image processing using computers emerged in the form of works by such photographers as Miwa Yanagi and Yasumasa Morimura. In other words, in Japan, there arose the peculiarly limited thinking that post-modern photography (photography not based on reality "as it is") = digital image processing (cosplay).

e. The 1990s, the "endless everyday" and the globalization of Japanese photography: The last decade of the 20th century following the bursting of the Japanese asset price bubble that had existed since the late 1980s is commonly referred to as the Lost Decade and was a time when Japanese society was seized by a strong sense of helplessness. However, it was during this same difficult period that the Japanese art and photography worlds globalized in the true sense of the word, a process that continues to this day. Photographers once again directed their gazes at the social reality around them, and in parallel with the re-evaluation of Shigeo Gocho that occurred at this time, a 1990s version of Conpora appeared. It is possible to position the everyday candid photography represented by such photographers as Masafumi Sanai, Katsumi Omori and Takashi Homma (2 above) as the first post-Conpora photography. It was also during this period that women photographers such as Tomoko Yoneda, Rinko Kawauchi, Rika Noguchi and Yuki Kimura first came to prominence outside the frame of "girlie photos."

Also around this time, Daido Moriyama established his own post-modern expression with the publication of the three volumes of *Daido Hysteric* (1993/94/97) before bursting onto the world stage in the 2000s. With this as a turning point, the history of Japanese photography since the 1970s itself became the subject of re-evaluation and new evaluation internationally.

f. Neo-Conpora: Finally, based on the diffusion of the digital photographic technology that developed irreversibly from the late 1990s and the new photographic environment of the networked society (social networking sites, Instagram etc.), an awareness of the issues surrounding 4 above was added to the preceding clauses d and e, as a result of which since the 2000s a form of post-Conpora photography has appeared as an atavistic expression of the original Conpora. Represented by Takashi Yasumura, this new digital expression of the neo-Conpora generation, as one might put it, is currently ongoing.

Translated from Japanese by Pamela Miki Associates

Giving life: The latent power of still images in Japanese subculture

—

Futoshi Hoshino

Throughout the history of postwar Japanese art, subculture has constantly been a major source of images. In the work of Takashi Murakami (b. 1962) and Makoto Aida (b. 1965), who have used these images strategically, and in the work of such contemporaries as Yoshitomo Nara (b. 1959) and Kenji Yanobe (b. 1965), and artists of following generations, connections with subculture can be identified either clearly or implicitly. Of course, such a phenomenon can probably also be observed in Western Europe and North America as well as in Asian countries that modernized at around the same time as Japan. But for artists born in postwar Japan, and in particular in the 1960s, subculture was something that existed not only as a counter to high culture including "fine art" (which is the kind of territory the term "subculture" usually refers to), but also as a given cultural resource, or in other words as part of the surrounding "landscape."

Here, I am using the term "Japanese subculture" to refer to the various media that have evolved in a unique way in Japan, such as manga, anime and video games. Certainly, these media themselves were not necessarily "invented" in Japan, and various sources exist in the form of Western cartoons/Franco-Belgian comics and Disney's animated films (in addition to which the worldview of the RPG games that developed in Japan was largely inspired by Western myths and fantasies). Despite this, the reason these media can be said to have evolved in a unique way in Japan is that the aforementioned manga, anime and video games were attended by various conditions or restrictions arising from their status as commercial media aimed at the masses. As we shall see below, they were unusual media that possessed both the opportunity for "condensation" by combining standard patterns and the opportunity for the explosive "spreading" of fan communities that arose as a result.

One factor that is central to this "condensation" by combining standard patterns and this explosive "spreading" via fan communities is the concept of "*kyara*" in Japanese manga and anime. As has already been pointed out by numerous commentators, this term, an abbreviation of *kyarakutaa*, has a meaning that is similar to but different from the English word "character" from which it derives.[1]

According to Inuhiko Yomota, in manga and anime, which consist of series of countless frames (i.e. pictures), the face of character X is by no means always depicted as the same face; yet, at the same time, as long as the identity of X is maintained, it is possible for that character's face to be depicted infinitely.[2] What is required in order to maintain this identity is the creation of so-called *kyara*. This contrasts sharply with live-action movies, for example, in which the identity of a character is carried by the face of the same actor. *Kyara* in manga and anime is none other than a form invented for bestowing a stable identity on a character in a work based on such creative necessity. More specifically, it is a peculiar grammar for reducing the features of characters to several broad patterns including the color and style of their hair, the size and contour of their eyes, and the presence or absence of glasses and accessories, and shaping the features of their character through the combination of these. Accordingly, from the point of view of realism, the external appearance of characters in Japanese manga and anime has often displayed absurd characteristics. It goes without saying that having girls with enormous eyeballs, extremely thin chins and green or pink hair occupying the same pictorial space is far from realistic. Within the world of manga and anime, however, such physical features are not regarded as abnormal. Rather, in the media of manga and anime, made up of series of countless drawings, such preposterous features arose necessarily from the expressive grammar used to maintain the identity of each character.

One can probably say that the recognition of Murakami, Aida, Nara and Yanobe overseas in the 1990s and 2000s was at least partially on the basis of this kind of parallax. Today, when Japanese anime and manga are almost immediately translated into English, French and other languages, the characterization technique outlined above is already widely known even outside Japan. However, it is probably certain that at the end of last century when such an environment did not yet exist, the *kyara*-like figures in the works of these artists were received as characters endowed with attributes different from those found in paintings up until then.

In addition to the above example of *kyara*, I would like to touch in a little more detail on the material conditions in which postwar Japanese manga and anime existed. As mentioned above, because Japanese manga and anime were commercial media aimed at the masses, they were attended by restrictions that were almost outrageous from the point of view of "fine art." One such restriction was the curtailment of the number of frames in television anime, a process known as "limited animation."

Limited animation refers to animation in which the amount of time and money required to create a work are greatly reduced by using a single still image together with a voice over, for example, or making only parts of a figure on screen move (the eyes, mouth, etc). It was first introduced by Osamu Tezuka (1928-1989) during the making of the television anime series *Astro Boy*, after which it continued to undergo its own unique creative evolution in the world of Japanese commercial animation, which is premised on televisation. Notable examples of its use include repeating the standard poses of the main characters numerous times during a broadcast and employing literary narration to complement still images. The full animation of Studio Ghibli that is familiar to many overseas viewers is actually the exception in Japanese anime, and the fact that the majority is made up of animation that effectively employed still images is important. As Thomas Lamarre points out, it is not uncommon for artists to make the connection that Hayao Miyazaki does between animation and the animism of ancient Japan when discussing their own work.[3] However, in Japanese anime created using the traditional method of limited animation, one can discern the paradoxical expressive grammar of using still, inanimate expression to give life to (i.e. animate) fictitious characters.

Whether it be *kyara* or limited animation, in the commercial media of manga and anime, various condensations of types and patterns arose that turned these restrictions into assets, as a result of which manga and anime spread into a form of communication centered on the younger generation through the medium of *kyara* images. Perhaps the most notable example of this is the popularized simulationism of "derivative works" of manga and anime. The various derivative works made by fans that flood the internet have transcended the simple dichotomy between original and copy and become a classic example of autonomously proliferating user generated contents (UGC).

And it goes without saying that one of these water veins without doubt flows into the territory of postwar Japanese art. Murakami, Aida, Nara and Yanobe are all artists of the generation that were quick to introduce into art the unique expressive grammar of manga and anime. Even though the creative intentions of each of these artist was certainly different, from the point of view of the conventional codes in traditional art, the characterization born out of commercial manga and anime— which is worlds apart from the kind of grasping of the decisive moment Lessing lauded in *Laocoon*—was something that functioned as an unmistakable foreign substance. The representation of Japanese *kyara* born out of various restrictions introduced into art the possibility of a new iconology for the purposes of giving life to still characters.

Translated from Japanese by Pamela Miki Associates

—

Notes

[1] Go Ito, *Tezuka is Dead* (Tokyo: NTT Publishing, 2005).

[2] Inuhiko Yomota, *Manga genron* (Tokyo: Chikumashobo, 1994).

[3] Thomas Lamarre, *The Anime Machine: A Media Theory of Animation* (Minneapolis: University of Minnesota, 2009).

Performance in Japan:
Between anti-establishment and popular culture
—

Emmanuelle de Montgazon

The participation of Japanese artists in the various mainstream global avant-garde movements of the 20th century contributed to some of its most important intellectual and cultural exchanges, resonating in particular with the North American art movements of the 1950s. The postwar era was particularly outstanding in terms of the increased number of artist collectives working across multiple domains, such as the Gutai Art Association, *Jikken Kobo* ("Experimental Workshop," 1951-1958), and literary and artistic collectives like *Kiroku Geijutsu no Kai* ("Documentary Arts Society") that sought to transcend popular genres and culture.

The 1960s, characterized by energetic activism in response to a tense socio-political context, was a period of transition. Neo-Dada artists and their shocking protest performances, Hi-Red Center, and Kansai-based group The Play staged both individual and collective acts across the entire country, especially in public space. As is well-known, a coterie of artists and intellectuals formed in Tokyo centered on the Sogetsu Art Center (SAC), which went on to become a place for the avant-garde to foment, as well as a meeting point for cross-disciplinary explorations into what was known as "intermedia." Between 1958 and 1971, the SAC promoted experimental approaches, serving as a point of contact for artists, musicians, designers, critics, authors, and performers to gather around their shared practices. The SAC was a place where life happened, a site for activities related to the Fluxus movement in Japan, the venue for experimental film screenings led by Takahiko Iimura, as well as the legendary location where experimental music performances and concerts focusing on the works of Toshi Ichiyanagi, John Cage, David Tudor, and Merce Cunningham were held. This was also the period that saw the emergence of the pioneering generation of "little theaters" with an intellectual, experimental character. Strongly influenced by the initiatives of the time, these small theaters sprung up as an act of resistance against the established *shingeki* (literally, "new drama") genre based on an imported brand of Western realism.

For the many artists who participated in Expo '70 in Osaka, as well as those who joined the extremely radical anti-Expo movement « Banpaku Hakai Katsudo », this dynamism provided a vital foundation for their practice. Expo '70, which saw some 64 million visitors, was the first time that popular culture, which developed by leaps and bounds, encountered more experimental approaches. The "festival whirlwind" that gave birth to these "children of the Expo" also revitalized the art world, and exerted an influence on its surroundings. This vitality in the art world became more evident after the Saison Group opened the Seibu Theater (later renamed the Parco Theater). Since 1973, the corporate group known as Saison has played a major role in terms of bringing pop culture — a mechanism for creating a consumer culture linked to the commercialization of what was popular and trendy — to Tokyo. It was also the parent company of the radio station J-Wave, which brought about a shift towards innovative forms of music. The Parco Theater, a small-scale facility with a capacity of about 500, quickly became a symbol of the relationship between "anti-establishment culture" and a commercial culture that was witnessing vertiginous growth: in other words, a curious relationship in which these two cultures grew and developed by exerting a reciprocal impact on each other. Just like the Osaka Expo, the Parco Theater served as an archetype of how everything happened across the entire urban landscape — associations and interactions between the anti-consumerist generation, as well as the appearance of products formulated by an extremely refined community of artists, musicians, and designers.

Throughout the era of the bubble economy during the 1980s, large corporate groups followed in the footsteps of Parco's initiatives. Spiral Hall opened in the chic Aoyama district in 1985, and Bunkamura opened in Shibuya in 1989. As a result, central Tokyo became a place of artistic vitality with a strong influence. The prolific creative activity of the time spread to a wide range of both public and private spaces, helping to generate an aesthetic that belonged to both popular and underground culture. The phenomenon saw an almost immediate response from abroad, something that was demonstrated by the success of YMO (Yellow Magic Orchestra, 1978-1984), the musical group that positioned itself somewhere between pop and experimental music. After 1981, the sound and aesthetic of techno pop transcended Japan's borders and became scattered abroad while also dispersing itself throughout Japanese society, becoming a true symbol of an era that privileged youth and urban culture. It was in this context that Japan saw the advent of diverse, liberated theatrical formats. In Shibuya, Shuji Terayama developed a kind of urban theater (*Shigaigeki*) in the streets together with his troupe, while little theaters (Shogekijo) emerged one after the other. The Kansai region, meanwhile, saw the birth of initiatives that struck a balance between performance and theater, with an emphasis on production values, including Dumb Type and Ideal Copy. In 1985, the accomplished modern-day observer Yasumasa Morimura embarked on his series of art-historical self-portraits where he would be dressed up as van Gogh, for instance, in the city of Osaka, located within the sphere of influence of the renowned popular theater troupe Takarazuka.

The period between 1991 and 2006 was one of economic decline following the collapse of the bubble economy, known as the "lost decade." Faced with this situation, artistic practice sought to reassess the notion of the collective as it played out in terms of the inter-relation between community approaches and individuals. Dumb Type staged participatory performances with a politically radical tone that also resonated with the spirit of community activism, and acquired a kind of mythical status after its leader, Teiji Furuhashi, died of AIDS in 1995. Subsequently, the Kyoto group Kyupi Kyupi, which began working with video, film, and performance, launched their career in 1996.

In the wake of the Great Hanshin earthquake of 1995, many artists articulated the necessity of imparting a sense of new value to their social realities, as seen in Shimabuku's *The Chance to Recover Our Humanity* (1995), or Tsuyoshi Ozawa's project Nasubi Gallery, which began in 1993 and consisted of a series of mobile, miniature galleries. A far cry from the wild enthusiasm of the avant-garde, this era was marked by a sense of artists being displaced and deprived of a space to call their own. As a result of decentralization policies, theaters emerged one after another (more than 1000 theaters and concert halls opened over the space of a decade), and people of substantial financial means who could serve as backers were appointed to top positions at these theaters. Although they had been constructed with finances dating from the bubble economy, these new spaces began operating right in the middle of a period of complete economic decline, hosting large-scale productions and internationally renowned theaters and dance companies (Merce Cunningham, Pina Bausch, Philippe Decouflé, and Peter Brook among others). Parallel to these large-scale activities, a mood of disenchantment emerged, where the commercial world and the underground seemed to become polarized.

The "little theater" genre saw the emergence of a genre of quiet drama (*Shizukana engeki*) embodied by Oriza Hirata. This sort of realist theater was based on the performance of daily conversation against a rarefied backdrop of stage devices.

Contemporary dance was led by radical, unique figures including Saburo Teshigawara and Kim Ito, who devised forms of dance rich in irony that were inspired by how a sense of the extraordinary lay concealed within everyday life.

In the field of music, noise music involving technologies that amplified feedback and created distortions and experimental electronic music occupied an important place at small spaces for live music (*Raibuhausu*). Active on this circuit were artists like Keiji Haino and Merzbow (Masami Akita), who were clearly influenced by the Dadaists and bruitism (the use of sounds taken from an extra-musical context). The growth of the small-scale music scene, which was largely housed in underground spaces, was the result of the increased dissemination of music through radio channels, as well as the larger number of record stores. It was an entirely natural development for this noise music scene to come into contact with the performance scene, and the force and energy of industrial music in particular. In a wider context, Canon ArtLab (a laboratory for artistic research by Canon Inc.) was engaged in various explorations, producing radically experimental works like those of Seiko Mikami that have now become the stuff of legend, on a prodigious scale worthy of special mention. Thanks to these alternative currents in relation to the predominance of popular culture, works of art that were clearly distinct from products like

J-pop and feature-length anime films went on to achieve international recognition. Although these currents resonated with the technology found in Japanese culture and the vertiginous progress it was making, they had emerged in a place that was far removed from that of kawaii ("cute") form-making, norms of female beauty, and sexual fetishism. Accordingly, the distinguishing feature of this era might be said to be the emergence of a new anti-establishment culture stemming from a critique of technology and the worship of the philosophy of man as a machine.

Even with the amplified sense of social uncertainty and a grave identity crisis lurking in the background that had come about as a result of technologies applied to the realm of everyday life, economic activity managed to regain a sense of momentum in 2006. Young people saw something of themselves in the notion of the "divided self" proposed by author Keiichiro Hirano. According to Hirano, each individual possesses multiple faces that become relativized in the face of social diversity, with the specter of job insecurity and the collapse of values in the background.

In spite of this, robust economic activity brought various cultural initiatives into being, and Japan demonstrated a willingness to enter into a dialogue with the world. It was around this time that the Tokyo Performing Arts Market (TPAM), Art Fair Tokyo, several biennials and triennials, and art festivals like Festival/Tokyo and Kyoto Experiment (KEX) were launched, leading many foreign artists to come to Japan. The structure of society took on a certain density, and artists rediscovered their cultural roots through fresh eyes, articulating a renewed relationship to the community and a desire to break out of a state of isolation. New forms of theater created by artists born in the 1970s emerged. Akira Takayama and Daisuke Miura paved the way towards a stripped-down, pseudo-documentary brand of theater that sought to blur the boundaries between reality and fiction, while Toshiki Okada created a kind of theatrical "writing" depicting fictional dystopias, set against a political and social context that transcended the individual. This questioning of identity can also be observed in the performative turn that has developed in recent years in the genre-crossing work of Fuyuki Yamakawa, or many female artists like Tabaimo and Miwa Yanagi. Yanagi has slowly departed from the framework of photography: in 2014, she conceptualized a unique, mobile stage-like device involving performances with gorgeous, three-dimensional effects inspired by Kenji Nakagami's literary triptych about the "untouchable" *burakumin* class that has suffered discrimination in contemporary Japanese society.

The tsunami of 2011 and the Fukushima disaster that followed had clear repercussions for artistic practices, and a strong impact on the world. Trends and currents in literature, theater, fashion, and music shifted towards an emphasis on the notion of a community that emerges in the gap between a highly developed network of social media and individual testimony. There was a renewed sense of political consciousness, which led to new forms of art realized through action.

This phenomenon was supported by the work of Chim↑Pom, which positioned itself exactly between installation and the articulation of dissent. Over a period of some 11 years, critical opinion of their work has sometimes been divided — something that owes itself to the way in which it defies convention while referring to social issues, producing a form of art that consists of action. From the relational device *Don't Follow the Wind*, installed in the no-go zone in Fukushima and inaccessible to outsiders, to *So See You Again Tomorrow, Too?*, a more recent exhibition held on the premises of a building in the Kabukicho area of Tokyo that was about to be demolished, Chim↑Pom's artistic gestures are a response to contemporary Japanese society, and the post-Fukushima era in particular. At the same time, their work demonstrates a return to an activism and actionism that could be found in the silence of what had already existed before. There has been an evident uptick in the number of art formats and collectives that attempt to impose a sense of organization onto individual or collective action: this phenomenon stems from how a new activist consciousness has had an impact on all sorts of artistic practices in the 'atomic era of the anthropocene'.

Ten Evenings

Ten Evenings, the title of a planned event at Centre Pompidou-Metz, is a reference to the *Nine Evenings: Theater and Engineering* series of performances organized by Billy Klüver in New York on October 23, 1966. The Centre Pompidou event addresses Japan's complex historical relationship to the United States and its impact on American culture and art, which served as a basis for how Japan constructed its own antithesis to Western modernity. Thanks to the dynamic exchanges that took place between Japan and the US during this period, a similar event called *Cross Talk/Intermedia* was held in Tokyo in 1969. This event attracted some 10,000 visitors to gather at the Yoyogi National Gymnasium to address the topic of the sprawling networks created by co-producers, industries, sound engineers, artists, and various structures and organizations, prefiguring the innovative artistic developments that would contribute to the success of Expo '70 in Osaka. *Cross Talk/Intermedia* also became symbolic of the important question of what constituted a Japanese identity.

    Ten Evenings, which alludes to this era while also posing a similar question applicable to our current age, was formulated as a program that continuously unfolds each month, from October 2017 through March 2018. Each event highlights artists and artist collectives, as well as their relationship to the plurality of our artistic and cultural heritage. By expressing the diversity of artists from various generations, *Ten Evenings* allows participants to experience the diverse approaches taken by artists in relation to our contemporary age. Tying all of this diversity together are the following two threads that help to steer the task at hand: the act of traversing and responding to the dense, turbulent currents of this era of endless rupture, as well as the creation of a unique, distinctive Japanese identity, both by relying on the living memories of international avant-garde movements.

Translated from Japanese by Darryl Jingwen Wee

—

Notes

[1] Made up of 14 artists, musicians, choreographers, designers, lighting designers, and poets, Jikken Kobo was established in 1951, and was active up until 1958. Influenced by the likes of John Cage, Martha Graham, Alexander Calder, and Isamu Noguchi, Jikken Kobo was formed around the notion of the genre-crossing artwork, based on other experiences related to ballet, recitals, and the perception of art.

[2] Some of the figures associated with the pioneering generation of avant-garde theater in the 1960s were Shuji Terayama (1935-1983), Tadashi Suzuki (1939-), Yukio Ninagawa (1935-2016), and Juro Kara (1940-).

[3] Julian Ross, "Site and Specificity in Japanese Expanded Cinema: Intermedia and its Development in the late-60's," Décadrage, issue ok21-22, winter 2012.

[4] Yoko Hayashi, "The Children of the Osaka World Expo: the symbolic generation of the Japanese art scene of the 1990s," in Éric Mézil (dir.), Donai yanen! = Et maintenant : la création contemporaine au Japon, cat. exp., Paris, Ensba, 1998.

[5] So See You Again Tomorrow, Too? was an activist event that featured a range of formats. In the fall of 2016, it brought together performers and musicians in various fields who had a strong following among their generation. Publicity was carried out only through social media, and a stand-alone, autonomous budget was secured to produce the project.

[6] A reference to a statement made by Kenji Kubota at the symposium Activism and Art in the Era of Fukushima, held at the Copenhagen art space, X and Beyond, on May 27, 2017.

[7] David Novak, Japanoise, Music at the Edge of Circulation, Duke University Press, 2013, p.24.

A — Strange Object, Post-human Body

Genpei AKASEGAWA (1937-2014), *Wind*, 1963/1985, electric fan, paper, string, 67 x 35 x 28 cm, Museum of Contemporary Art, Tokyo © Centre Pompidou-Metz / Photo Jacqueline Trichard / 2017 /Exposition Japanorama (pp.60-61)

Comme des Garçons (1969-; **Rei KAWAKUBO**: 1942-), *Comme des Garçons*, 1982, gelatin silver print, 60 x 60 cm, Photography: Peter Lindbergh, Collection of the artist © Centre Pompidou-Metz / Photo Jacqueline Trichard / 2017 / Exposition Japanorama (pp.60-61)

Comme des Garçons, *Ensemble*, from collection autumn-winter 2001-2002, 2001, Mode Museum Provincie Antwerpen-Momu, Antwerp

Comme des Garçons, *Shoes*, from collection autumn-winter 2001-2002, 2001, Mode Museum Provincie Antwerpen-Momu, Antwerp

Comme des Garçons, *Robe*, from collection spring-summer 2012-2013, 2012, Isolde Pringiers Collection, Brussels

Comme des Garçons, *Robe-cloak*, from collection autumn-winter 2012-2013, 2012, Isolde Pringiers Collection, Brussels

Dumb Type (1984-), *Dumb type Archive*, 2017, book, Collection of the artist

Dumb Type, Extract from *Pleasure Life* (1988), *pH* (1990), *S/N* (1994), *OR* (1997), *Memorandum* (1999), *Voyage* (2002), 2017, video (color, sound), 10 min, Collection of the artist, Courtesy of Dumb Type (p.68)

Dumb type, *Glass Table*, 2017, glass table, video (color, sound), 71.5 x 213.5 x 74.2 cm, Collection of the artist

Tatsumi HIJIKATA (1928-1986), *Tatsumi Hijikata and Japanese People: Rebellion of the Body*, 1968, video (black and white, sound), 13 min, Video: Hiroshi NAKAMURA, Collection of Tatsumi Hijikata Archive, Keio University Art Center, Tokyo

Tatsumi HIJIKATA, *Tatsumi Hijikata and Japanese People : Rebellion of the Body*, 1968, gelatin silver print, 16.3 x 24.7 cm, Photograph: Ryozen TORII, Collection of Tatsumi Hijikata Archive, Keio University Art Center, Tokyo, Courtesy of Tatsumi Hijikata Archive, Keio University Art Center, Tokyo (p.63)

Minoru HIRATA (1930-2018), *Akasegawa Genpei's Morphology of Revenge (a.k.a. 1,000-Yen Note Painting), at Hi Red Center's 5th Mixer Plan exhibition at Shinjuku Dai-Ichi Gallery,* 1963/2017, gelatin silver print, Image size : 33.5 x 22.2 cm, Paper size : 35.7 x 27.8 cm, HM Archive, Courtesy of Taka Ishii Gallery Photography / Film, Tokyo

Minoru HIRATA, *Hi Red Center's Cleaning Event (officially known as Be Clean! and Campaign to Promote Cleanliness and Order in the Metropolitan Area)*, 1964/2017, gelatin silver print, Image size: 22.2 x 33.5 cm, Paper size: 27.8 x 35.7 cm, HM Archive, Courtesy of Taka Ishii Gallery Photography / Film, Tokyo (p.62)

Minoru HIRATA, *Hi Red Center's Cleaning Event (officially known as Be Clean ! and Campaign to Promote Cleanliness and Order in the Metropolitan Area)*, 1964/2017, gelatin silver print, Image size : 33.5 x 22.2 cm, Paper size : 35.7

x 27.8 cm, HM Archive, Courtesy of Taka Ishii Gallery Photography / Film, Tokyo

Eikoh HOSOE (1933-), *"Kamaitachi" #17*, 1965/c.2010, gelatin silver print, Image: 30.4 x 45.1 cm, Paper: 40.5 x 50.4 cm, Collection of the artist, Courtesy of Taka Ishii Gallery Photography / Film, Tokyo (p.63)

Eikoh HOSOE, *"Kamaitachi" #8*, 1965/c.2010, gelatin silver print, Image: 45 x 32.4 cm, Paper: 50.4 x 40.4 cm, Collection of the artist, Courtesy of Taka Ishii Gallery Photography / Film, Tokyo

Eikoh HOSOE, *unpublished photo from photograph collection "Kamaitachi", at the foot of Mt.Tsukuba*, 1968/2017, gelatin silver print, Image: 30.2 x 45.2 cm, Paper: 40.3 x 50.3 cm, Collection of the artist, Courtesy of Taka Ishii Gallery Photography / Film, Tokyo

Tomoaki ISHIHARA (1959-), *I.S.M. (H)*, 1989, styrofoam, cowhide, 115 x 110 x 180 cm, Toyota Municipal Museum of Art, Aichi, Courtesy of Toyota Municipal Museum of Art, Aichi (p.64)

Tetsumi KUDO (1935 - 1990), *Your Portrait—Chrysalis in the Cocoon,* 1967, wadding plastic, polyester, black light, 161 x 87 x 78 cm, Centre Pompidou, Musée national d'art moderne, Paris

Tetsumi KUDO, *Homage to the Young Generation - The Cocoon Opens*, 1968, baby carriage, polyester, electronic flash, sound source, 120 x 100 x 150 cm, Museum of Contemporary Art, Tokyo, Courtesy of Museum of Contemporary Art, Tokyo © ADAGP, Paris & JASPER, Tokyo. 2020 E3778 (p.65)

Tetsumi KUDO, *Portrait of Artist in the Crisis*, 1975, perforated plate of hardboard mounted on a flat frame and on which is fixed a metal cage with a turnstile and a water tank containing various elements: a freezer thermometer, a plastic cup laboratory, two metal needles, wool knitting, three synthetic resin moldings, a cigarette, 29 x 45 x 32 cm, Centre national des arts plastiques, Paris

Yuko MOHRI (1980-), *Parade*, 2011-2017, mixed media, dimensions variable, Centre Pompidou, Musée national d'art moderne, Paris © Centre Pompidou-Metz / Photo Jacqueline Trichard / 2017 / Exposition Japanorama (p.68)

Mariko MORI (1967-), *Link of the Moon (Miko no Inori),* 1996, video(color, sound), 5 min, Museum of Contemporary Art, Tokyo, Courtesy of Museum of Contemporary Art, Tokyo (p.64)

Yasumasa MORIMURA (1951-), *A Requiem: Theater of Creativity. Self Portrait as Marcel Duchamp (Based on the photo by Julian Wasser)*, from "New Requiem" series, 2010, c-print, 150 x 187.5 cm, Galeria Juana de Aizpuru, Madrid, Courtesy of Galeria Juana de Aizpuru, Madrid (p.64)

Yukio NAKAGAWA (1918-2012), *Flowery Priestess*, 1973, c-print (carnation, glass), 180.2 x 130 x 2.5 cm, Photo: Naomi Maki, Collection of Fondation Cartier d'art contemporain, Paris © YUKIO NAKAGAWA (p.65)

Yukio NAKAGAWA, *Sacred Book*, 1994 (print: 2004), c-print (carnation, glass), image: 94.7 x 120 cm (image size), 21st Century Museum of Contemporary Art, Kanazawa, Ishikawa

Kodai NAKAHARA (1961-), *Viridian Adaptor + Kodai's Morpho II*, 1989, wool, plywood, dimensions variable, Toyota Municipal Museum of Art, Aichi, Courtesy of Toyota Municipal Museum of Art, Aichi (p.67)

Natsuyuki NAKANISHI (1935-2016), *Cloths Pegs Assert Churning Action*, 1963, strings, clothespins on canvas, 6 pieces (right and left): 116.5 x 91 cm each, center: 41 x 31.5 cm, *4 pieces of them were exhibited, Museum of Contemporary Art, Tokyo, Courtesy of Museum of Contemporary Art, Tokyo (p.65)

Motohiko ODANI (1972-), *Double Edged of Thought (Dress 2)*, 1997, hair, dress:172 x 67 x 3 cm, 21st Century Museum of Contemporary Art, Kanazawa, Ishikawa

Motohiko ODANI, *Double Edged of Thought (Dress 2)*, 1997, c-print, photograph:23.5 × 18.5 cm, 21st Century Museum of Contemporary Art, Kanazawa, Ishikawa

Motohiko ODANI, *Phantom-Limb*, 1997, c-print, acrylic frame, each 148 × 111 × 2.7 cm (5 pieces), 21st Century Museum of Contemporary Art, Kanazawa, Ishikawa, Courtesy of 21st Century Museum of Contemporary Art, Kanazawa © ODANI Motohiko (p.66)

Motohiko ODANI, *Rompers*, 2003, video, 2'52", music: PIRAMI, 21st Century Museum of Contemporary Art, Kanazawa, Ishikawa

Kazuo OHNO (1906-2010), Extract from *The Portrait of Mr.O* (1969), *Mandala of Mr.O* (1971), *Mr.O's Book of the Dead* (1973), *Admiring La Argentina* (1977, the first performance), 2017, video, sound, Videography: Video Information Center, Photography: Hiroaki Tsukamoto, Kazuo Ohno Dance Studio | NPO Dance Archive Network, Tokyo, Courtesy of Kazuo Ohno Dance Studio | NPO Dance Archive Network (p.63)

Yukimasa OKUMURA (1947-), *Logo*, 1980, block copy, 25.5 x 30.5 cm, TSTJ Inc., Tokyo

Yukimasa OKUMURA, *Yellow Magic Orchestra World Tour'80 From TOKIO To TOKYO*, 1980, brochure, 24.8 x 21 cm, TSTJ Inc., Tokyo

Yukimasa OKUMURA, *Yellow Magic Orchestra World Tour'80 From TOKIO To TOKYO*, 1980, CD jacket, 12.7 x 14.2 cm, TSTJ Inc., Tokyo

Yukimasa OKUMURA, *BGM*, 1981, CD jacket, 11 x 15.5 cm, TSTJ Inc.

Yukimasa OKUMURA, *Yellow Magic Orchestra World Tou'80 From TOKIO To TOKYO*, 1981, leaflet, 14.8 x 21 cm, TSTJ Inc., Tokyo

Yukimasa OKUMURA, *Yellow Magic Orchestra World Tour'80 From TOKIO To TOKYO*, 1981, sticker, 11.7 x 16.6 cm, TSTJ Inc., Tokyo

Yukimasa OKUMURA, *YMO*, 1981, *YMO exhibition, ticket*, 17 x 6.5 cm, TSTJ Inc., Tokyo

Yukimasa OKUMURA, *LDK studio*, 1982, 24.7 x 21 cm each, TSTJ Inc., Tokyo

Yukimasa OKUMURA, *S·F·X*, 1984, original poster, 72.8 x 51.5 cm, TSTJ Inc., Tokyo

Yukimasa OKUMURA, *S·F·X artwork A*, 1984, block copy, 30.3 × 25.3 cm, TSTJ Inc., Tokyo

Yukimasa OKUMURA, *S·F·X artwork B*, 1984, block copy, 30.4 × 25.2 cm, TSTJ Inc., Tokyo

Yukimasa OKUMURA, *S·F·X artwork C*, 1984, block copy, 30.3 × 25.3 cm, TSTJ Inc., Tokyo

Yukimasa OKUMURA, *S·F·X artwork D*, 1984, block copy, 35.5 × 29.7 cm, TSTJ Inc., Tokyo

Yukimasa OKUMURA, *S·F·X artwork E*, 1984, block copy, 30 × 25.3 cm, TSTJ Inc., Tokyo

Yukimasa OKUMURA, *S·F·X artwork F*, 1984, block copy, 30.4 × 25.5 cm, TSTJ Inc., Tokyo

Yukimasa OKUMURA, *S·F·X artwork G*, 1984, block copy, 22.2 × 30.5 cm, TSTJ Inc., Tokyo

Yukimasa OKUMURA, *Winter Live 81*, 2013, stage model, table: 16 x 100 x 62 cm, stage: 46.6 x 100 x 62 cm, TSTJ Inc., Tokyo

Katsuhiro OTOMO (1954-), *AKIRA*, 1982-90, print on paper, 21 boards, Kodansha, Tokyo (p.69)

Katsuhiro OTOMO, *GENGA exhibition catalogue*, 2012, print on paper, 3

boards, Kodansha, Tokyo

Rhizomatiks (2006-), ***Perfume, at Cannes Lions International Festival of Creativity***, 2013, video (color, sound), 3', Collection and courtesy of the artist (p.69)

Rhizomatiks, ***chains***, 2016, video (color, sound), Collection of the artist

Shozo SHIMAMOTO (1928-2013) ***Work (Holes)***, c.1950, paint, pencil on newspaper, 194 x 130.6 cm, Museum of Contemporary Art, Tokyo © Centre Pompidou-Metz / Photo Jacqueline Trichard / 2017 /Exposition Japanorama (pp.60-61)

Sputniko! (1985-), ***Menstruation Machine – Takashi's Take***, 2010, video (color, sound), 3'24", Collection of the Artist, Courtesy of the Artist (p.66)

Sputniko!, ***The Moonwalk Machine – Selena's Step***, 2013, video (color, sound), 4'30", Collection of the Artist

Masayoshi SUKITA (1938-), ***Yellow Magic Orchestra***, 1979, photo print (LP jacket of "Solid State Survivor", 1979), Collection of the artist

Masayoshi SUKITA, ***Yellow Magic Orchestra***, 1979, photo print (LP jacket of "Nice Age", 1980), Collection of the artist

Masayoshi SUKITA, ***Yellow Magic Orchestra: Posters, London***, 1979, photo print, Collection of the artist

Masayoshi SUKITA, ***Yellow Magic Orchestra***, 1979, photo print, Collection of the artist

Masayoshi SUKITA, ***Yellow Magic Orchestra***, 1979, photo print, Collection of the artist

Masayoshi SUKITA, ***Yellow Magic Orchestra (Air Version)***, 1980, photo print (advertising image for Fuji cassette), Collection of the artist

Masayoshi SUKITA, ***Yellow Magic Orchestra (Air Version)***, 1980, photo print (advertising image for Fuji cassette), Collection of the artist

Masayoshi SUKITA, ***Yellow Magic Orchestra (Air Version)***, 1980, photo print (advertising image for Fuji cassette), Collection of the artist

Atsuko TANAKA (1932-2005), ***Work (Bell),*** 1955/1981, bell, notch, dimension variable, Museum of Contemporary Art, Tokyo

Atsuko TANAKA, ***Plan for Work (The Bell)***, 1955, ink on paper, wood, 39.7 × 27.5 cm, Museum of Contemporary Art, Tokyo

Atsuko TANAKA, ***Denkifuku (Robe électrique)***, 1956/1999, color bulbs, tube bulbs with 8 colors, felt, cable, electricity, adhesive tape, metal, painted wood, electric case, circuit breaker, dimmer switch, 165 x 90 x 90 cm, Centre Pompidou, Musée national d'art moderne, Paris © Centre Pompidou-Metz / Photo Jacqueline Trichard / 2017 /Exposition Japanorama (p.62)

YMO (1978-) ***Solid State Survivor***, 1979, LP Jacket, 31.4 x 31.4 cm, Private collection, Courtesy / Photography: Masayoshi Sukita (p.69)

YMO, ***Yellow Magic Orchestra***, 1979, LP Jacket, 31.4 x 31.4 cm, Private collection

YMO, ***Fuji Cassette CF video (Technopolis 25 version)***, 1980, video (color, sound), 1'09", FUJIFILM, Tokyo

YMO, ***Fuji Cassette CF video (Tokyo Technopolis version)***, 1980, video (color, sound), 1'20", FUJIFILM, Tokyo

YMO, ***Public Pressure***, 1980, LP Jacket, 31.4 x 31.4 cm, Private collection

YMO, ***X∞Multiplies***, 1980, LP Jacket, 31.4 x 31.4 cm, Private collection

YMO, ***Fuji Cassette CF video (Air version)***, 1981, video (color, sound), 0'30", FUJIFILM, Tokyo

YMO, ***BGM,*** 1981, LP Jacket, 31.4 x 31.4 cm, Private collection

YMO, ***Technodelic***, 1981, LP Jacket, 31.4 x 31.4 cm, Private collection

YMO, ***NAUGHTY BOYS***, 1983, LP Jacket, 31.4 x 31.4 cm, Private collection

YMO, *SERVICE*, 1983, LP Jacket, 31.4 x 31.4 cm, Private collection
YMO, *Zoshoku Ningyo (multiply dolls)*, 2007, plaster, 38 x 11 x 6 cm, 38 x 12 x 6 cm, 38 x 11.5 x 6 cm (each), Private collection

B   Pop Art: before/after the 1980s

Makoto AIDA (1965-), *No One Knows the Title (War Picture Returns)*, 1996, four-panel folding screens / enamel, vinyl tablecloth on fusuma (sliding door), hinges, 178.4 x 272.4 cm, Private collection, Courtesy of Mizuma Art Gallery (p.80)
Genpei AKASEGAWA (1937-2014), *Model 1,000 Yen Notes I*, 1963, letterpress print on quality paper, 7.4 x 16.1 cm, Private Collection
ANREALAGE (2003-; **Kunihiko MORINAGA**: 1980-), *Ensemble from 2011 A/W Collection "LOW"*, 2011, 180 x 50 x 40 cm, Collection and courtesy of the artist (p.83)
ANREALAGE, *Ensemble from 2016 S/S Collection "REFLECT"*, 2016, 180 x 10 x 40 cm, Collection of the artist
ANREALAGE, *Ensemble from 2017 A/W Collection "ROLL"*, 2017, 180 x 60 x 60 cm, Collection of the artist
ANREALAGE, Extract from *2011 A/W Collection "LOW"*, *2016 S/S Collection "REFLECT"*, and *2017 A/W Collection "ROLL"*, 2017, video (color, sound), 9 min, Collection of the artist
Yayoi DEKI (1977-), *Mimichin,* 1998, acrylic on board, 145.5 x 103 cm, Takahashi Collection, Tokyo, Courtesy of ANOMALY (p.83)
Katsuhiko HIBINO (1958-), *PRESENT SHOE*, 1982, acrylic, color pencil, sumi ink, gesso, corrugated cardboard, cardboard, 72.8 x 103 cm, The Museum of Fine Arts, Gifu
Katsuhiko HIBINO, *PRESENT SOCCER*, 1982, acrylic, color pencil, sumi ink, gesso, corrugated cardboard, cardboard, newspaper, 72.8 x 103 cm, Collection and courtesy of The Museum of Fine Arts, Gifu (p.77)
Katsuhiko HIBINO, *SWEATY JACKET*, 1982, acrylic, color pencil, sumi ink, cardboard, plastic, kite string, wire, 106.7 x 83 x 22 cm, The Museum of Fine Arts, Gifu
Minoru HIRATA (1930-2018), *Nakanishi Natsuyuki's Clothespins Assert Churning Action, for Hi Red Center's 6th Mixer Plan event, Tokyo*, 1963/2017, gelatin silver print, Image size: 33.5 x 22.2 cm, Paper size: 35.7 x 27.8 cm, HM Archive, Courtesy of Taka Ishii Gallery Photography/Film, Tokyo
Minoru HIRATA, *Shining Clothespins (Nakanishi Natsuyuki's clothespins on a model at the artist's studio)*, 1963/2017, gelatin silver print, Image size: 33.5 x 22.2 cm, Paper size: 35.7 x 27.8 cm, HM Archive, Courtesy of Taka Ishii Gallery Photography/Film, Tokyo
Minoru HIRATA, *Hi Red Center's Dropping Event, at Ikenobo Kaikan*, 1964/2017, gelatin silver print, Image size: 33.5 x 22.2 cm, Paper size: 35.7 x 27.8 cm, HM Archive, Courtesy of Taka Ishii Gallery Photography/Film, Tokyo
Minoru HIRATA, *Hi Red Center's Dropping Event, at Ikenobo Kaikan*, 1964/2017, gelatin silver print, Image size: 33.5 x 22.2 cm, Paper size: 35.7 x 27.8 cm, HM Archive, Courtesy of Taka Ishii Gallery Photography/Film, Tokyo
Minoru HIRATA, *Jasper Johns opening the door at Hi Red Center's Closing Event, at Naiqua Gallery*, 1964/2017, Image size: 33.5 x 22.2 cm, Paper size: 35.7 x 27.8 cm, gelatin silver print, HM Archive, Courtesy of Taka Ishii Gallery Photography/Film, Tokyo
Minoru HIRATA, *Akiyama Yutokutaishi's Glicoman*, 1967/2017, gelatin silver print, Image size: 33.5 x 22.2 cm, Paper size: 35.7 x 27.8 cm, HM Archive, Courtesy

of Taka Ishii Gallery Photography/Film, Tokyo

Minoru HIRATA, *Expo'70 Destruction Joint-Struggle Group's Anti-Expo Event, on the rooftop of Kyoto University's lecture hall*, 1969/2017, gelatin silver print, Image size: 22.2 x 33.5 cm
Paper size: 27.8 x 35.7 cm, HM Archive, Courtesy of Taka Ishii Gallery Photography/ Film, Tokyo

Minoru HIRATA, *Banzai Party's "Peace and Love Banzai",* 1970/2017, gelatin silver print, Image size: 22.2 x 33.5 cm, Paper size: 27.8 x 35.7 cm, HM Archive, Courtesy of Taka Ishii Gallery Photography/Film, Tokyo

Minoru HIRATA, *K.M.'s Challenge*, 1970-71/2017, gelatin silver print, Image size: 33.5 x 22.2 cm, Paper size: 35.7 x 27.8 cm, HM Archive, Courtesy of Taka Ishii Gallery Photography/Film, Tokyo

Taro IZUMI (1976-), *Cannot see the shadow of the rainbow*, 2015, video (color, sound), 14'16", Take Ninagawa, Tokyo, Courtesy of Take Ninagawa, Tokyo (p. 83)

Teppei KANEUJI (1978-), *White Discharge*, 2012, found objects, resin, glue, 132 x 50 x 59 cm, Fondation Guy & Myriam Ullens, Geneva, Courtesy of the artist (p.79)

Izumi KATO (1969-), *Untitled*, 2010, wood, oil, acrylic, stone, iron, 166 x 230 x 230 cm, Galerie Perrotin (Paris), Photo : Clarie Dorn © 2010 Izumi Kato. Courtesy of the Artist and Perrotin (p.84)

Izumi KATO, *Untitled*, 2016, oil on canvas, 74.5 x 24.5 cm, Take Ninagawa, Tokyo

Izumi KATO, *Untitled*, 2017, oil on canvas, 56 x 106 cm, Take Ninagawa, Tokyo

Izumi KATO, *Untitled*, 2017, oil on canvas, 50 x 133.5 cm, Take Ninagawa, Tokyo

Tsunehisa KIMURA (1928-2008), *The City Welcomes a Bracing Morning*, 1978, photo montage, 40.2 x 20.6 cm, Tokyo Photographic Art Museum, Tokyo

Tsunehisa KIMURA, *Howling at the Pig*, 1980, photo montage, 40.8 x 28.6 cm, Tokyo Photographic Art Museum, Tokyo, Courtesy of Tokyo Photographic Art Museum, Tokyo (p.74))

Tsunehisa KIMURA, *Title Unknown*, n.d., photo montage, 38 x 31.8 cm, Tokyo Photographic Art Museum, Tokyo

Haruka KOJIN (1983-), *Relectwo*, 2008/2017, artificial flowers, acrylic, wire, dimensions variable, São Paulo Museum of Modern Art / Museum of Contemporary Art Tokyo © Centre Pompidou-Metz / Photo Jacqueline Trichard / 2017 /Exposition Japanorama (p.84)

Yayoi KUSAMA (1929-), *The Spirit is about to Part*, 1975, watercolor, pastel, collage on paper, 39.9 x 54.4 cm, Museum of Contemporary Art, Tokyo

Yayoi KUSAMA, *I who Committed Suicide*, 1977, ink, watercolor, ball-point pen, collage on paper, 39.5 x 54 cm, Museum of Contemporary Art, Tokyo

Yayoi KUSAMA, *Tidal Waves of War*, 1977, watercolor, pastel, collage on paper, 97.5 x 78.5 cm, Museum of Contemporary Art, Tokyo

Yayoi KUSAMA, *Fireflies on the Water*, 2000, mirror, metal, electric light bulb, wood acrylic plate, water, 442.4 x 442.4 x 320 cm, Centre national des arts plastiques, Paris © YAYOI KUSAMA, Courtesy Ota Fine Arts (p.82)

Yayoi KUSAMA, *After School*, 2003, pen and watercolor on cardboard, 36.5 x 26 cm, Centre Pompidou, Musée national d'art moderne, Paris

Yayoi KUSAMA, *The Snow melts, Spring is there,* 2003, pen and watercolor on cardboard, 36 x 25.5 cm, Centre Pompidou, Musée national d'art moderne, Paris

Kumi MACHIDA (1970-), *Visitor*, 2004, sumi, pigments and mineral pigments on kumohada linen paper, 90.6 x 116.7 cm, Takahashi Collection, Tokyo © Kumi MACHIDA, Courtesy of Nishimura Gallery (p.83)

Takashi MURAKAMI (1962-), *Polyrhythm Red*, 1989, acrylic, wooden plate, Tamiya model (American infantry, scale: 1/35), 98 x 60.7 x 3.5 cm, Takahashi Collection, Tokyo

Takashi MURAKAMI, *Cosmos*, 1998, acrylic on canvas mounted on board, 300 x 450 cm (3 panels), Collection and courtesy of 21st Century Museum of Contemporary Art, Kanazawa, Ishikawa © 1998 Takashi Murakami / Kaikai Kiki Co., Ltd. All Rights Reserved. (p.81)

Takashi MURAKAMI, *And then and then and then and then.........(Red),* 2001, offset printing, 50 x 50 cm, Museum of Contemporary Art, Tokyo

Takashi MURAKAMI, *Mushroom Bomb PINK*, 2001, offset printing, 50 x 50 cm, Museum of Contemporary Art, Tokyo

Hiroshi NAKAMURA (1932-), *Circular Train A (Telescope Train)*, 1968, oil on canvas, 182 x 227.5 cm, Collection and courtesy of Museum of Contemporary Art, Tokyo (p.75)

Mika NINAGAWA (1972-), *Tokyo Douchu*, 2017, video (color, sound), Collection of the artist © mika ninagawa/Roppongi Art Night 2017, Courtesy of Tomio Koyama Gallery, Tokyo (p.85)

Shinro OHTAKE (1955-), *Cape (from ZYAPANAИORAMA series)*, 2003, charcoal, acrylic, paper, 100 x 70 cm, Take Ninagawa, Tokyo

Shinro OHTAKE, *Nightscape (from ZYAPAИORAMA series)*, 2003, charcoal, acrylic, paper, 100 x 70 cm, Take Ninagawa, Tokyo

Shinro OHTAKE, *Scrapbook #68, 2014.2.14 - 2016.5.25*, 2014-2016, mixed media artist book, 20kg, 704 pages, 41 x 39 x 50 cm, Collection and courtesy of Take Ninagawa, Tokyo (p.76)

Kyoko OKAZAKI (1963-), *River's edge*, 1993-94, reprint on paper, Takarajima-sha, Tokyo, Courtesy of Takarajima-sha, Tokyo (p.85)

Kyoko OKAZAKI, *Helter Skelter*, 1995-96, reprint on paper, Shoden-sha, Tokyo

TABAIMO (1975-), *Haunted House*, 2003, video installation, dimension variable, 4'00", Fondation Cartier pour l'art contemporain © Tabaimo / Courtesy of Gallery Koyanagi (p.74)

Aya TAKANO (1976-), *A city in which saunter dangerous wandering*, 2002, ink and watercolor on paper, 25.5 x 21 cm, Galerie Perrotin, Paris

Aya TAKANO, *Untitled*, 2002, acrylic on canvas, wood, 65 x 50cm, Galerie Perrotin, Paris

Aya TAKANO, *Milk of tender love*, 2003, acrylic on canvas, 162 x 131 cm, Galerie Perrotin, Paris, Courtesy of Kaikai Kiki Gallery, Tokyo (p.83)

Aya TAKANO, *Untitled*, 2003, acrylic on canvas, wood, 41 x 32 cm, Galerie Perrotin, Paris

Aya TAKANO, *Untitled*, 2012, watercolor and pencil on paper, 21 x 29.7 cm, Galerie Perrotin, Paris

Aya TAKANO, *Pervert*, n.d., ink and watercolor on paper, 21 x 19 cm, Galerie Perrotin, Paris

Keiichi TANAAMI (1936-), *Commercial War*, 1971, video (color, sound), 4'30", NANZUKA, Tokyo

Keiichi TANAAMI, *Goodbye Marilyn*, 1971, video (color, sound), 4'52", NANZUKA, Tokyo

Keiichi TANAAMI, *OH! YOKO!,* 1973, video (color, sound), 4'00", NANZUKA, Tokyo

Keiichi TANAAMI, *untitled_collagebook03_06*, 1973, marker pen, ink, magazine scrap collage on drawing paper, 45 x 54 cm, NANZUKA, Tokyo

Keiichi TANAAMI, *untitled_collagebook03_07*, 1973, marker pen, ink, magazine scrap collage on drawing paper, 45 x 54 cm, Collection and courtesy of NANZUKA, Tokyo (p.72)

Keiichi TANAAMI, *Crayon Angel*, 1975, video (color, sound), 3'00", NANZUKA, Tokyo

Keiichi TANAAMI, *Sweet Friday*, 1975, video (color, sound), 3'00", NANZUKA, Tokyo

Tiger TATEISHI (1941-1998), *The Alamo Sphinx*, 1966, oil on canvas, 130.3 x 162 cm, Collection and courtesy of Museum of Contemporary Art, Tokyo (p.75)

Harumi YAMAGUCHI (1941-), *Poster of PARCO*, 1973, 103 x 72.8 cm, NANZU-KA, Tokyo

Harumi YAMAGUCHI, *Poster of PARCO*, 1973, 103 x 72.8 cm, NANZUKA, Tokyo

Harumi YAMAGUCHI, *Hand Picking the Shirt*, 1974, acrylic on board , 48 x 63 cm, NANZUKA, Tokyo

Harumi YAMAGUCHI, *Turtleneck*, 1974, acrylic on board, 43.8 x 56.5 cm, NANZUKA, Tokyo

Harumi YAMAGUCHI, *Flower Print*, 1974, acrylic on board, 45 x 60.5 cm, NANZUKA, Tokyo

Harumi YAMAGUCHI, *Poster of PARCO*, 1974, 103 x 72.8 cm, NANZUKA, Tokyo

Harumi YAMAGUCHI, *Poster of PARCO*, 1974, 103 x 72.8 cm, NANZUKA, Tokyo

Harumi YAMAGUCHI, *Fur Coat and Hat*, 1975, acrylic on board, 51.5 x 61 cm, NANZUKA, Tokyo

Harumi YAMAGUCHI, *Best Friends*, 1975, acrylic on board, 36.4 x 51.5 cm, NANZUKA, Tokyo

Harumi YAMAGUCHI, *Hand to Forehand*, 1975, acrylic on board, 51.5 x 72.7 cm, NANZUKA, Tokyo

Harumi YAMAGUCHI, *Love Letter*, 1975, acrylic on board, 36.4 x 51.5 cm, NANZUKA, Tokyo

Harumi YAMAGUCHI, *Coca Cola*, 1976, acrylic on board, 47.3 x 64.6 cm, NANZU-KA, Tokyo

Harumi YAMAGUCHI, *Telephone*, 1976, acrylic on board, 51.5 x 51.2 cm, NANZUKA, Tokyo

Harumi YAMAGUCHI, *Jumping with Foot Fins*, 1977, acrylic on board, 52.5 x 71.2 cm, NANZUKA, Tokyo

Harumi YAMAGUCHI, *Dryer*, 1977, acrylic on board, 46.3 x 65 cm, NANZUKA, Tokyo

Harumi YAMAGUCHI, *Women*, 1977, Acrylic on board, 44 x 58 cm, NANZUKA, Tokyo

Harumi YAMAGUCHI, *Poster of PARCO*, 1977, 103 x 145.6 cm, NANZUKA, Tokyo

Harumi YAMAGUCHI, *Poster of PARCO*, 1977, 103 x 145.6 cm, NANZUKA, Tokyo

Harumi YAMAGUCHI, *From a High Angle*, 1977, acrylic on board, 72.7 x 51.3 cm, NANZUKA, Tokyo

Harumi YAMAGUCHI, *Lying on Ice*, 1977, acrylic on board, 59.8 x 51.5 cm, NANZUKA, Tokyo

Harumi YAMAGUCHI, *Carribean Sunset*, 1981, acrylic on board, 46.8 x 61 cm, NANZUKA, Tokyo

Harumi YAMAGUCHI, *Poster of PARCO*, 1981, 103 x 72.8 cm, NANZUKA, Tokyo

Harumi YAMAGUCHI, *Poster of PARCO*, 1982, 103 x 72.8 cm, NANZUKA, Tokyo

Harumi YAMAGUCHI, *Suspender Swimsuit*, 1983, acrylic on board, 65 x 51.5 cm, Collection and courtesy of NANZUKA, Tokyo (p.77)

Harumi YAMAGUCHI, *Poster of PARCO*, 1983, 103 x 72.8 cm, NANZUKA, Tokyo

Harumi YAMAGUCHI, *Red Blouson*, 1985, acrylic on board, 51.5 x 42 cm, NANZUKA, Tokyo

Harumi YAMAGUCHI, *Big Nude*, 1985, acrylic on board, 60 x 43 cm, NANZUKA, Tokyo

Harumi YAMAGUCHI, *Poster of PARCO*, n.d., 103 x 72.8 cm, NANZUKA, Tokyo

Harumi YAMAGUCHI, *Poster of PARCO*, n.d., 103 x 72.8 cm, NANZUKA, Tokyo

Harumi YAMAGUCHI, *Poster of PARCO*, n.d., 103 x 72.8 cm, NANZUKA, Tokyo

Miwa YANAGI (1967-), *Elevator Girl: Eternal City I*, 1998, digital print, 90 x 160 cm, FABA (Fondacion Almine y Bernard Ruiz-Picasso para el Arte), Brussels

Miwa YANAGI, *My Grandmothers: YUKA*, 2000, digital print, 100 x 100 cm, Collection and courtesy of FABA (Fondacion Almine y Bernard Ruiz-Picasso para el Arte), Brussels © MIWA YANAGI (p.78)

Kenji YANOBE (1965-), *Sweet Harmonizer II*, 1995, metal, plastic, textile, perfume, motor, automatic change machine, 160 x 130 x 320 cm, Musée d'art contemporain de Marseille, Marseille

Kenji YANOBE, *E.E. Pod 1*, 1996, geiger, steel, water, food, others, battery, 150 x 130 x 120 cm, Galerie Perrotin, Paris

Kenji YANOBE, *Atom Suit Project: Reactor Chernobyl*, 1997, color photography, frame, 100 x 100 cm, Galerie Perrotin, Paris, Photographer: Seiji Toyanoga

Kenji YANOBE, *Atom Suit Project: Desert*, 1998, matte, 49.8 x 59.8 cm, Private collection, Photographer: Russel Liebman

Kenji YANOBE, *Atom Suit Project: The World Fair in Osaka 1*, 1998, color photography, frame, 50 x 50 cm, Galerie Perrotin, Paris, Photographer: Seiji Toyanoga, Courtesy of ANOMALY, Tokyo (p.79)

Kenji YANOBE, *Atom Suit Project: The World Fair in Osaka 2,* 1998, color photography, frame, 100 x 100 cm, Galerie Perrotin, Paris, Photographer: Seiji Toyanoga

Kenji YANOBE, *Soap Bubbles Project: Portrait 2 Blue*, 2000, steel, bubble, machine, plastic, hairs, 76 x 76 x 62 cm, Galerie Perrotin, Paris

Tadanori YOKOO (1936-), *TADANORI YOKOO*, 1965, silkscreen on paper, 103 x 72.8 cm, Museum of Contemporary Art, Tokyo

Tadanori YOKOO, *Bride*, 1966, acrylic on canvas, 53 x 45.5 cm, Museum of Contemporary Art, Tokyo

Tadanori YOKOO, *Motorcycle*, 1966/2002, acrylic on canvas, 53 x 45.5 cm, Private collection, Courtesy of Yokoo's Circus Co., Ltd. (p.73)

Tadanori YOKOO, *Recruiting Members for Tenjo Sajiki, Tenjo Sajiki*, 1967, silkscreen on paper, 103 x 72.8 cm, Museum of Contemporary Art, Tokyo

Tadanori YOKOO, *Eikoh Hosoe Photographic Exhibition; Tatsumi Hijikata and Japanese ;The Book of Kamaitachi, For new human, Gendai Shichosya*, 1968, silkscreen on paper, 103 x 72.8 cm, Museum of Contemporary Art, Tokyo

Tadanori YOKOO, *Yakuza Movies, Sogetsu Art Center*, 1968, silkscreen on paper, 103 x 72.8 cm, Museum of Contemporary Art, Tokyo

Tadanori YOKOO, *Amazon*, 1989, offset print, 102.6 x 72.1 cm, Centre national des arts plastiques, Paris

Tadanori YOKOO, *Céramique Rado*, 1989, offset print, 102.6 x 72.1 cm, Centre national des arts plastiques, Paris

Tadanori YOKOO, *Fancy Danse*, 1989, offset print, 102.6 x 72.1 cm, Centre national des arts plastiques, Paris

Tadanori YOKOO, *L'histoire de fantôme – Kaiin no uma*, 1989, offset print, 102.6 x 72.1 cm, Centre national des arts plastiques, Paris

Tadanori YOKOO, *Pop Art, Mon Amour Maison d'Ailleurs*, 2016, 128 x 89.5 cm, Collection of the artist

Tadanori YOKOO, *JASRAC*, n.d., silkscreen on paper, 103 x 72.8 cm, Collection of the artist

Yuichi **YOKOYAMA** (1967-) *Color Engineering*, 2004, ink on paper, 55.6 x 78.8 cm, Collection and courtesy of NANZUKA, Tokyo (p.72)

Yuichi **YOKOYAMA**, *Color Engineering episode 5*, 2004, ink on paper, 13 x 54.6 cm, NANZUKA, Tokyo

Yuichi **YOKOYAMA**, *Color Engineering episode 5*, 2004, ink on paper, 23.4 x 37.6 cm, NANZUKA, Tokyo

Yuichi **YOKOYAMA**, *Color Engineering episode 6*, 2004, ink on paper, 38 x 45 cm, NANZUKA, Tokyo

Yuichi **YOKOYAMA**, *Color Engineering episode 6*, 2004, ink on paper, 47.7 x 62 cm, NANZUKA, Tokyo

Yuichi **YOKOYAMA**, *Color Engineering episode 6*, 2004, ink on paper, 37.5 x 11.3 cm, NANZUKA, Tokyo

Yuichi **YOKOYAMA**, *Color Engineering episode 11*, 2004, ink on paper, 10.7 x 53.3 cm, NANZUKA, Tokyo

Yuichi **YOKOYAMA**, *Color Engineering episode 11*, 2004, ink on paper, 26.2 x 51.6 cm, NANZUKA, Tokyo

Yuichi **YOKOYAMA**, *Color Engineering episode 11*, 2004, sumi ink on paper, 25.7 x 24 cm, NANZUKA, Tokyo

Yuichi **YOKOYAMA**, *Color Engineering episode 11*, 2004, ink on paper, 10.6 x 24.7 cm, NANZUKA, Tokyo

Yuichi **YOKOYAMA**, *Color Engineering episode 12*, 2004, acrylic paint and ink on paper, 16 x 39 cm, NANZUKA, Tokyo

Yuichi **YOKOYAMA**, *Color Engineering episode 12*, 2004, acrylic paint and ink on paper, 18.2 x 37.5 cm, NANZUKA, Tokyo

Yuichi **YOKOYAMA**, *Color Engineering episode 12*, 2004, acrylic paint and ink on paper, 21.5 x 41.5 cm, NANZUKA, Tokyo

Yuichi **YOKOYAMA**, *Color Engineering episode 12*, 2004, acrylic paint and ink on paper, 17.8 x 37.7 cm, NANZUKA, Tokyo

Yuichi **YOKOYAMA**, *Color Engineering episode 14*, 2004, sumi ink on paper, 37.6 x 14.7 cm, NANZUKA, Tokyo

Yuichi **YOKOYAMA**, *Color Engineering episode 15*, 2004, ink on paper, 11.8 x 70 cm, NANZUKA, Tokyo

Yuichi **YOKOYAMA**, *Color Engineering episode 15*, 2004, sumi ink on paper, 9.6 x 37.3 cm, NANZUKA, Tokyo

Yuichi **YOKOYAMA**, *Color Engineering episode 15*, 2004, sumi ink on paper, 10 x 37.2 cm, NANZUKA, Tokyo

Yuichi **YOKOYAMA**, *Color Engineering episode 15*, 2004, ink on paper, 11.5 x 37 cm, NANZUKA, Tokyo

Yuichi **YOKOYAMA**, *Color Engineering episode 15*, 2004, ink and sumi ink on paper, 9.6 x 24.8 cm, NANZUKA, Tokyo

Yuichi **YOKOYAMA**, *Color Engineering episode 15*, 2004, ink on paper, 10.7 x 20 cm, NANZUKA, Tokyo

Yuichi **YOKOYAMA**, *Color Engineering episode 15*, 2004, ink on paper, 11.5 x 9.4 cm, NANZUKA, Tokyo

Yuichi **YOKOYAMA**, *Color Engineering episode 17*, 2004, acrylic paint on paper, 6.9 x 13.4 cm, NANZUKA, Tokyo

Yuichi **YOKOYAMA**, *Color Engineering episode 17*, 2004, acrylic paint on paper, 10.6 x 22.3 cm, NANZUKA, Tokyo

Yuichi **YOKOYAMA**, *Color Engineering episode 17*, 2004, acrylic paint on paper,

7 x 10 cm, NANZUKA, Tokyo

Yuichi YOKOYAMA, *Color Engineering episode 17*, 2004, acrylic paint on paper, 10.6 x 22.3 cm, NANZUKA, Tokyo

C Collaboration/Participation/Sharing

Atelier Bow-Wow+Kaijima Lab, University of Tsukuba, *Momonoura Village Public Drawing*, 2017, architectural drawing, 84.1 x 118.9 cm, Collection of the architects, Courtesy of the architects (p.93)

Fluxus (Mieko Shiomi), *FLUXUS maciuNAS V TRE FLUXUS laudatio ScriPTa Pro GEoRge No.10*, 1976, offset on paper, 58.4 x 44.4[p], Musée d'art contemporain de Lyon

Kazuhiko HACHIYA (1966-), *M-02 [Möwe, replica of plane of Nausica, Hayao Miyazaki's Film]*, version of 2016, 21st Century Museum of Contemporary Art, Kanazawa, Courtesy of 21st Century Museum of Contemporary Art, Kanazawa (p.92)

Kumamoto Artpolis Tohoku Support Group (Toyo ITO, Hideki KATSURA, Kaoru SUEHIRO, Masashi SOGABE), *Home-for-All, Sendai, Miyagi*, 2011, ensemble of the documents, version of 2012, video, Courtesy of Toyo Ito & Associates, Architects (p.93)

Toyoo ITO, Sou FUJIMOTO, Kumiko INUI, Akihisa HIRATA, Naoya HATAKEYA-MA, *Home-for-All*, 2012, 100 x 100 x 100 cm or less, document/scaned data, Collection of the artist

Yoko ONO (1933-), *Grapefruits*, 1964, offset, overall (closed) 13.8 x 13.8 x 3.2 cm, Bibliothèque Kandinsky, Centre Pompidou, Paris © Centre Pompidou Metz / Photo Jacqueline Trichard / 2017 / Exposition Japanorama(p.88)

Yoko ONO, *Eyeblink (Fluxfilm n°9)*, 1966, 16 mm film, 1', Centre Pompidou, Paris (p.88)

Yoko ONO, *Mend Piece for John*, 1968, The Library of Museums of Strasbourg (p.88)

THE PLAY (1967-), *Voyage: Happening in An Egg*, 1968.8.1, poster, 350×235mm, Collection of the artist

THE PLAY, *Voyage: Happening in An Egg*, 1968.8.1, back side of the poster, 197×133mm, Collection of the artist

THE PLAY, *Voyage: Happening in An Egg*, 19688.1, marine chart, 143×208mm, Collection of the artist

THE PLAY, *Voyage: Happening in An Egg*, 1968.8.1, document photo, 210×145mm, Collection of the artist

THE PLAY, *Voyage: Happening in An Egg*, 1968.8.1, document photo, 174×117mm, Collection of the artist

THE PLAY, *Voyage: Happening in An Egg*, 1968.8.1, document photo, 140×100mm, Collection of the artist

THE PLAY, *Voyage: Happening in An Egg*, 1968, poster, Collection of the artist

THE PLAY, *SHEEP*, 1970.8.23-28, poster, 274×392mm, Collection of the artist

THE PLAY, *SHEEP*, 1970.8.23-28, map, 177×125mm, Collection of the artist

THE PLAY, *SHEEP*, 1970, document photo, Collection of the artist

THE PLAY, *SHEEP*, 1970, document photo, Collection of the artist

THE PLAY, *SHEEP*, 1970, document photo, Collection of the artist

THE PLAY, *THE BRIDGE*, 1973.8.10-19, 8.20-22, plan, 325×245mm, Collection of the artist,

THE PLAY, *THE BRIDGE*, 1973.8.10-19, 8.20-22, document photo, 161×247mm, Collection of the artist

THE PLAY, *THE BRIDGE*, 1973.8.10-19, 8.20-22, document photo, 174×113mm, Collection of the artist

THE PLAY, THE BRIDGE, 1973.8.10-19, 8.20-22, document photo, 247×161mm, Collection of the artist

THE PLAY, *THUNDER*, 1977-1986, activity log, Collection of the artist, Courtesy of the artist (p.89)

THE PLAY, *THUNDER*, 1977-1986, activity log, Collection of the artist

THE PLAY, *THUNDER*, 1977-1986, activity log, Collection of the artist

THE PLAY, *THUNDER*, 1977-1986, activity log, Collection of the artist

THE PLAY, *THUNDER*, 1977-1986, activity log, Collection of the artist

THE PLAY, *THUNDER*, 1977-1986, activity log, Collection of the artist

THE PLAY, *THUNDER*, 1977-1986, activity log, Collection of the artist

THE PLAY, *THUNDER*, 1977-1986, activity log, Collection of the artist

THE PLAY, *THUNDER*, 1977-1986, activity log, Collection of the artist

THE PLAY, *THUNDER*, 1977-1986, activity log, Collection of the artist

THE PLAY, *THUNDER*, 1977-1986, document photo, Collection of the artist

THE PLAY, *THUNDER 1*, 1977, poster, Collection of the artist

THE PLAY, *THUNDER 2*, 1978, poster, Collection of the artist

THE PLAY, *THUNDER 3*, 1979, poster, Collection of the artist

THE PLAY, *THUNDER 4*, 1980, poster, Collection of the artist

THE PLAY, *THUNDER 5*, 1981, poster, Collection of the artist

THE PLAY, *THUNDER 6*, 1982, poster, Collection of the artist

THE PLAY, *THUNDER 7*, 1983, poster, Collection of the artist

THE PLAY, *THUNDER 8*, 1984, poster, Collection of the artist

THE PLAY, *THUNDER 9*, 1985, poster, Collection of the artist

THE PLAY, *THUNDER 10*, 1986, poster, Collection of the artist

THE PLAY, *Working Room=Model of meaning*, 1981.3.7-21, plan, 206×142mm, Collection of the artist

THE PLAY, *Working Room=Model of meaning*, 1981.3.7-21, document photo, 223×137mm, Collection of the artist

THE PLAY, *Working Room=Model of meaning*, 1981, poster, Collection of the artist

THE PLAY, *Working Room=Model of meaning*, 1981, document photo, Collection of the artist

THE PLAY, *CLOCK: A Shaft of Light of 70 million years*, 1990.5.12-20, plan, 208×296mm, Collection of the artist

THE PLAY, *CLOCK: A Shaft of Light of 70 million years*, 1990.5.12-20, document photo, 175×114mm, Collection of the artist

THE PLAY, *CLOCK: A Shaft of Light of 70 million years*, 1990, poster, Collection of the artist

THE PLAY, *CLOCK: A Shaft of Light of 70 million years*, 1990, document photo, Collection of the artist

THE PLAY, *CLOCK: A Shaft of Light of 70 million years*, 1990, document photo, Collection of the artist

The PLAY, Document Photo, 1960-70s, photograph /or video as it is mentionned in the video list, Collection of the artist, Courtesy of the artist

THE PLAY, *La Seine /CURRENT OF CONTEMPORARY ART*, 2012.6.5, poster, 297×420mm, Collection of the artist

THE PLAY, *La Seine /CURRENT OF CONTEMPORARY ART*, 2012.6.5, map, 153×124mm, Collection of the artist

THE PLAY, *La Seine /CURRENT OF CONTEMPORARY ART*, 2012.6.5, document photo, 210×134mm, Collection of the artist

THE PLAY, *La Seine /CURRENT OF CONTEMPORARY ART*, 2012.6.5, document photo, 210×142mm, Collection of the artist

SANAA (Kazuyo Sejima and Ryue Nishizawa), *21st Century Museum of Contemporary Art*, Kanazawa, model, 2004, FRAC Centre (Orléans), Courtesy of SANAA (p.93)

Shimabuku (1969-), *The Chance to Recover Our Humanity, 1995 Suma Kobe*, 1995, photograph/ print, Collection of the artist (p.90)

Shimabuku, *Then, I Decided to Give a Tour of Tokyo to the Octopus from Akashi*, 2000, video, 6'56", Collection of the artist, Courtesy of the artist

Mieko SHIOMI (1938-), *Spatial Poem N°2*, 1965, Musée d'art contemporain de Lyon (p.89)

Mieko SHIOMI, *Bottled Music #1 - #14*, 1993, bottles, caption panels, board, instructions, Museum of Contemporary Art, Tokyo

Mieko SHIOMI, *Disappearing Music for Face (Fluxfilm n°4)*, 1966, video, 10', Centre Pompidou, Paris

Mieko SHIOMI, *Endless Box*, 1963/1990, paper, 8.5 x 15.7 x 15.8 cm, Museum of Contemporary Art, Tokyo

Mieko SHIOMI, *Event and Games*, 1963-64/2005, paper, 5 x 17 x 14 cm, Museum of Contemporary Art, Tokyo

Mieko SHIOMI, *Invitation Letters of 'Spacial Poem No.1-9'*, 1965-75, ten types papers, 27.7 x 22 cm, Museum of Contemporary Art, Tokyo

Mieko SHIOMI, *SHADOW EVENT NO. Y*, 1993, booklet with shadow film (edition hundertmark), 10.8 x 15.3 x 0.4 cm, Museum of Contemporary Art, Tokyo

Mieko SHIOMI, *Spacial Poem No.2 Direction Event - Flux Atlas*, 1966, paper, 36.7 x 82.2 x 2.2 cm, Museum of Contemporary Art, Tokyo, Courtesy of Museum of Contemporary Art, Tokyo

Mieko SHIOMI, *Spacial Poem No.3 Falling Event - a fluxcalender (Reflux edition)*, 1968/1992, paper, 17 x 13.3 x 3.3 cm, Museum of Contemporary Art, Tokyo

Koki TANAKA (1975-), *A Piano Played by Five Pianists at Once (First Attempt)*, 2012, video HD, 57', Collection of the artist, Commissioned by The University Art Galleries, University of California, Irvine, Courtesy of the artist, Vitamin Creative Space, Guangzhou and Aoyama Meguro, Tokyo © Centre Pompidou Metz / Photo Jacqueline Trichard / 2017 / Exposition Japanorama (p.91)

Koki TANAKA, *A behavioral statement (or an unconscious protest)*, 2013, video HD, 8', Collection of the artist © Centre Pompidou Metz / Photo Jacqueline Trichard / 2017 / Exposition Japanorama

Koki TANAKA, *A pottery produced by 5 potters at once (silent attempt)*, 2013, video HD, 75', Collection of the artist © Centre Pompidou Metz / Photo Jacqueline Trichard / 2017 / Exposition Japanorama

Kosuke TSUMURA (1959-), *Coat "Final Home"*, c. 1994, polyester, nylon and paper, env. 150 x 150 cm, Collection of the artist, Courtesy of the Artist (p.88)

wah document (2006-), *wah27 "Bath on the ground"*, 2008, photograph, 80 x 110cm, Courtesy of the artist (p.93)

wah document, *wah27 "Bath on the ground"*, 2008, drawing on paper, 30 x 21cm, Courtesy of the artist (p.92)

wah document, *wah47 "Lifting a house"*, 2010, drawing on paper, 32 x 21cm,

Collection of the artist

wah document, *wah47 "Lifting a house",* 2010, video (color, sound), 2', Collection of the artist

wah document, *wah55 "Making a boat, Going to an uninhabited island !!",* 2010, photograph, 90 x 135cm, Collection of the artist

wah document, *wah55 "Making a boat, Going to an uninhabited island !!",* 2010, drawing on paper, 32 x 21cm, Collection of the artist

wah document, *wah document— Idea Conference,* 2017, video (color, sound), 5', Collection of the artist

Tokujin YOSHIOKA (1967-), *Honey-pop,* 2001, paraffin paper, 83 x 80 x 74 cm, Centre Pompidou, Musée national d'art moderne, Paris, Courtesy of the artist (p.92)

D   **Poetics of Resistance**

Chim ↑Pom (2005-), *SUPER RAT (DIORAMA),* 2008, 5 rats (stuffed after being caught in Shibuya), diorama of town of Shibuya, video, monitor, etc, 136 x 87 x 87 cm, Private Collection, Photo: Yoshimitsu Umekawa (p.103)

Chim ↑Pom, *Level 7 feat. 'Myth of Tomorrow',* 2011, video, 4'32", MUJIN-TO Production (Tokyo)

Chim ↑Pom, *SUPER RAT,* 2011 - 12, video, MUJIN-TO Production (Tokyo), Courtesy of the artist and MUJIN-TO Production"

Sou FUJIMOTO (1971-), *Residential treatment center for emotionally disturbed children,* 2004-2006, plan and photograph, Collection of the architect, Photograph: (c) Daici Ano, Plan: (c) Sou Fujimoto Architects (p.100)

Hideko FUKUSHIMA (1927-1997), *Wings,* 1950, oil on canvas, 92 x 74 cm, Museum of Contemporary Art, Tokyo, Courtesy of Museum of Contemporary Art, Tokyo (p.98)

Junya ISHIGAMI (1974-), *Balloon,* 2007, video (color, silent), 2'50", Collection of the architect, Courtesy of the Artist © junya.ishigami+associates (p.101)

Zon ITO (1971-), *Traveling in The Shallows,* 2000, embroidery on fabric, wooden panel, 90 x 135 cm, Private collection (p.100)

Zon ITO, *Slaver Twinkled in-.,* 2001, embroidery in cloth, wooden frame, 300 x 300 cm, Takahashi Collection (Tokyo)

Tomoko KASHIKI (1982-), *Shadow Play,* 2009, acrylic, cotton, wooden panel, 102 x 173 cm, Takahashi Collection (Tokyo), Copyright Tomoko Kashiki, Courtesy of Ota Fine Arts (p.99)

Harue KOGA (1895-1933), *Sea,* 1929, oil on canvas, 130 x 162.5 cm, National Museum of Modern Art, Tokyo, Courtesy of National Museum of Modern Art, Tokyo © Centre Pompidou Metz / Photo Jacqueline Trichard / 2017 / Exposition Japanorama (p.96-97)

Mame Kurogouchi (2010-; **Maiko KUROGOUCHI** 1985-), *Personal Memory 2014AW,* 2014, 3 sets with some texts, Collection of the artist (p.100)

Mame Kurogouchi, *Personal Memory 2014AW,* 2014, Collection of the artist

Mame Kurogouchi, *Personal Memory 2014AW,* 2014, Collection of the artist

Koji NAKAZONO (1989-2015), *Untitled,* 2012, oil on canvas, 194 x 194.5 cm, Museum of Contemporary Art, Tokyo, Courtesy of Museum of Contemporary Art Tokyo (p.99)

Yoshitomo NARA (1959-), *Sayon,* 2006, acrylic on canvas, 146 x 112.5 cm, Museum of Contemporary Art, Tokyo, Courtesy of Museum of Contemporary Art, Tokyo © Yoshitomo Nara © Centre Pompidou Metz / Photo Jacqueline Trichard / 2017 / Exposition Japanorama (p.96-97)

Yoshitomo NARA, *In the White Room II*, 1995, acrylic on cotton, 100 x 100 cm, Collection of the Japan Foundation © Yoshitomo Nara © Centre Pompidou Metz / Photo Jacqueline Trichard / 2017 / Exposition Japanorama (p.96-97)

Yoshitomo NARA, *In the Deepest Puddle II*, 1995, acrylic on cotton, 120 x 110 cm, Takahashi Collection (Tokyo)

Yoshitomo NARA, *Ocean Child (in the floating world)*, 1999, reworked wood-cut, Fuji xerox copy (16 works), 41.5 x 29.5 cm, Takahashi Collection (Tokyo)

Yoshitomo NARA, *Rescue Puppy (in the floating world)*, 1999, reworked woodcut, Fuji xerox copy (16 works), 29.5 x 41.5 cm, Takahashi Collection (Tokyo)

Yoshitomo NARA, *Human Face Dog*, 1989, acrylic on paper, 34.5 x 49.5 cm, Takahashi Collection (Tokyo)

Tsuyoshi OZAWA (1965-), *Jizoing: Panmunjon, July 2, 1992*, 1992, photograph, 24.5 x 24.5 cm, Collection of the artist, Courtesy of the Artist (p.101)

Tsuyoshi OZAWA, *Jizoing, Teheran, August 24, 1988*, 1988, photograph, 24.5 x 24.5 cm, Collection of the artist

Tsuyoshi OZAWA, *Jizoing, The Grand Shrines of Ise, April 2, 1989*, 1989, photograph, 24.5 x 24.5 cm, Collection of the artist

Tsuyoshi OZAWA, *Jizoing, Lhasa (Festival), August 21, 1993*, 1993, photograph, 48 x 24 cm, Collection of the artist

Tsuyoshi OZAWA, *Jizoing, Mt. Fuji, August 9, 1995*, 1995, photograph, 48 x 24 cm, Collection of the artist

Tsuyoshi OZAWA, *Jizoing; Kamikuisshiki Village, August 10, 1995*, 1995, photograph, 48 x 24 cm, Collection of the artist

Hiroshi SUGITO (1970-), *connecting man no.2*, 2006, acrylic on paper, 59 x 230 cm, Sammlung Peters-Messer (Germany) (p.100)

Yuken TERUYA (1973-), *You-I You-I*, 2002, pigment (Okinawan bingata) on linen, 180 x 140 cm, Collection of Okinawa Prefectural Museum o& Art Museum, Courtesy the Artist and Okinawa Prefectural Museum of Art, Photo: Yoshikazu Nema (p.98)

Yuken TERUYA, *Notice-Forest: McDonald's bag*, 2017, paper bag, glue, 4.75 x 7 x 11.5 cm, Collection of the artist

Fuyuki YAMAKAWA (1973-), *The Voice-Over*, 1997-2008, 35', computer, video projector, old type TV, old type radio, etc, 700 x 700 x 400 cm (Installation size), Museum of Contemporary Art, Tokyo, Courtesy of the artist (p.102)

E   Floating Subjectivity/Private Documentary

Nobuyoshi ARAKI (1940-), *Sentimental Journey*, 1971/2012, gelatin silver print, image size: 21.9 x 33 cm, paper size: 27.7 x 35.5 cm, Collection of the artist, Courtesy of Taka Ishii Gallery, Tokyo (p.111)

Nobuyoshi ARAKI, *Sentimental Journey*, 1971/2013, gelatin silver print, image size: 21.9 x 33 cm, paper size: 27.7 x 35.5 cm, Collection of the artist, Courtesy of Taka Ishii Gallery, Tokyo

Nobuyoshi ARAKI, *Sentimental Journey*, 1971/2014, gelatin silver print, image size: 21.9 x 33 cm, paper size: 27.7 x 35.5 cm, Collection of the artist, Courtesy of Taka Ishii Gallery, Tokyo

Nobuyoshi ARAKI, *Sentimental Journey*, 1971/2015, gelatin silver print, image size: 21.9 x 33 cm, paper size: 27.7 x 35.5 cm, Collection of the artist, Courtesy of Taka Ishii Gallery, Tokyo

Nobuyoshi ARAKI, *Winter Journey*, 1971-1990 /2005, gelatin silver print, image size: 27 x 40.6 cm, paper size: 35 x 43 cm, Collection of the artist, Courtesy of Taka Ishii Gallery, Tokyo

Nobuyoshi ARAKI, *Winter Journey*, 1971-1990 /2006, gelatin silver print, image size: 27 x 40.6 cm, paper size: 35 x 44 cm, Collection of the artist, Courtesy of Taka Ishii Gallery, Tokyo

Finger Pointing Worker, *Pointing at Fukuichi Live Cam*, 2011, color video, sound, 24'40", Collection of **Kota Takeuchi**, Courtesy of SNOW Contemporary (p.112)

Hikaru FUJII (1976-), *Documentary about Fukushima*, 2011, color video, sound, 8'12", Collection of the artist, Courtesy of the artist (p.112)

Naoya HATAKEYAMA (1958-), *Underground #6205*, 1998, c-print, image size: 49 x 49 cm, paper size: 55 x 55 cm, Collection of the artist, Courtesy of Taka Ishii Gallery, Tokyo

Naoya HATAKEYAMA, *Rikuzentakata / 2013.10.20 Kesen-cho*, 2013/2015, c-print, 38 x 47 cm, Collection of the artist, Courtesy of Taka Ishii Gallery, Tokyo

Naoya HATAKEYAMA, *Rikuzentakata / 2011.5.1 Yonesaki-cho*, 2011/2015, c-print, image size: 38 x 47 cm, Collection of the artist, Courtesy of Taka Ishii Gallery, Tokyo (p.112)

HATRA (2010-; **Keisuke NAGAMI** 1987-), *HATRA AW 2011 "ASYMMETRY HOODIE"*, 2011, cotton, H83 cm W45 cm, Collection of the artist © Centre Pompidou Metz / Photo Jacqueline Trichard / 2017 / Exposition Japanorama (p.114)

HATRA, *HATRA AW2012 "VT-MYNA"*, 2012, polyester, H88 cm W45 cm, Collection of the artist (p.114)

HATRA, *HATRA SS2014 "OX SHIRT HOODIE"*, 2014, cotton, H86 cm W45 cm, Collection of the artist

HATRA, *HATRA AW2011 "FLEECE PANEL LONG JACKET"*, 2011, cotton, wool, polyurethane, H90 cm W45 cm, Collection of the artist

HATRA, *HATRA AW2011 "WAVE PANTS"*, 2011, TENCEL®, nylon, polyurethane, H85 cm W35 cm, Collection of the artist © Centre Pompidou Metz / Photo Jacqueline Trichard / 2017 / Exposition Japanorama (p.114)

HATRA, *HATRA AW2011 "WAVE PANTS SLIM"*, 2011, polyester, H85 cm W35 cm, Collection of the artist

HATRA, *HATRA AW2011 "SILNECK SHIRT"*, 2017, cotton, polyester, H90 cm W42 cm, Collection of the artist

HATRA, *HATRA AW2011 "WAVE SLEEVE BAG"*, 2011, polyester, H100 cm W45 cm, Collection of the artist

HATRA, *HATRA AW2011 "FLEECE PANEL PANTS"*, 2011, cotton, TENCEL®, nylon, polyurethane, H95 cm W43 cm, Collection of the artist

HATRA, *HATRA AW2011 "WHALE NECK FARMER"*, 2011, cotton, H45 cm W45 cm, Collection of the artist

HATRA, *HATRA Autumn/Winter 2011*, video (color, sound), 3', Collection of the artist

Takashi HOMMA (1962-), *Shonan International Village 1, Kanagawa*, 1998, photograph, 1000 x 1260 mm, Collection of the artist

Takashi HOMMA, *Boy 1, Keio Tama Center, Tokyo*, 1998, photograph, 1000 x 1260 mm, Collection of the artist, Courtesy of the artist (p.106)

Takashi HOMMA, *Shonan International Village, Kanagawa*, 1997, photograph,

1000 x 1260 mm, Collection of the artist

Takashi HOMMA, *Urayasu Marina East 21, Chiba*, 1995, photograph, 1000 x 1260 mm, Collection of the artist

Takashi HOMMA, *Boy 7, Urayasu, Chiba*, 1998, photograph, 570 x 470 mm, Collection of the artist

Takashi HOMMA, *Girl 1, Shonan International Village 1, Kanagawa*, 1995, photograph, 570 x 470 mm, Collection of the artist

Takashi HOMMA, *Makuhari Bay Town,Chiba*, 1995, photograph, 470 x 570 mm, Collection of the artist

Takashi HOMMA, *Boy 2, Tokyo Joypolis, Tokyo*, 1998, photograph, 470 x 570 mm, Collection of the artist

Takashi HOMMA, *Boy 4, Sagamiono, Kanagawa*, 1996, photograph, 470 x 570 mm, Collection of the artist

Takashi HOMMA, *Tama New Town,Tokyo*, 1998, photograph, 470 x 570 mm, Collection of the artist

Takashi HOMMA, *Rainbow Bridge, Odaiba,Tokyo*, 1995, photograph, 470 x 570 mm, Collection of the artist

Takashi HOMMA, *Love Hotel UFO,Chiba*, 1995, photograph, 470 x 570 mm, Collection of the artist

Takashi HOMMA, *Parking Lot, Tokorozawa, Saitama*, 1995, photograph, 470 x 570 mm, Collection of the artist

Takashi HOMMA, *Nerima, Tokyo*, photograph, 470 x 570 mm, Collection of the artist

Eikoh HOSOE (1933-), *Simon: A Private Landscape*, 1971/2012, photograph, gelatin silver print (d.o.p), image size: 35.4 x 45.4 cm, paper size: 40.3 x 50.7 cm, Collection of the artist, Courtesy of Taka Ishii Gallery, Tokyo

Eikoh HOSOE, *Simon: A Private Landscape*, 1971/2012, photograph, gelatin silver print (d.o.p), image size: 45.4 x 39 cm, paper size: 50.6 x 40.5 cm, Collection of the artist, Courtesy of Taka Ishii Gallery, Tokyo

Eikoh HOSOE, *Simon: A Private Landscape*, 1971, photograph, gelatin silver print (d.o.p), 29.1 x 227 cm, Collection of the artist, Courtesy of Taka Ishii Gallery, Tokyo

On KAWARA (1932-2014), *DEC 18, 1992 "TODAY" Series No.46*, 1992, acrylic on canvas and carton box containing a page of New York Post (18th, December 1992), 66 x 91.5 x 4.5 cm, Carré d'art de Nîmes © Centre Pompidou Metz / Photo Jacqueline Trichard / 2017 / Exposition Japanorama (p.107)

On KAWARA, *Nov.5, 1988*, 1988, Liquitex on canvas and carton box containing a page of New York Post (5th, November 1988), 67 x 91.5 x 4.5 cm, CNAP Lambert Collection © Centre Pompidou Metz / Photo Jacqueline Trichard / 2017 / Exposition Japanorama (p.107)

Rinko KAWAUCHI (1972-), *Untitled from Illuminance*, 2009, c-print, Meessen De Clercq (Brussels, Belgium)

Rinko KAWAUCHI, *Untitled from Illuminance*, 2009, c-print, Meessen De Clercq (Brussels, Belgium)

Rinko KAWAUCHI, *Untitled from Illuminance*, 2009, c-print, Meessen De Clercq (Brussels, Belgium)

Rinko KAWAUCHI, *Untitled from Illuminance*, 2009, c-print, 101 x 101 cm, Meessen De Clercq (Brussels, Belgium)

Rinko KAWAUCHI, *Untitled from Illuminance*, 2007, c-print, 50 x50 cm, Meessen De Clercq (Brussels, Belgium)

Rinko KAWAUCHI, *Untitled from Illuminance*, 2009, c-print, 50 x50 cm, Meessen De Clercq (Brussels, Belgium)

Rinko KAWAUCHI, *Untitled from Illuminance*, 2009, c-print, 24.7 x 24.7 cm, Meessen De Clercq (Brussels, Belgium)

Rinko KAWAUCHI, *Untitled from Illuminance*, 2009, c-print, 24.7 x 24.7 cm, Meessen De Clercq (Brussels, Belgium)

Rinko KAWAUCHI, *Untitled from Illuminance*, 2009, c-print, 24.7 x 24.7 cm, Meessen De Clercq (Brussels, Belgium)

Rinko KAWAUCHI, *Untitled from Illuminance*, 2009, c-print, 24.7 x 24.7 cm, Meessen De Clercq (Brussels, Belgium)

Rinko KAWAUCHI, *Untitled from Illuminance*, 2009, c-print, 24.7 x 24.7 cm, Meessen De Clercq (Brussels, Belgium)

Rinko KAWAUCHI, *Untitled from Illuminance*, 2007, c-print, 101 x 101 cm, Meessen De Clercq (Brussels, Belgium)

Rinko KAWAUCHI, *Untitled from Illuminance*, 2007, c-print, 101 x 101 cm, Collection of the artist, Courtesy of the artist (p.115)

Tetsuaki MATSUE (1977-) *Tokyo Drifter*, documentary film (HD cam, color), sound, 72', Collection of the artist, Courtesy of the artist (p.114)

Daido MORIYAMA (1938-), *Nikko Toshogu*, 1977, gelatin silver print, 25.3 x 30.8 cm, 19.5 x 29.5 cm (hors marge), Centre Pompidou, Paris

Daido MORIYAMA, *provoke no.2*, 1968/2017, gelatin silver print, paper size: 35.6 x 43.2 cm, Collection of the artist, Courtesy of Taka Ishii Gallery, Tokyo (p.110)

Daido MORIYAMA, *provoke no.2*, 1968/2017, gelatin silver print, paper size: 35.6 x 43.2 cm, Collection of the artist, Courtesy of Taka Ishii Gallery, Tokyo

Daido MORIYAMA, *provoke no.2*, 1968/2017, gelatin silver print, paper size: 35.6 x 43.2 cm, Collection of the artist, Courtesy of Taka Ishii Gallery, Tokyo

Daido MORIYAMA, *provoke no.2*, 1968/2017, gelatin silver print, paper size: 35.6 x 43.2 cm, Collection of the artist, Courtesy of Taka Ishii Gallery, Tokyo

Daido MORIYAMA, *Shinjuku*, 2002/2008, gelatin silver print, image size: 55.5 x 83.8 cm, paper size: 60.1 x 90 cm, Collection of the artist, Courtesy of Taka Ishii Gallery, Tokyo

Daido MORIYAMA, *Shinjuku*, 2002/2008, gelatin silver print, image size: 84 x 55.6 cm, paper size: 90.2 x 60.1 cm, Collection of the artist, Courtesy of Taka Ishii Gallery, Tokyo

Takuma NAKAHIRA (1938-2015), *Untitled*, 2005, chromogenic print, 90 x 60 cm © Gen Nakahira, Courtesy of Osiris (p.109)

Takuma NAKAHIRA, *Documentary*, 2005, chromogenic print, 90 x 60 cm

Takuma NAKAHIRA, *Documentary*, 2008, chromogenic print, 90 x 60 cm

Takuma NAKAHIRA, *For a Language to Come*, 1970, slideshow with 79 photos © Gen Nakahira, Courtesy of Osiris (p.108-109)

Ikko NARAHARA (1931-2020), *Domains, Garden of Scilence*, 1958/1977, gelatin silver print, 32.5 x 21.8 cm, Collection of Narahara Ikko Archives, Courtesy of Taka Ishii Gallery Photography / Film (p.108)

Ikko NARAHARA, *Domains, within the Walls #2-3*, 1956/1977, gelatin silver print, 35.5 x 27.7 cm, Collection of the artist, Courtesy of Taka Ishii Gallery, Tokyo

Ikko NARAHARA, *Domains, within the Walls #2-11*, 1956/2018, gelatin silver print, 35.5 x 27.7 cm, Collection of the artist, Courtesy of Taka Ishii Gallery, Tokyo

Ikko NARAHARA, *Domains, within the Walls #2-20*, 1956/2017, gelatin silver print, 35.5 x 27.7 cm, Collection of the artist, Courtesy of Taka Ishii Gallery, Tokyo

Ikko NARAHARA, *Domains, Garden of Silence*, 1958, gelatin silver print, 32.7 x 22 cm, Collection of the artist, Courtesy of Taka Ishii Gallery, Tokyo

Hiraki SAWA (1977-), *Spotter*, 2003, single channel video, 7'40", Private collection, Courtesy of the artist and Ota Fine Arts (p.115)

Lieko SHIGA (1980-), ***RASEN KAIGAN***, 2008-, c-print, 81 x 120 cm, Collection of the artist

Lieko SHIGA, ***RASEN KAIGAN***, 2008-, c-print, 81 x 120 cm, Collection of the artist, Courtesy of the artist (p.113)

Lieko SHIGA, ***RASEN KAIGAN***, 2008-, c-print, 104 x 160 cm, Collection of the artist

Lieko SHIGA, ***RASEN KAIGAN***, 2008-, c-print, 54 x 100 cm, Collection of the artist

Lieko SHIGA, ***RASEN KAIGAN***, 2008-, c-print, 94 x 125 cm, Collection of the artist

---

F   **Materiality and Minimalism**

Koji ENOKURA (1942-1995), ***A Stain No.1***, 1975, silkscreen (waste oil), 75.5 x 106.8 cm, Museum of Contemporary Art, Tokyo

Koji ENOKURA, ***STORY & MEMORY (P.W.-No.112)***, 1993, gelatin silver print, left 26.3 x 33.7 cm right 26 x 33.7 cm (diptych), Museum of Contemporary Art, Tokyo

Koji ENOKURA, STORY & MEMORY (P.W.-No.113), 1993, gelatin silver print, left 25.5 x 33.3 cm right 26.1 x 34.0 cm (diptych), Museum of Contemporary Art, Tokyo

Koji ENOKURA, *Untitled*, 1980, oil on cotton, 220 x 440 x 80 cm, Private collection, Courtesy of Tokyo Gallery (Tokyo) (p.123)

Ryoji IKEDA (1966-), ***data.tron***, 2007, audio-visual installation, materials: DLP projector, computer, speaker, dimensions variable, Courtesy of Yamaguchi Center for Arts and Media [YCAM], concept, composition: Ryoji Ikeda, computer graphics, programming: Shohei Matsukawa, co-produced by Le Fresnoy Studio National des Arts Contemporains and Forma, 2007 © Ryoji Ikeda, photo by Ryuichi Maruo (p.122)

Ryoji IKEDA, ***the transcendental (ϖ) [n°1-2d]***, 2017, aluminum, pigment print, 100 x 100 x 10 cm, galerie Almine Rech (Paris) © Centre Pompidou Metz / Photo Jacqueline Trichard / 2017 / Exposition Japanorama (p.118-119)

Tadashi KAWAMATA (1953-), ***Tree Huts in Place Vendome***, 2013, wood, dimensions variable, Centre Pompidou, Paris, Courtesy of Centre Pompidou, Paris (p.123)

Susumu KOSHIMIZU (1944-), ***Relief '80-8***, 1980, wood, 162.5 x 97 x 6.5 cm each (a pair), Museum of Contemporary Art, Tokyo, Courtesy of Museum of Contemporary Art, Tokyo (p.118-119)

LEE Ufan (1936-), ***Relatum (Formerly Phenomena and Perception B)***, 1968/2017, steel plaque and stones, 220 x 280 x 60 cm, Courtesy of the artist and kamel mennour, Paris/London © Centre Pompidou-Metz / Photo Jacqueline Trichard © Lee Ufan, Courtesy of the artist and kamel mennour, Paris/London (p.118-119)

Tatsuo MIYAJIMA (1957-), ***Moon in the ground no.2***, 2015, stainless steel, light emitting diode, IC, electric wire, H17 × W150 × D150 cm, SCAI THE BATHHOUSE (Tokyo), Courtesy of SCAI THE BATHHOUSE (p.122)

Tomoharu MURAKAMI (1938-), ***Untitled***, 1981, oil on canvas, 162 x 130 cm, Private collection © Tomoharu Murakami, Courtesy of Shigeru Yokota Gallery (p.121)

Kohei NAWA (1975-), ***Force***, 2015, mixed media, dimensions variable, ZKM Karlsruhe, Courtesy of the artist (p.125)

Hitoshi NOMURA (1945-), ***'moon' score***, 1975-79, gelatin silver print on file, 31.1 x 25.5 x 5.5 cm each (6 photo files), The National Museum of Modern Art, Tokyo

Hitoshi NOMURA, ***'moon' score***, 1975-79, LP, LP record: φ 30 jacket: 31.5 x 31.5 cm, The National Museum of Modern Art, Tokyo

Hitoshi NOMURA, ***'moon' score 1977.1.1,*** 1980, gelatin silver print, 82.5 x 100.5

cm, The National Museum of Modern Art, Tokyo

Hitoshi NOMURA, *'moon' score 1978.1.12*, 1980, gelatin silver print, 82.5 x 100.5 cm, The National Museum of Modern Art, Tokyo

Hitoshi NOMURA, *'moon' score 1979.1.1*, 1980, gelatin silver print (set of 4), 82.5 x 100.5 cm, The National Museum of Modern Art, Tokyo, Courtesy of The National Museum of Modern Art, Tokyo, Photo: MOMAT/DNPartcom (p.120)

Hitoshi NOMURA, *'moon' score 1980.1.1*, 1980, gelatin silver print, 82.5 x 100.5 cm, The National Museum of Modern Art, Tokyo

Kishio SUGA (1944-), *Protrusion HZ-87*, 1987, oil paint on wood, 153 x 125 cm, Gallery Yonetsu

Kishio SUGA, *Law of Peripheral Units*, 1997/2017, metallic tubes, stones, strings, dimensions variable, The National Museum of Modern Art (The Centre Pompidou), Courtesy of Tomio Koyama Gallery (p.124)

Hiroshi SUGIMOTO (1948-), *Mediterranean Sea, La Galère from the series of Ten Seascape*, 1989, gelatin silver print, 67 x 84 cm, Musée d'art contemporain de Lyon, Courtesy of Musée d'art contemporain de Lyon (p.120)

Hiroshi SUGIMOTO, *Sea of Okhotsk, Hokkaido from the series of Ten Seascape*, 1989, gelatin silver print, 67 x 84 cm, Musée d'art contemporain de Lyon, Courtesy of Musée d'art contemporain de Lyon (p.120)

Hiroshi SUGIMOTO, *North Sea, Berriedale from the series of Ten Seascape*, 1990, gelatin silver print, 67 x 84 cm, Musée d'art contemporain de Lyon, Courtesy of Musée d'art contemporain de Lyon (p.120)

Hiroshi SUGIMOTO, *Mirtoan Sea, Sounion I from the series of Ten Seascape*, 1990, gelatin silver print, 67 x 84 cm, Musée d'art contemporain de Lyon, Courtesy of Musée d'art contemporain de Lyon (p.120)

Hiroshi SUGIMOTO, *Marmar Sea, Silivli from the series of Ten Seascape*, 1991, gelatin silver print, 67 x 84 cm, Musée d'art contemporain de Lyon, Courtesy of Musée d'art contemporain de Lyon

Noboru TAKAYAMA (1944-), *Underground Zoo (Part)*, 1969/2003, railway ties (set of 7 pieces), 250 x 23 x 14 cm each, approx. 310 x 250 x H187 cm (installation size), Centre Pompidou, Paris, Courtesy of Kamakura Gallery, Photography: Uchida Yoshitaka © Centre Pompidou Metz / Photo Jacqueline Trichard / 2017 / Exposition Japanorama (p.118-119)

Yohji YAMAMOTO (1972-; Yohji YAMAMOTO 1943-), *Women's jacket*, 1990/1991 AW, textile, wool, 103 x 62 x 6 cm (size 36), Centraal Museum (Utrecht, Netherlands) © Centre Pompidou Metz / Photo Jacqueline Trichard / 2017 / Exposition Japanorama (p.121)

Yohji YAMAMOTO, *Women's shirts blouse*, 1989/1990 SS, cotton, size 36, Centraal Museum (Utrecht, Netherlands)

Yohji YAMAMOTO, *Women's jacket*, 1989, textile, linen, Centraal Museum (Utrecht, Netherlands)

Expo'70 Archive, video (color, sound), extracted from *DVD-SET of 40th anniversary of Expo'70* (2010, Geneon Universal) ("Opening Remarks", "Art in Plaza", "Tree of Life", "Toshiba IHI Pavilion, Mitsui Group Pavilion, Textile Pavilion", "Introduction – Opening"), 15'51", Courtesy of Osaka Prefectural Expo'70 Commemorative Park Office

Installation view: © Centre Pompidou Metz / Photo Jacqueline Trichard / 2017 / Exposition Japanorama

Editorial Superviser

Yuko Hasegawa
Yuko Hasegawa is a Professor of curatorial theory and
practice, and modern and contemporary art history at
Graduate School of Global Arts, Tokyo University of the
Arts, Director of the 21st Century Museum of Contemporary Art, Kanazawa, and Artistic Director of Inujima
House Art Project. She has curated on numerous bien-
nales in Istanbul (2001), Shanghai (2002), São Paulo
(2010), Sharjah (2013), Moscow (2017), and Thailand
(2021). The exhibitions she curated to introduce Jap-
anese arts include *Japanorama: A New Vision on Art
Since 1970*, Centre Pompidou-Metz (2017); *Fukami:
Une Plongée dans l'Esthétique Japonaise*, Hôtel Salo-
mon de Rothschild, Paris (2018); solo exhibitions of Japanese contemporary artists: Kishio Suga, Atsuko Tanaka,
Ryoji Ikeda, DumbType, Rhizomatiks, and SANAA. Her
publications include "A New Ecology and Art: on the
Clouds ⇄ Forests exhibition," in *Journal of Global Arts
Studies and Curatorial Practices*, Tokyo University of the
Arts, (2020); "Grotesque and cruel imagery in Japanese
gender expression: Nobuyoshi Araki, Makoto Aida,
and Fuyuko Matsui," in *The Persistence of Taste: Art,
Museums and Everyday Life After Bourdieu*, Routledge
(2018); "Performativity in the Work of Female Japanese
Artists in the 1950s–1960s and the 1990s," in *Modern
Women: Women Artists at The Museum of Modern Art*,
MoMA (2010); and *Kazuyo Sejima + Ryue Nishizawa:
SANAA*, Phaidon Press (2006).

Contributors

Emma Lavigne
Predident, Palais de Tokyo. She has been for five years
director of the Centre Pompidou-Metz, where she
orgaized a whole saison devoted to Japanese art and
architecture in 2017.

Yasuo Kobayashi
Professor Emeritus, University of Tokyo. His research
interests are studies of culture and representation and
philosophy.

Yoshitaka Mōri
Professor, Tokyo University of the Arts. His research interests are postmodern culture, media, art, the city and
transnationalism.

Keisuke Kitano
Professor, Ritsumeikan University. His research interests
are film theory, media theory, contemporary art theory.

Manabu Miki
Writer, editor, color researcher, and software planner.

Kenji Kajiya
Professor, University of Tokyo. His research interests include Japanese and American art since 1945, the history
and theory of archives, and oral history interviews on
Japanese art.

Akio Miyazawa
Professor, Waseda University. His research interests are
performing arts.

Minoru Shimizu
Professor, Doshisha University. His research interests are
contemporary art theory.

Futoshi Hoshino
Associate Professor, University of Tokyo. His research interests are aesthetics, critical theory, and interdisciplinary
cultural studies.

Emmanuelle de Montgazon
Independent Curator, art consultant. She is currently Director of Ryoji Ikeda Studio and is working on overseas
projects for Hiroshi Sugimoto among others.

*

Junya Utsumi (J. U.)
Miki Okubo (M. O.)
Anna Kato (A. K.)
Seiha Kurosawa (S. K.)
Yohji Suzuki (Y. S.)
Lee Kyung-rim (K. L.)
Rei Kagitani (R. K.)

Translators
Kenjiro Matsuda
Pamela Miki Associates
Tsutomu Nakano
Darryl Jingwen Wee

Editorial assistants
Kotaro Shimada
Mio Harada

Published by wind rose – suiseisha, Tokyo, 2021.
Printed by Seikosha Printing Co., Ltd., Tokyo.
Designed by Junichi Munetoshi.
ISBN978-4-8010-0511-2